Java™ Extreme Programming Cookbook

Eric M. Burke and Brian M. Coyner

O'REILLY®

Beijing · Cambridge · Farnham · Köln · Paris · Sebastopol · Taipei · Tokyo

Java™ Extreme Programming Cookbook
by Eric M. Burke and Brian M. Coyner

Published by O'Reilly & Associates, Inc., 1005 Gravenstein Highway North, Sebastopol, CA 95472.

O'Reilly & Associates books may be purchased for educational, business, or sales promotional use. Online editions are also available for most titles (*safari.oreilly.com*). For more information, contact our corporate/institutional sales department: (800) 998-9938 or *corporate@oreilly.com*.

Editor:	Mike Loukides
Production Editor:	Colleen Gorman
Cover Designer:	Hanna Dyer
Interior Designer:	Bret Kerr

Printing History:

March 2003:	First Edition.

ISBN: 0-596-00387-0

[M]

For Jennifer, Aidan, and Tanner

—Eric M. Burke

For Mom and Dad

—Brian M. Coyner

Table of Contents

Preface

Anyone involved with the open source community or using open source software knows there are tons of tools available on the market. Keeping up with these tools, and knowing which tools to use and how to use them, is an intimidating road to travel. We hope to simplify your journey by showing concise, useful recipes for some of the more popular open source Java tools on the market today.

We show you tools like JUnit, JUnitPerf, Mock Objects (more of a concept), and Cactus for testing Java code. We show how to generate EJB files using XDoclet, too. All tools discussed in this book are completely executable through Ant, allowing for a complete and stable build environment on any Java-enabled platform.

This is also a book about Extreme Programming (XP), which led us to choose the tools that we did. The XP software development approach does not depend on a particular set of tools; however, the right tools certainly make following XP practices easier. For instance, test-first development is a cornerstone of XP, so most of the tools in this book are testing frameworks. XP also demands continuous integration, which is where Ant fits in. We are big fans of automation, so we cover the XDoclet code generator as well as describe ways to automate deployment to Tomcat and JBoss.

Audience

This book is for Java programmers who are interested in creating a stable, efficient, and testable development environment using open source tools. We do not assume any prior knowledge of XP or the tools covered in this book, although we do assume that you know Java. The chapters generally open with simple recipes and progress to more advanced topics.

About the Recipes

This book is a collection of solutions and discussions to real-world Java programming problems. The recipes include topics such as writing JUnit tests, packaging and deploying server-side tests to application servers, and generating custom code using XDoclet. Each recipe follows the same format. A problem and brief solution is presented, followed by in-depth discussion.

You can find the code online at *http://www.oreilly.com/catalog/jextprockbk/*.

Organization

This book consists of 11 chapters, as follows:

Chapter 1, *XP Tools*
> This chapter provides a quick overview of each tool covered in this book. It also explains how the tool selection relates to XP.

Chapter 2, *XP Overview*
> This chapter explains many key concepts of XP.

Chapter 3, *Ant*
> This chapter is a beginner's overview to Ant, a portable Java alternative to *make* utilities.

Chapter 4, *JUnit*
> This chapter provides in-depth coverage of JUnit, the most popular testing framework available for Java.

Chapter 5, *HttpUnit*
> This chapter shows how to use HttpUnit for testing web applications.

Chapter 6, *Mock Objects*
> This chapter explains techniques for using mock objects for advanced testing.

Chapter 7, *Cactus*
> This chapter describes how to test servlets, filters, and JSPs running in a servlet container. This is the only tool in this book devoted to *in-container testing* (tests that execute in a running server).

Chapter 8, *JUnitPerf*
> This chapter shows how to use JUnitPerf, a simple and effective tool for writing performance tests around existing JUnit tests. This chapter also discusses how to use JUnitPerfDoclet, which is a custom XDoclet code generator created specifically for this book.

Chapter 9, *XDoclet*
> This chapter shows how to use the XDoclet code generator. In addition to showing how to generate EJB code, we show how to create a custom code generator from the ground up. This code generator is used to generate JUnitPerf tests and is aptly name JUnitPerfDoclet.

Chapter 10, *Tomcat and JBoss*

This chapter shows how to incorporate Tomcat and JBoss into an XP build environment. Tomcat is the official reference implementation of the servlet specification and JBoss is arguably the most popular open source EJB container.

Chapter 11, *Additional Topics*

This chapter introduces additional open source tools that are gaining popularity but were not quite ready for their own chapters.

Conventions Used in This Book

The following typographical conventions are used in this book:

Italic

Used for Unix and Windows commands, filenames and directory names, emphasis, and first use of a technical term.

`Constant width`

Used in code examples and to show the contents of files. Also used for Java class names, Ant task names, tags, attributes, and environment variable names appearing in the text.

`Constant width italic`

Used as a placeholder to indicate an item that should be replaced with an actual value in your program.

`Constant width bold`

Used for user input in text and in examples showing both input and output.

Comments and Questions

Please address comments and questions concerning this book to the publisher:

O'Reilly & Associates, Inc.
1005 Gravenstein Highway North
Sebastopol, CA 95472
(800) 998-9938 (in the United States or Canada)
(707) 829-0515 (international/local)
(707) 829-0104 (fax)

There is a web page for this book, which lists errata, examples, or any additional information. You can access this page at:

http://www.oreilly.com/catalog/jextprockbk/

To comment or ask technical questions about this book, send email to:

bookquestions@oreilly.com

For information about books, conferences, Resource Centers, and the O'Reilly Network, see the O'Reilly web site at:

http://www.oreilly.com

Acknowledgments

This is my third book, and I find myself consistently underestimating how much time it takes to write these things. I have to extend a big thanks to Brian for helping bring this book to completion. Without his help, I don't think I could have done this.

My family is the most important part of my life, and I want to thank Jennifer, Aidan, and Tanner for supporting and inspiring me, even though I spend way too many hours working. I love you all.

—Eric Burke, December 2002

I would like to thank Eric for bringing me on board to write this book. Without his support and trust, I would not have received this wonderful opportunity.

My Mom and Dad have provided years of support and encouragement. I appreciate everything you have done for me, and I love you both very much. Without you I would not be where I am today.

And Grandpa, you are in my heart and prayers every day. You would be so proud. I wish you were here to see this.

—Brian Coyner, December 2002

We both want to thank our editor, Mike Loukides, for helping mold this book into reality. An infinite amount of thanks goes to the tech reviewers: Kyle Cordes, Kevin Stanley, Bob Lee, Brian Button, Mark Volkmann, Mario Aquino, Mike Clark, Ara Abrahamian, and Derek Lane.

CHAPTER 1

XP Tools

This is a book about open source Java tools that complement Extreme Programming (XP) practices. In this chapter, we outline the relationship between programming tools and XP, followed by a brief introduction to the tools covered in this book. Our approach to tool selection and software development revolves around three key concepts: automation, regression testing, and consistency among developers. First, let's explain how tools relate to XP.

Java and XP

XP is a set of principles and practices that guide software development. It is an agile process in that it makes every effort to eliminate unnecessary work, instead focusing on tasks that deliver value to the customer.* XP is built upon four principles: simplicity, communication, feedback, and courage, all described in Chapter 2. The four XP principles have nothing to do with programming languages and tools. Although this book shows a set of Java tools that work nicely with XP, you are not limited to Java and these tools. XP is a language-independent software development approach.

While XP works with any language, we believe it works well with Java for a few reasons. Most important is the speed with which Java compiles. XP relies on test-first development in which programmers write tests for code before they write the code. For each new feature, you should write a test and then watch the test run and fail. You should then add the feature, compile, and watch the test run successfully. This implies that you must write a little code, compile, and run the tests frequently, perhaps dozens of times each day. Because Java compiles quickly, it is well suited to the test-first approach.

The second reason Java is a good choice for XP development is Java's wealth of tools supporting unit testing and continuous integration. JUnit, covered in Chapter 4,

---

* Check out *http://www.agilealliance.com* to learn more about agile processes.

provides a lightweight framework for writing automated unit tests. Ant, the premier build tool for Java, makes continuous integration possible even when working with large development teams. You will also find more specialized testing tools such as Cactus and HttpUnit for server-side testing.

Java's power and simplicity also make it a good language when writing code using XP. Many features of the tools outlined in this book, such as Ant tasks and JUnit's test suites, are built upon Java's reflection capability. Java's relatively easy syntax makes it easier to maintain code written by other team members, which is important for XP's concepts of pair programming, refactoring, and collective code ownership.

Tools and Philosophies

Creating great software is an art. If you ask a dozen programmers to solve a particular problem, you are likely to get a dozen radically different solutions. If you observe how these programmers reach their solutions, you will note that each programmer has her own favorite set of tools. One programmer may start by designing the application architecture using a UML CASE tool. Another may use wizards included with a fancy IDE, while another is perfectly content to use Emacs or vi.

Differences in opinion also manifest themselves at the team and company level. Some companies feel most comfortable with enterprise class commercial tools, while others are perfectly happy to build their development environment using a variety of open source tools. XP works regardless of which tools you choose, provided that your tools support continuous integration and automated unit testing. These concepts are detailed in the next chapter.

 We are very skeptical of the term "enterprise class." This tends to be a marketing ploy, and actually means "the features you really need," such as integrated support for free tools like JUnit, Ant, and CVS.

The IDE Philosophy

Many commercial IDEs focus very heavily on graphical "wizards" that help you automatically generate code, hide complexity from beginners, and deploy to application servers. If you choose such a tool, make sure it also allows for command-line operation so you can support continuous integration and automated unit testing. If you are forced to use the graphical wizards, you will be locked into that vendor's product and unable to automate your processes. We strongly recommend XDoclet, Covered in Chapter 9, for automated code generation. This is a free alternative to wizard-based code generation and does not lock you into a particular vendor's product.*

---

* XDoclet allows you to generate any kind of code and thus works with any application server.

This book does not cover commercial development environments and tools. Instead, we show how you can use free tools to build your own development environment and support XP practices. Perhaps in a sign of things to come, more and more commercial development environments now provide direct support for the open source tools covered in this book. With free IDEs like Eclipse and Netbeans growing in popularity and functionality, you will soon be hard-pressed to justify spending thousands of dollars per developer for functionality you can get for free.[*]

Minimum Tool Requirements

Regardless of whether you choose to use open source or commercial tools, XP works most effectively when your tool selection supports the concepts mentioned at the beginning of this chapter. These three concepts are automation, regression testing, and consistency among developers.

Automation

XP requires automation. In an XP project, programmers are constantly pairing up with one another and working on code from any given part of the application. The system is coded in small steps, with many builds occurring each day. You simply cannot be successful if each programmer must remember a series of manual steps in order to compile, deploy, and test different parts of the application.

People often talk about "one-button testing" in XP, meaning that you should be able to click a single button—or type a simple command like **ant junit**—in order to compile everything, deploy to the app server, and run all tests.

Automation also applies to repetitive, mundane coding tasks. You increase your chances of success by identifying repeating patterns and then writing or using tools to automatically generate code. Automation reduces chances for human error and makes coding more enjoyable because you don't have to spend so much time on the boring stuff.

Regression testing

Automated regression testing is the building block that makes XP possible, and we will spend a lot more time talking about it in the next chapter. Testing, most notably unit testing, is tightly coupled with an automated build process. In XP, each new feature is implemented along with a complementary unit test. When bugs are encountered, a test is written to expose the bug before the bug is fixed. Once the bug is fixed, the test passes.

---

[*] Both authors use IntelliJ IDEA, a commercial IDE available at *http://www.intellij.com*. Although it costs around $400, we feel its refactoring support easily adds enough productivity to justify the cost.

Tools must make it easy for programmers to write and run tests. If tests require anything more than a simple command to run, programmers will not run the tests as often as they should. JUnit makes it easy to write basic unit tests, and more specialized testing frameworks make it possible to write tests for web applications and other types of code. JUnit has been integrated with Ant for a long time, and most recent IDEs make it easy to run JUnit tests by clicking on a menu and selecting "run tests."

Consistency among developers

In a true XP environment, developers are constantly shuffling from machine-to-machine, working with new programming partners, and making changes to code throughout a system. To combat the chaos that might otherwise occur, it is essential that tools make every developer's personal build environment identical to other team members' environments. If Alex types **ant junit** and all tests pass, Andy and Rachel should also expect all tests to run when they type the same command on their own computers.

Providing a consistent environment seems obvious, but many IDEs do not support consistent configuration across a team of developers. In many cases, each developer must build his own personal project file. In this world it becomes very difficult to ensure that Andy and Rachel are using the same versions of the various JAR files for a project. Andy may be using an older version of *xalan.jar* than everyone else on the team. He may then commit changes that break the build for everyone else on the team for a few hours while they figure out the root of the problem.

Open Source Toolkit

Open source tools have been with us for a long time, but did not always enjoy widespread acceptance within the corporate environment. This has all changed in the past few years, as free tools became increasingly powerful and popular. In many cases, open source tools have no commercial equivalent. In others, commercial tools have embraced open source tools due to popular demand—although you may have to purchase the most expensive enterprise edition to get these features. This is ironic because Ant and JUnit are free.

In this section, we introduce the tools used throughout this book. While we have no reason to suggest that you avoid commercial tools, we believe you can achieve the same end result without an expensive investment in tools.

Version Control

Version control tools are an essential building block of any software development project, so much so that we assume you are familiar with the basic concepts. We do not cover any specific tool in this book; however, we do want to spend a few moments pointing out how tools like CVS fit into an XP toolkit.

CVS keeps a master copy of each file on a shared directory or server, known as the repository. The repository keeps a history of all changes to each file, allowing you to view a history of changes, recover previous revisions of files, and mark particular revisions with tag names. In a nutshell, tools like CVS allow an entire team to update and maintain files in a predictable, repeatable way.

Each programmer has a copy of the entire code base on his computer, and makes changes locally without affecting other programmers. When the current task is complete, the programmer commits the modified files back to the CVS repository. The newly revised files are then visible to other programmers, who can choose to update to the new revisions whenever they are ready.

Regardless of whether you are using CVS or some other tool, two key principles always apply. These principles are:

- Work in small steps.
- Stay in sync with the shared repository.

Because of the pair programming required by XP, working in small steps is a necessity. You cannot switch programming partners several times per day if you work on tasks that take several days to complete. A key to XP success is your ability to break down a project into smaller tasks that can be completed within a few hours. Working in small steps also helps when using CVS (or any other version control tool) because your personal workspace does not get too far out of sync with the repository.

With CVS, multiple programmers on the team may work on the same files concurrently. When this happens, you must merge changes and resolve conflicts before committing your modified code to the repository. The best way to minimize potential for conflicts is to perform frequent updates. If a programmer does not get the latest code for days and weeks at a time, she increases the likelihood of conflict with work done by other team members.

While CVS allows concurrent edits to the same files, other version control tools force programmers to lock files before making changes. While exclusive locking seems safer than concurrent editing, it can impede development if other team members are unable to make changes. Again, working in small steps is the best way to avoid problems when working with locking version control tools. If each programmer only locks a few files at a time, the likelihood of lock contention is greatly reduced.

Ant

Ant, covered in Chapter 3, is a Java replacement for platform-specific *make* utilities. Instead of a Makefile, Ant uses an XML buildfile typically named *build.xml*. This buildfile defines how source code is compiled, JAR files are built, EAR files are deployed to servers, and unit tests are executed. Ant controls all aspects of the software build process and guarantees that all developers have a common baseline environment.

In the XP model, all programmers on the team share code. Programmers work in pairs that constantly shuffle. XP shuns the idea of certain individuals owning different frameworks within a system. Instead, any programmer is allowed to work on any piece of code in the application in order to finish tasks. Shared code spreads knowledge and makes it easier for people to swap programming partners. Sharing code also coerces people into writing tests, because those tests provide a safety net when working in unfamiliar territory.

Ant is important to XP because you cannot afford to have each developer compiling different parts of the system using different system configurations. Individual classpath settings might mean that code compiles for one team member, but fails to compile for everyone else. Ant eliminates this class of problem by defining a consistent build environment for all developers.

Ant buildfiles consist of targets and tasks. Targets define how developers use the buildfile, and tasks perform the actual work, such as compiling code or running tests. You generally begin by writing a basic Ant buildfile with the following targets:

prepare
> Creates the output directories which will contain the generated *.class* files.

compile
> Compiles all Java source code into the executable.

clean
> Removes the build directory and all generated files, such as *.class* files.

junit
> Searches for all unit tests in the directory structure and runs them. Tests are files following the *Test*.java* naming convention.*

This is a good start, and will certainly be expanded upon later. A critical feature of this Ant buildfile is the fact that it should define its own classpath internally. This way, individual developers' environment variable settings do not cause unpredictable builds for other developers. You should add the Ant buildfile to your version control tool and write a few simple classes to confirm that it runs successfully.

The other developers on the team then get the Ant buildfile from the version control repository and use it on their own computers. We also recommend that you place all required JAR files into version control,† thus allowing the Ant buildfile to reference those JAR files from a standard location.

---

* You can adopt whatever naming convention you wish; we chose *Test*.java* for this book.

† You normally don't put generated code into CVS, but third-party JAR files are not generated by you. Instead, they are resources required to build your software, just like source files.

JUnit

Automated unit testing is one of the most important facets of XP and a central theme throughout this book. JUnit tests are written by programmers and are designed to test individual modules. They must be designed to execute without human interaction. JUnit is not intended to be a complete framework for all types of testing. In particular, JUnit is not well-suited for high-level integration testing.

Instead, JUnit is a programmer-level framework for writing unit tests in Java. Programmers extend from the TestCase base class and write individual unit tests following a simple naming convention. These tests are then organized into test suites and executed using a text or graphical test runner.

JUnit is a simple framework for writing tests, and it is easily extended. In fact, JUnit is the starting point for several of the other testing tools covered in this book. From one perspective, the JUnit API is a framework for building other, more sophisticated testing frameworks and tools.

Tools like CVS, JUnit, and Ant become more powerful when everyone on the team uses them consistently. You might want to talk to the other programmers on your team and come up with a set of guidelines for adding new features to your application. The following list shows one such approach for adding a new feature to a system:

1. Update your PC with the latest source files from the CVS repository. This minimizes the chance of conflicts once you are finished.
2. Write a unit test using JUnit. Try to execute one facet of the new functionality that does not yet exist. Or, write a test to expose a bug that you are trying to fix.
3. Run the test using JUnit and Ant by typing **ant junit**. The junit Ant target is defined with a dependency on the compile target, so all code is automatically compiled.
4. After watching the test fail, write some code to make the test pass.
5. Run the test again by typing **ant junit**. Repeat steps 2–5 until the task is complete and all tests pass. The task is complete when you have written tests for anything you think might break and all tests pass.
6. Perform another CVS update to ensure you are up-to-date with all recent changes. This is a critical step because the CVS repository may have changed while you were working on your task.
7. Run **ant clean junit** in order to perform a full build.
8. If all code compiles and all tests pass, commit changes to CVS and move to the next task. Otherwise, go back and fix whatever broke before committing changes to CVS.

It is important for every developer to follow these steps, because you are using XP and practicing pair programming. Each of the team members takes turn pair programming with another person and each of you is allowed to make changes to any part of the code. Because you are all constantly updating a shared code base, you rely on the suite of automated unit tests along with a consistent build environment to immediately catch errors.

Provided everyone follows the process, it is generally easy to fix problems when a test starts failing. Because all tests passed before you made your changes, you can assume that the most recent change broke the test. If you work in small steps, the problem is usually (but not always!) easy to fix.

On the other hand, things get really ugly when a programmer commits changes to CVS without first running the tests. If that programmer's change broke a test, then all other programmers on the team begin to see test failures. They assume that they broke the test, and waste time debugging their own code. For a team of ten programmers, this may mean that ten programmers spend one hour each tracking down the problem, only to find that it wasn't their fault in the first place. Had that first programmer run the tests locally, he may have been able to fix the problem in a few minutes rather than wasting ten hours.*

HttpUnit and Cactus

HttpUnit, covered in Chapter 5, is a framework for testing web applications. HttpUnit isn't built with JUnit; however, you do use JUnit when testing with HttpUnit. Http-Unit tests execute entirely on the client machine and access a web server by sending HTTP requests. In this fashion, HttpUnit simulates a web browser hitting a web site. Although you typically use JUnit when working with HttpUnit, the tests you write are more correctly considered "functional" tests rather than "unit" tests. This is because HttpUnit can only test a web application from the outside view, instead of unit-testing individual classes and methods.

A closely related tool is Cactus, covered in Chapter 7. Cactus is significantly more complicated than HttpUnit, and is built on top of JUnit. Cactus tests allow for true unit testing of web applications, with specific types of tests for servlets, JSPs, and servlet filters. Unlike HttpUnit, Cactus tests execute on both client and server—simultaneously. The client portion of the test acts something like a web browser, issuing requests to the server portion of the test that acts more like a unit test. The server then sends a response back to the client portion that then interprets the results.

Cactus can also make use of the HttpUnit library for parsing the HTML output from web applications. We'll see how this works in Chapter 7.

---

* If the shared code base breaks frequently, programmers may begin to ignore the errors. This causes a snowball effect when they quit running tests and check in even more bad code. Pair programming helps avoid these breakdowns in diligence.

JUnitPerf

JUnitPerf, as you might expect, is a performance-testing tool built on top of JUnit. In Chapter 8, we show how to use JUnitPerf to ensure that unit tests execute within certain time limits and can handle expected usage loads. JUnitPerf does not help you find performance problems. Instead, it ensures that tests run within predefined performance limits.

You will often use JUnitPerf to complement commercial profiling tools. You may use a profiling tool to isolate performance bottlenecks in your code. Once you have fixed the bottleneck, you write a JUnitPerf test to ensure the code runs within acceptable time limits. The JUnitPerf test is then automated, and will fail if someone changes code and makes the code slow again. At this point, you probably go back to the profiling tool to locate the cause of the problem.

Application Servers

We round out our overview of tools with a brief mention of two open source server tools, JBoss and Tomcat. JBoss is a free application server supporting EJB, while Tomcat is a servlet and JSP container. The recipes in this book do not show how to use these tools in detail. Instead, we describe how to configure JBoss and Tomcat in order to support automated testing and continuous integration.

The kind of automation we are interested in occurs when you compile code and run tests. As mentioned earlier, you should strive for a simple command that compiles your code and then runs all of your tests. When working with an application server, typing a command like **ant junit** may actually do the following:

1. Compile all code.
2. Build a WAR file.
3. Start Tomcat if it is not already running.
4. Deploy the new WAR file.
5. Run all unit tests, including those written using HttpUnit.
6. Display a summary of the test results.

Setting Up a Build Server

At some point, your team will probably decide to create a build server. This is a shared machine that performs a clean build of the software on a continuous basis. The build server ensures that your application always compiles and that all tests run. The build server is easy to set up if you have been using CVS and Ant all along. For the most part, the build server operates exactly like each developer's PC. At various intervals throughout the day, the build server gets a clean copy of the code, builds the application, and runs the test suite.

Over time, however, you may want to make the build server more sophisticated. For instance, you might want the build server to monitor the CVS repository for changes. The build can start after some files have changed, but should not do so immediately. Instead, it should wait for a brief period of inactivity. The server can then get a clean copy of the sources using a timestamp from sometime during the inactive period. This process ensures that the build server is not getting code while programmers are committing changes to the repository.

You might also want to keep a change log of who changes what between each build, in order to notify the correct developers whenever the build succeeds or fails. We have found that notifying the entire team whenever a build fails is not a good idea because people begin to ignore the messages. With a change log, you can notify only those people who actually made changes. The developer process then begins to look like this:

- Make a change, following all of the steps outlined earlier.[*]
- Commit changes to CVS.
- Wait for an email from the build server indicating whether the build succeeds or fails.

There is a tool that does everything just described. It is called Cruise Control, and is available at *http://cruisecontrol.sourceforge.net*. Cruise Control works in conjunction with Ant, CVS, and JUnit to perform continuous builds on a server machine. The exact mechanics of setting up a build server vary widely depending on what version-control tool you use, whether you are using Linux or Windows, and what steps are required to build your particular application. The important thing to keep in mind is that builds should become a seamless part of everyday activity on an XP project, ensuring that developers can work without constantly stopping to figure out how to compile software and integrate changes with other team members.

---

[*] In theory, the build shouldn't break if every developer follows the process before checking in code. We have found, however, that people occasionally "break the build" no matter how careful they are. An automated build server helps catch problems right away.

CHAPTER 2

XP Overview

This chapter provides a quick introduction to the key programming-related XP activities. These activities are the aspects of XP that affect programmers the most.

XP encompasses much more than programming techniques. XP is a complete approach to software development, including strategies for planning, gathering user requirements, and everything else necessary to develop complete applications. Understanding these strategies is essential if you wish to base an entire project on XP.

What Is XP?

XP is based on four key principles: simplicity, communication, feedback, and courage. This section introduces each principle, and the remainder of this chapter touches on each concept where appropriate.

Simplicity

Simplicity is the heart of XP. Applying the principle of simplicity affects everything you do, and profoundly impacts your ability to successfully apply XP. Focusing on simple designs minimizes the risk of spending a long time designing sophisticated frameworks that the customer may not want. Keeping code simple makes changing code easier as the requirements inevitably change. In addition, adopting simple techniques for communicating requirements and tracking progress maximizes chances that the team will actually follow the process. Most importantly, focusing on simple solutions to today's problems minimizes the cost of change over time. Figure 2-1 shows that the intended result of XP practices is to tame the cost of change curve, making it increase much less over time than we would otherwise expect.

Traditional theory argues that software becomes increasingly expensive to change over the lifetime of a project. The theory is that it is ten times harder to fix a mistake of requirements when you are in the design phase, and 100 times harder to make changes late in a project during the coding phase. There are many reasons. For one,

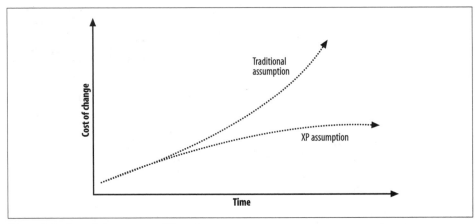

Figure 2-1. Cost of change on an XP project

there is more code to change as time goes on. If the design is not simple, one change can affect many other parts of the system. Over time, as more and more programmers change the system, it becomes increasingly complex and hard to understand.

The XP approach recognizes that the cost of change *generally* increases like one would expect, but this increase is not *inevitable*. If you constantly refactor and keep your code simple, you can avoid ever-increasing complexity. Writing a full suite of unit tests is another tool at your disposal, as described later in this chapter. With complete regression testing, you have the ability to make big changes late in the development cycle with confidence. Without these tests, the cost of change does increase because you have to manually test everything else that you may have just broken.

There are other forces in XP projects that balance the rising cost of change. For example, collective code ownership and pair programming ensure that the longer an XP project goes, the better and deeper understanding the whole team has of the whole system.

Communication

Communication comes in many forms. For programmers, code communicates best when it is simple. If it is too complex, you should strive to simplify it until the code is understandable. Although source code comments are a good way to describe code, self-documenting code is a more reliable form of documentation because comments often become out of sync with source code.

Unit tests are another form of communication. XP requires that unit tests be written for a vast majority of the code in a system. Since the unit tests exercise the classes and methods in your application, source code for the tests become a critical part of the system's documentation. Unit tests communicate the design of a class effectively, because the tests show concrete examples of how to exercise the class's functionality.

Programmers constantly communicate with one another because they program in pairs. Pair programming means that two programmers sit at a single computer for all coding tasks; the two share a keyboard, mouse, and CPU. One does the typing while the other thinks about design issues, offers suggestions for additional tests, and validates ideas. The two roles swap often; there is no set observer in a pair.

The customer and programmer also communicate constantly. XP requires an on-site customer to convey the requirements to the team. The customer decides which features are most important, and is always available to answer questions.

Feedback

Having an on-site customer is a great way to get immediate feedback about the project status. XP encourages short release cycles, generally no longer than two weeks. Consider the problems when the customer only sees new releases of your software every few months or so. With that much time in between major feature releases, customers cannot offer real-time feedback to the programming team. Months of work may be thrown away because customers changed their minds, or because the programmers did not deliver what was expected.

With a short release cycle, the customer is able to evaluate each new feature as it is developed, minimizing the necessity to rework and helping the programmers focus on what is most important to the customer. The customer always defines which features are the most important, so the most valuable features are delivered early in the project. Customers are assured that they can cancel the project at any time and have a working system with the features that they value the most.

Code can offer feedback to programmers, and this is where good software development tools shine. In XP, you use unit tests to get immediate feedback on the quality of your code. You run all of the unit tests after each change to source code. A broken test provides immediate feedback that the most recent change caused something in the system to break. After fixing the problem, you check your change into version control and build the entire system, perhaps using a tool like Ant.

Courage

The concepts that were just described seem like common sense, so you might be wondering why it takes so much courage to try out XP. For managers, the concept of pair programming can be hard to accept—it seems like productivity will drop by 50%, because only half of the programmers are writing code at any given time. It takes courage to trust that pair programming improves quality without slowing down progress.[*]

---

[*] Check out *http://www.pairprogramming.com* for more information on the benefits of pair programming.

Focusing on simplicity is one of the hardest facets of XP for programmers to adopt. It takes courage to implement the feature the customer is asking for today using a simple approach, because you probably want to build in flexibility to account for tomorrow's features, as well. Avoid this temptation. You cannot afford to work on sophisticated frameworks for weeks or months while the customer waits for the next release of your application.* When this happens, the customer does not receive any feedback that you are making progress. You do not receive feedback from the customer that you are even working on the right feature!

Now, let's look at several specific concepts behind XP in more detail.

Coding

Coding is an art, and XP acknowledges that. Your success at XP depends largely on your love of coding. Without good code, the exponential cost of change as shown in Figure 2-1 is inevitable. Let's look at some specific ways that XP helps keep code simple.

One of the most frustrating misconceptions about XP is that it is a chaotic approach to software development that caters to hackers. The opposite is true. XP works best with meticulous, detail-oriented programmers who take great pride in their code.

Simplicity

Just getting code to work is not good enough, because the first solution you come up with is hardly ever the simplest possible solution. Your methods may be too long, which makes them harder to test. You may have duplicated functionality, or you may have tightly coupled classes. Complex code is hard to understand and hard to modify, because every little change may break something else in the system. As a system grows, complexity can become overwhelming to the point where your only remaining option is to start over.

When compared to beginners, expert programmers typically implement superior solutions using fewer lines of code. This is a hint that simplicity is harder than complexity, and takes time to master.

Simple code is self-documenting because you pick meaningful names, your methods are concise, and your classes have clearly defined responsibilities. Simple code is hard to achieve, and relies on knowledge in the areas of object-oriented programming, design patterns, and other facets of software engineering.

---

* The best frameworks usually evolve instead of being designed from scratch. Let refactoring be the mechanism for framework development.

Comments

If code is self-documenting, do you need source code comments? In short, there will always be cases where you need comments, but you should never write comments simply for the sake of commenting. If the meaning of a method is completely obvious, you do not need a comment. An abundance of comments in code is often an indication that the code is unclear and in need of refactoring. Let's look at a method that needs a comment, and see how to eliminate this need.

```
/**
 * Sets the value of x.
 * @param x the horizontal position in pixels.
 */
public void setX(int x) {
    this.x = x;
}
```

This method needs a comment because the meaning of "x" is not entirely clear. Over time, the comment might not be kept in sync if someone changes the method's implementation or signature. But what if we rename things to make the code more clear? How about this:

```
public void setXPixelPosition(int xPixelPosition) {
    this.xPixelPosition = xPixelPosition;
}
```

This code no longer needs a comment because it is self-documenting. As a result, we end up typing a little bit more for the method declaration, but save a few lines of comments. This helps us out in the long run because we don't have to spend time and effort keeping the comment in sync with the code. Long method names do not degrade performance in any appreciable way, and are easy to use thanks to code-completion features found in any modern IDE.

Pair Programming

As mentioned earlier, XP teams work in pairs. These pairs of programmers share a single computer, keyboard, and mouse. Having dual monitors is a good idea because both programmers can then see the screen clearly, although this is not a requirement. Desks should be configured so that two people can sit side-by-side comfortably, and the entire team should work in the same room.

Here is how pair programming works:

1. You pick out a user story* for your next task.
2. You ask for help from another programmer.

---

* A *user story* is a requirement from the customer. Stories are typically written on index cards, and the customer decides which stories are the most important.

3. The two of you work together on a small piece of functionality.
   - Try to work on small tasks that take a few hours.
   - After the immediate task is complete, pick a different partner or offer to help someone else.

By working on small tasks, partners rotate frequently. This method facilitates communication between team members and spreads knowledge. As mentioned earlier, writing simple code is hard, and experienced programmers are generally better at it. By pairing people together, beginners can gain valuable coding experience from the experts.

Pair programming is critical because XP requires a very high degree of discipline in order to be successful. As we will learn in the next section, programmers must write unit tests for each new feature added to the application. Writing tests takes a great deal of patience and self-discipline, so having a partner often keeps you honest. When you start to get lazy about writing tests, it is the partner's job to grab the keyboard and take over.

When you have control of the keyboard, you are thinking about the code at a very fine-grained level of detail. When you are not the partner doing the typing, you have time to think about the problem at a higher level of abstraction. The observer should look for ways to simplify the code, and think about additional unit tests. Your job is to help your partner think through problems and ultimately write better code.

Collective Code Ownership

XP teams do not practice individual code ownership. Every team member is able to work on any piece of code in the application, depending upon the current task. The ability to work on any piece of code in an application makes sense when pairs of programmers are constantly shuffling and re-pairing throughout the day. Over time, most of the programmers see and work on code throughout the application.

Collective code ownership works because you can always ask someone else for help when you work on unfamiliar classes. It also works because you have a safety net of unit tests. If you make a change that breaks something, a unit test should catch the error before you and your partner integrate the change into the build. The tests also serve as great documentation when you are working with unfamiliar code.

Collective ownership facilitates communication among team members, avoiding situations where the entire team depends on the one person who understands the custom table sorting and filtering framework. The shared ownership model also encourages higher quality, because programmers know that other team members will soon be looking at their code and potentially making changes.

Coding Standards

Collective code ownership and pair programming ensure that all team members are constantly looking at each other's code. This is problematic when some programmers follow radically different coding conventions. Your team should agree on a consistent set of coding conventions in order to minimize the learning curve when looking at each other's code.

Picking coding conventions can turn into a bitter argument, as programmers become very attached to their personal style. It's ironic, because code style has absolutely no bearing on the functionality of the compiled application.

 Consider using a code-formatting tool that automatically formats code according to your team standards.

If everyone on your team is agreeable, coding standards might be a non-issue. Otherwise, either try to hammer out an agreement or select an industry standard set of conventions such as the JavaSoft coding guidelines.* You might be able to win people over by adopting standards written by a neutral party.

Code Inspections

Code inspections are a great technique for validating the quality of code. In typical projects, programmers work in isolation for several weeks, and then present their code to a group of peers for a formal inspection meeting. People often talk about how great code inspections are, but procrastinate until the last minute. At this point, it is generally too late to inspect everything and it might be too late to make changes if you find problems.

Code inspections are a valuable tool, so why not inspect code constantly? XP teams do not rely on formal code inspections, primarily because all of the code is constantly reviewed as it is developed by pairs of programmers. As programmers migrate to new partners and work on different parts of the system, code is constantly enhanced and refactored by people other than the original author.

Unit Testing

A unit test is a programmer-written test for a single piece of functionality in an application. Unit tests should be fine grained, testing small numbers of closely-related methods and classes. Unit tests should not test high-level application functionality.

---

* The examples in this book follow JavaSoft coding guidelines, available at *http://java.sun.com/docs/codeconv/html/CodeConvTOC.doc.html/*.

Testing application functionality is called *acceptance testing*, and acceptance tests should be designed by people who understand the business problem better than the programmers.

Why Test?

XP cannot be done without unit testing. Unit tests build confidence that the code works correctly. Tests also provide the safety net enabling pairs of programmers to make changes to any piece of code in the system without fear. Making changes to code written by someone else takes courage, because you might not be familiar with all of the ins-and-outs of the original solution.

Imagine a scenario in which you are presented with a legacy payroll application consisting of 50,000 lines of code and zero unit tests. You have been asked to change the way that part-time employee salaries are computed, due to a recent change in the tax laws. After making the change, how can you be confident that you did not introduce a bug somewhere else in the system? In a traditional model, you hand the application to a quality assurance team that manually tests everything they can think of.* Hopefully, everybody gets the correct paycheck next month.

Now imagine the XP scenario. If the original development team used XP, each class would have a suite of automated unit tests. Before you make your change, you run all of the unit tests to ensure they pass. You then write a new unit test for your new payroll calculation feature. This new test fails, because you have not written the new feature yet. You then implement the new feature and run all of the tests again.

Once all of the tests pass, you check in your code and feel confident that you did not break something else while making the improvement.† This is called test-driven development, and it is how XP teams operate.

Who Writes Unit Tests?

Programmers write unit tests. Unit tests are designed to test individual methods and classes, and are too technical for nonprogrammers to write. It is assumed that programmers know their code better than anyone else, and should be able to anticipate more of the problems that might occur.

Not all programmers are good at anticipating problems. This is another example of the benefit of pair programming. While one partner writes code, the other is thinking of devious ways to break the code. These ideas turn into additional unit tests.

---

* Most companies would like to have dedicated QA teams, but few of these teams seem to exist. XP requires that programmers take on more responsibility for testing their own code.

† This confidence is justified because of the extensive test suite.

What Tests Are Written?

Unit tests should be written for any code that is hard to understand, and for any method that has a nontrivial implementation. You should write tests for anything that might break, which could mean just about everything.

So what don't you test? This comes down to a judgment call. Having pairs of people working together increases the likelihood that tests are actually written, and gives one team member time to think about more tests while the other writes the code. Some would argue that tests do not have to be written for absolutely trivial code, but keep in mind that today's trivial code has a tendency to change over time, and you will be thankful that you have tests in place when those changes occur.

There will always be scenarios where you simply cannot write tests. GUI code is notoriously difficult to test, although Chapter 4 offers recipes for testing Swing GUIs using JUnit. In these cases, your programming partner should push you to think hard and make sure you really cannot think of a way to write a test.

Testing New Features

XP teams write tests before each new feature is added to the system. Here is the test-driven process:

1. Run the suite of unit tests for the entire project, ensuring that they all pass.
2. Write a unit test for the new feature.
3. You probably have to stub out the implementation in order to get your test to compile.
4. Run the test and observe its failure.
5. Implement the new feature.
6. Run the test again and observe its success.

At this point, you have tested one facet of your new feature. You and your programming partner should now think of another test, and follow this process:

1. Write another test for some aspect of the new function that might break, such as an illegal method argument.
2. Run all of your tests.
3. Fix the code if necessary, and repeat until you cannot think of any more tests.

Once your new feature is fully tested, it is time to run the entire suite of unit tests for the entire project. Regression testing ensures that your new code did not inadvertently break someone else's code. If some other test fails, you immediately know that you just broke it. You must fix all of the tests before you can commit your changes to the repository.

Testing Bugs

You also write unit tests when bugs are reported. The process is simple:

1. Write a test that exposes the bug.
2. Run the test suite and observe the test failure.
3. Fix the bug.
4. Run the test suite again, observing the test succeeding.

This is simple and highly effective. Bugs commonly occur in the most complicated parts of your system, so these tests are often the most valuable tests you come up with. It is very likely that the same bug will occur later, but the next time will be covered because of the test you just wrote.

How Do You Write Tests?

All tests must be pass/fail style tests. This means that you should never rely on a guru to interpret the test results. Consider this test output:

```
Now Testing Person.java:
First Name: Tanner
Last Name: Burke
Age: 1
```

Did this test pass or fail? You cannot know unless you are a "guru" who knows the system inside and out, and know what to look for. Or you have to dig through source code to find out what those lines of text are supposed to be. Here is a much-improved form of test output:

```
Now Testing Person.java:
    Failure: Expected Age 2, but was 1 instead.
```

Once all of your tests are pass/fail, you can group them together into test suites. Here is some imaginary output from a test suite:

```
Now Testing Person.java:
    Failure: Expected Age 2, but was 1 instead
Now Testing Account.java:
    Passed!
Now Testing Deposit.java:
    Passed!
Summary: 2 tests passed, 1 failed.
```

This is a lot better! Now we can set up our Ant buildfile to run the entire test suite as part of our hourly build, so we have immediate feedback if any test fails. We can even instruct Ant to mail the test results to the entire team should any test fail.

Writing effective tests takes practice, just like any other skill. Here are a few tips for writing effective tests:

- Test for boundary conditions. For instance, check the minimum and maximum indices for arrays and lists. Also check indices that are just out of range.
- Test for illegal inputs to methods.
- Test for null strings and empty strings. Also test strings containing unexpected whitespace.

Unit Tests Always Pass

The entire suite of unit tests must always pass at 100% before any code is checked in to the source repository. This ensures that each programming pair can develop new features with confidence. Why? Because when you change some code and a test starts to fail, you know that it was your change that caused the failure. On the other hand, if only 98% of the unit tests passed before you started making changes, how can you be confident that your changes are not causing some of the tests to fail?

Testing Improves Design

Writing good unit tests forces you to think more about your design. For GUIs, you must keep business logic clearly separated from GUI code if you have any hope of testing it. In this respect, the tests force you to write independent, modular code.

Writing tests also leads you to write simpler methods. Methods that perform four calculations are hard to test. But testing four methods, each of which performs a single calculation, is straightforward. Not only is the testing easier when your methods are concise—the methods become easier to read because they are short.

Acceptance Testing

When you need to test high-level application functionality, turn to acceptance testing. This sort of testing is driven by the customer, although they will probably need help from a programmer to implement the tests.

Unit or Acceptance Tests?

If you find that your unit tests require lots of complex initialization logic, or they have numerous dependencies that are making it hard for you to change code without rewriting your tests, you may have actually written acceptance tests, rather than unit tests.

Unit tests should test very fine-grained functionality, such as individual classes and methods. As your unit tests grow more and more complex, they start to take on the flavor of acceptance tests instead of unit tests. While these kinds of tests are valuable, it is hard to ensure that they run at 100% success because they have so many dependencies.

Like unit tests, acceptance tests should be designed to pass or fail, and they should be as automated as possible. Unlike unit tests, however, acceptance tests do not have to pass at 100%. Since programmers do not run the suite of acceptance tests with each and every change, it is likely that acceptance tests will occasionally fail. It is also likely that the acceptance tests will be created before all of the functionality is written.

The customer uses acceptance tests for quality assurance and release planning. When the customer deems that the critical acceptance tests are passing to their satisfaction, which is probably 100%, the application can be considered finished.

Refactoring

Refactoring* is the practice of improving the design of code without breaking its functionality. In order to keep code simple and prevent the cost of making changes from skyrocketing, you must constantly refactor. This keeps your code as simple as possible.

Here is a simple refactoring. Suppose you have this code:

```
public class Person {
    private String firstName;
    public void setFirst(String n) {
        this.firstName = n;
    }
}
```

This code can be improved by picking a better argument name, changing n to firstName:

```
public class Person {
    private String firstName;
    public void setFirst(String firstName) {
        this.firstName = firstName;
    }
}
```

The code can be improved even further by renaming the method to setFirstName():

```
public class Person {
    private String firstName;
    public void setFirstName(String firstName) {
        this.firstName = firstName;
    }
}
```

The method has been refactored and is now more easily understandable. Of course, changing the method name requires you to change all references to the method

---

* See *Refactoring: Improving the Design of Existing Code* by Martin Fowler, et al. (Addison-Wesley).

throughout your application. This is where a good IDE can help out, because it can identify all usages and update the calls automatically.

Goals

You refactor code to make it simpler. Each individual refactoring introduces a small improvement; however, these small improvements add up over time. By constantly striving to keep code as concise and as simple as possible the cost of making changes to an application does not rise so dramatically over time.

Removing duplication is another goal of refactoring that deserves mention. Duplicated logic is almost always harder to maintain because changes must be made to more than one part of the system as it evolves. We have found that duplicated logic is often a signal that code should be refactored and simplified.

Without refactoring, complexity inevitably increases as more and more features are tacked onto a system. Increasing complexity is known as entropy, and is a fundamental reason why the cost of change increases over time. Our goal is to stave off entropy as long as possible through constant refactoring.

When to Refactor

You should refactor constantly, throughout the lifetime of a project. Your customer and manager will not ask you to refactor your code, just like they probably won't ask you to write unit tests. Instead, this is a practice that must be engrained into your daily routine. Each time you fix a bug or add a new feature, look for overly complex code. Look for chunks of logic that are duplicated and refactor them into a shared method. Try to rename methods and arguments so they make sense, and try to migrate poorly designed code towards better usage of design patterns.

Writing unit tests is a great way to identify portions of code that need refactoring. When you write tests for a class, your test is a client of that class. You will have first-hand experience using the class, and will be the first to realize when the API is overly complicated. Use this opportunity to refactor the API and make it simple to use.

How to Refactor

Refactoring works hand-in-hand with automated unit testing. Before you refactor code, make sure you have a working unit test on hand. Assuming that the test works before the refactoring effort, it should also work after you are done refactoring. This process is similar to any new feature or bug fix that you put into the system:

1. Make sure you have a working unit test for the feature you are about to refactor.
2. Do the refactoring, or a portion of the refactoring.
3. Run the test again to ensure you did not break anything.
4. Repeat steps 2–4 until you are finished with the refactoring.

Refactoring Tools

Most new IDEs on the market offer rudimentary support for refactoring, and this is constantly improving. Some key features to look for include:

- The ability to rapidly find usages for fields, methods, and classes. This ability makes it easier for you to determine what will break if you start changing things.

- The ability to automatically rename fields, methods, classes, and other entities. All references to those items should be updated automatically.

- The ability to automatically convert a selected block of code into a method call. This is called *Extract Method* in most refactoring tools.

These are just the tip of the iceberg. Many tools already do much more than this.

Design

XP does not encourage a lot of up-front design. Instead, the XP approach recognizes that humans cannot accurately design every single feature of an application before writing code. So why not design a little bit right away and then write the code immediately? As a result, your customer can get his or her hands on some working software right away.

XP practitioners typically obsess about good design, taking it much more seriously than other developers. They simply have a different point of view on when to do it—all the time, instead of all at the beginning.

Design Today's Features

Customers define which features are most important, and programmers work on those features first. As each new feature is implemented, the application is delivered to customers and they have the opportunity to offer immediate feedback.

In this customer-centric delivery model, we do not have time to spend months and months of time doing detailed design and analysis. We also cannot afford to develop complex frameworks to accommodate every anticipated feature. If we did either of these things, we would not be able to deliver working code (and thus get feedback) to the customer in a timely fashion.

Figure 2-2 shows the relationship between time-to-customer and the likelihood that the finished product does not meet expectations. Stated simply, the longer you work in a vacuum without getting feedback from your customer, the higher the probability is that you will develop the wrong features.

This is where courage comes back into the picture. The best developers may have the most trouble accepting the fact that they should not worry so much about framework development. Instead, they should worry more about writing exactly what the

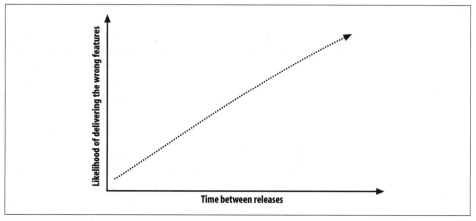

Figure 2-2. Strive for short release cycles

customer wants today, along with extensive unit tests. The code may or may not be reusable, but we can resolve that later using refactoring techniques.

Simple Design

People on XP teams use a lot of index cards and whiteboards. Since you are only working on one small feature at a time, you rarely have to develop complex design models. Instead, you come up with a good design for the feature you are working on, and then you write your unit tests and code.

When you move on to the next feature, you do additional design work if necessary. The original design documents are generally not useful, because code can change and people rarely bother to keep design documents in sync with code, anyway. The code itself is the most reliable design document in existence. The next best thing is the unit tests, because they show how to use your code.

UML

Unified Modeling Language (UML) can be used on XP projects, but only to the extent that it helps you deliver requested features to customers. A UML class diagram can make it far easier to visualize the static relationship between classes, and a sequence diagram can make dynamic behavior much easier to see. The point is to make programming tasks easier, and nothing more. If you need to use UML to design the feature you are working on right now, then by all means work on that UML. But far too many project teams spend inordinate amounts of time perfecting diagram after diagram, only to find that the customer changed his mind after seeing the finished product.

UML tools

If you really want up-to-date UML diagrams, consider tools like JBuilder Enterprise Studio, Together Control Center, or Rational XDE. These types of tools can reverse-engineer your code and produce UML diagrams. These tools ensure that the diagrams stay in sync with your code. XP encourages you to throw away UML diagrams once you have written your code. With these tools, you can generate correct, current UML any time it is needed.

Whiteboards and scratch paper

You don't need fancy, expensive UML diagramming tools. A stack of index cards, a whiteboard, or even a scrap of paper can serve as a surprisingly effective design tool. Here is the process:

1. Draw a diagram.
2. Write a unit test.
3. Write some code.
4. Repeat steps 2–3 until the feature is complete.
5. Throw away the diagram.

This may seem silly, but think back to the last project you worked on where a lot of diagrams were created. When you encountered a bug in the application, did you generally turn to diagrams first, or look at the code? XP assumes that most programmers rely on the code, because diagrams do not present enough detail and manually updated diagrams are almost always out of date with respect to the actual code.

Throwing away diagrams does not imply that you throw away the "design." The design itself is embodied in the working code, and can only be thrown away if the code is erased.

Builds

A good build environment is essential to XP teams. Constant refactoring, collective code ownership, and ever-changing pair programming teams require that each developer have the ability to reliably build the software using an identical configuration. If this is not the case, then tests that pass for one developer may fail for everyone else.

Continuous Integration

Continuous integration means that XP teams build the software application frequently, often several times per day. In fact, the Cruise Control tool (mentioned in Chapter 1) performs a complete build of the application after every check-in to version control.

After you and your programming partner have finished a task, you should integrate your changes with the shared source code repository. This means that you check in your changes to your version control tool, run a complete build, and run all of the unit tests. If any tests fail, you fix them right away.

Since you probably build your application many times per day, you won't have any trouble when it comes time to deliver a build to your customer. For this task, you might want to define a script that copies the latest build to a "stable" build directory of some sort. This gives the customers a stable playground from which to run and test the application while the programmers continue with their day-to-day coding and builds.

There is no reason why automated builds should not go all the way to a customer deliverable. For example, if you are building a shrink-wrap product, going all the way to an installation CD image is not a bad idea. The desire to create completely automated build processes is very much in tune with the desire to create automated test suites. Taking manual, human-controlled steps out of the process improves quality and lets you focus on delivering features to customers rather than working on mundane software compilation steps.

Small Tasks

Continuous integration works best when pairs of programmers work on small tasks. Once each task is tested and implemented, it should be integrated with the main build as soon as possible. This is the best way to ensure that all of the team members are in sync with one another.

When programmers get sidetracked on large, complex tasks, they fall out of sync with the rest of the team. You should avoid situations where you have dozens of files checked out for days and weeks at a time. If this happens often, it may be an indication that you are not integrating often enough. Or, it may suggest that changes to one class are forcing changes in many other classes throughout the system. It could be time for some refactoring to break the dependencies.

CHAPTER 3
Ant

3.0 Introduction

Ant is a portable, Java-based build tool designed to support software builds—and many other tasks—on any platform supporting Java. An XML file known as a *build-file* specifies which *tasks* Ant follows when building your project. Ant ships with well over 100 tasks that perform operations ranging from compiling code to playing sound files when a build finishes. Java classes implement Ant tasks that can do anything Java can do. The Ant API is open and designed for extensibility; you can write your own custom tasks if the need arises.

A good build tool like Ant is critical to any successful XP implementation. You cannot expect a team of programmers to constantly refactor their code, run unit tests, and integrate their changes without a fast, predictable build environment. Consider the problems that occur when one of the programmers on a team has a newer version of a JAR file on his classpath. Unit tests may pass on his machine, but fail for everyone else. Ant helps avoid this sort of problem by clearly defining the files the project depends on, and the steps are followed to perform the build.

Build times must be kept to a minimum and Ant excels in this area. XP assumes that programmers write a lot of small, incremental pieces of code. Programmers must compile and run all unit tests after making each small change; therefore, the build needs to be fast. When builds are slow, programmers are discouraged from the constant refactoring and testing that XP demands. Ant helps performance in several ways:

- Most tasks only do their work if files are out of date. For example, code is only compiled when *.java* files are newer than their corresponding *.class* files.

- In most cases, individual build steps execute in the same JVM. Ant is written in Java and efficiently invokes many tools, such as the Java compiler, through direct method calls rather than spawning new processes.

- Ant tasks use a simple pattern-matching syntax to locate files quickly, allowing you to write buildfiles that perform work on the correct subset of a source tree for the job at hand.

Ant is available from the Apache Software Foundation at *http://jakarta.apache.org/ant*. Because Ant has so many tasks, the recipes in this chapter cannot describe them all. Instead, we show the most common aspects of Ant buildfiles followed by specific discussion of the tasks most directly related to XP.

3.1 Writing a Basic Buildfile

Problem

You want to write a basic Ant buildfile.

Solution

Example 3-1 lists a simple Ant buildfile that you may use as a boilerplate for your own projects.

Example 3-1. Boilerplate Ant buildfile

```xml
<?xml version="1.0"?>
<project name="Template Buildfile" default="compile" basedir=".">
  <property name="dir.src" value="src"/>
  <property name="dir.build" value="build"/>
  <property name="dir.dist" value="dist"/>

  <!-- Creates the output directories -->
  <target name="prepare">
    <mkdir dir="${dir.build}"/>
    <mkdir dir="${dir.dist}"/>
  </target>

  <target name="clean"
          description="Remove all generated files.">
    <delete dir="${dir.build}"/>
    <delete dir="${dir.dist}"/>
  </target>

  <target name="compile" depends="prepare"
          description="Compile all source code.">
    <javac srcdir="${dir.src}" destdir="${dir.build}"/>
  </target>

  <target name="jar" depends="compile"
          description="Generates oreilly.jar in the 'dist' directory.">
    <jar jarfile="${dir.dist}/oreilly.jar"
         basedir="${dir.build}"/>
  </target>
</project>
```

Discussion

You generally call this file *build.xml*, and can put it anywhere you like. In our example, the buildfile is found in the directory containing the *src* directory. The <project> tag is found in all buildfiles:

```
<project name="Template Buildfile" default="compile" basedir=".">
```

The project name should be something descriptive, as this may show up when you run Ant from other tools. The default attribute specifies which target is invoked when the user types **ant**. Finally, the basedir attribute specifies the directory from which all paths are relative to. Regardless of where you invoke Ant, "." is the directory containing the buildfile.

 Although you can put *build.xml* anywhere, we encounter the fewest difficulties when it is placed at the root of the project tree.

To invoke other targets, you type something like **ant *jar*** or **ant *clean compile***. If the buildfile were called *myproj.xml*, you would type **ant -buildfile *myproj.xml* clean**.

The remainder of our buildfile consists of tasks and targets. The end user invokes targets by name; tasks perform the actual work. The property task, for example, defines name/value pairs to avoid hardcoding throughout the buildfile:

```
<property name="dir.src" value="src"/>
```

The prepare target is a convention used in nearly every buildfile:

```
<target name="prepare">
  <mkdir dir="${dir.build}"/>
  <mkdir dir="${dir.dist}"/>
</target>
```

This creates the output directories relative to the project's base directory. If the directories already exist, the mkdir task ignores the request. Our example shows how the prepare target comes into action via target dependencies:

```
<target name="compile" depends="prepare"
        description="Compile all source code.">
  <javac srcdir="${dir.src}" destdir="${dir.build}"/>
</target>
```

Since the compile target depends on prepare, the output directories are always created before the compiler runs. Like other Ant tasks, the javac task only performs work if it has to. In this case, it only compiles *.java* files that are newer than their corresponding *.class* files.

It is important to note that checking timestamps on files results in fast builds, but does not catch logical dependencies between files. For instance, changing methods in a base class will not trigger a recompile on derived classes. For this reason, it is a good idea to type **ant clean compile** frequently. If you are using a version control tool like CVS, perform a clean compile just before checking in code so you don't "break the build" for other developers.

See Also

Ant ships with an optional task called depend that calculates dependencies based on references found inside of *.class* files, rather than merely checking file timestamps. You might also want to consider using IBM's Jikes compiler, since it is generally considered to be faster than Sun's *javac* compiler and it can provide better errors and warnings. See the Ant documentation for the javac task to learn how to use Jikes with Ant.

3.2   Running Ant

Problem

You want to run Ant.

Solution

The complete command-line syntax is as follows:

```
ant [options] [target [target2 [target3] ...]]
```

Discussion

Table 3-1 lists all of the Ant command-line options. This table applies to Ant Version 1.5.1.

Table 3-1. Ant command-line options

Option	Description
-buildfile *file* -f *file* -file *file*	Specify which buildfile to use. If omitted, Ant searches for a file named *build.xml*.
-D*property=value*	Pass name/value pairs as properties.
-debug	Write debugging information as the build progresses.
-diagnostics	Write diagnostic information as the build progresses.
-emacs	Write the log file in a way that Emacs understands.

Table 3-1. Ant command-line options (continued)

Option	Description
-find *file*	Locate a buildfile. Start searching in this directory, then the parent directory, and so on until the file is found or the filesystem root is reached.
-help	Show these options.
-inputhandler *classname*	Use a custom input handler class.
-listener *classname*	Use a custom build listener class.
-logfile *file* -l *file*	Send messages to the specified file instead of the console.
-logger *classname*	Use a custom logger class.
-projecthelp	Show a list of all targets in the buildfile.
-propertyfile *name*	Load all of the properties in the specified file. Properties specified with –D take precedence.
-quiet -q	Suppress much of the output.
-verbose -v	Write more information as the build progresses.
-version	Show the version of Ant.

See Also

Type **ant -help** to see the Ant options.

3.3   Providing Help

Problem

You want to provide help messages in your buildfiles.

Solution

Include a description attribute on the <project> and <target> tags. Also consider writing a help target, and use XML comments throughout the buildfile.

Discussion

Example 3-2 shows several techniques for providing additional help in Ant build-files. In this example, the help target is listed as the default target and is executed when the user types **ant** at the command line.

Example 3-2. Various ways to provide help

```xml
<?xml version="1.0"?>

<!-- You can document the buildfile using XML comments -->
<project name="My Big Project" default="help" basedir=".">
  <description>Shows how to provide help in an Ant buildfile.</description>

  <property name="dir.src" value="src"/>

  <target name="help">
    <echo message="This buildfile shows how to get help."/>
    <echo>(Type 'ant -projecthelp' for more info)</echo>
    <echo><![CDATA[
      Here is a block of text
      that you want to format
      in a very specific way!]]></echo>
  </target>

  <!-- Here is an example of a subtarget -->
  <target name="prepare">
    <mkdir dir="${dir.build}"/>
    <mkdir dir="${dir.dist}"/>
  </target>

  <!-- Here is an example of a main target -->
  <target name="clean"
          description="Remove all generated files.">
    <delete dir="${dir.build}"/>
    <delete dir="${dir.dist}"/>
  </target>

  <target name="compile" depends="prepare"
          description="Compile all source code.">
    <javac srcdir="${dir.src}" destdir="${dir.build}"/>
  </target>
</project>
```

The `help` target uses the `echo` task to print some usage information for Ant beginners. It reminds the user of the -projecthelp option, and uses an XML CDATA section to format a paragraph of text. CDATA sections are useful whenever you want to preserve linefeeds, spaces, and other characters precisely. CDATA is also useful because it allows you to print special XML characters like "<" without using entities like "<".

Providing target descriptions is very useful:

```xml
<target name="clean"
        description="Remove all generated files.">
```

These descriptions are displayed when the user types **ant -projecthelp**. Targets with descriptions are displayed as main targets, while those without descriptions are called subtargets, and are only displayed if you also include the **–verbose** command-line flag.

Because of the distinction between main targets and subtargets, you should only define `description` attributes for targets you want the user to actually use.

See Also

Recipe 3.6 shows how to use the `fail` task to abort the build if a property is not set.

3.4   Using Environment Variables

Problem

You want to obtain and use environment variables within Ant. This is a way to avoid hardcoding values in buildfiles.

Solution

Use a special form of the `<property>` task:[*]

```
<?xml version="1.0"?>
<project name="envSample" default="deploy" basedir=".">
  <!-- Set up the 'env' prefix for environment variables -->
  <property environment="env"/>

  <!-- Abort the build if TOMCAT_HOME is not set -->
  <target name="checkTomcatHome" unless="env.TOMCAT_HOME">
    <fail message="TOMCAT_HOME must be set!"/>
  </target>

  <target name="compile">
    ... compile the code
  </target>

  <!-- Deploy the WAR file to TOMCAT_HOME/webapps -->
  <target name="deploy" depends="checkTomcatHome,compile">
    <echo>Deploying to ${env.TOMCAT_HOME}</echo>
    <copy file="myapp.war" todir="${env.TOMCAT_HOME}/webapps"/>
  </target>

</project>
```

Discussion

Although most operating systems support the concept of environment variables, not all do. As a result, Sun deprecated Java's `System.getEnv( )` method, which used to return the values of environment variables. Undeterred by this restriction, Ant's programmers added the ability to obtain environment variables using the technique shown here.

---

[*] This technique only works with Ant 1.3 and later.

Use the property task's environment attribute to define a prefix, conventionally "env". Then use this prefix when referencing environment variables in other parts of a buildfile, as if you are referencing any normal Ant property. Our example Ant buildfile uses the TOMCAT_HOME environment variable to deploy a Web Application Archive (WAR) file to the correct directory.

Our example takes this technique to the next level by verifying that TOMCAT_HOME is actually set before attempting to deploy the WAR file. This is done in the checkTomcatHome target:

```
<target name="checkTomcatHome" unless="env.TOMCAT_HOME">
  <fail message="TOMCAT_HOME must be set!"/>
</target>
```

Any other target requiring TOMCAT_HOME should list checkTomcatHome as a dependency:

```
<target name="deploy" depends="checkTomcatHome,compile">
```

Environment variables should be used sparingly, but are particularly valuable when deploying to servers like Tomcat that might be installed in different locations depending on who is running the buildfile.

Portability is the main limitation with this technique. Since the underlying Java libraries no longer support System.getEnv( ), Ant must rely on Runtime.exec( ) to execute platform-specific commands when obtaining environment variables. While this is supported for Unix, Windows, and several other operating systems, you should definitely test things out if your buildfiles must run on some other platform.

Properties Files

An alternative to both environment variables, and the system properties approach described in Recipe 3.5 is a properties file that each developer uses to tell the build process about their environment. You might want to name the file *local.properties*. Advantages include:

- All developer-specific settings are in one place—it's a file you don't check in to source control.
- It's cross-platform.
- It's easy to edit, and the settings "stay put."
- It's easy for two or more developers to diff their settings.

You load it with <property file="local.properties">.

See Also

See the Ant user manual for the property core task.

3.5   Passing Arguments to a Buildfile

Problem

You want to pass system properties to a buildfile. Java system properties are a more portable alternative to environment variables.

Solution

Pass the system properties to Ant using the **-D** command-line argument. For example:

```
ant -Dprop1="My Property" run
```

Within the buildfile, refer to the property using Ant's ${prop1} syntax. You can specify default values for properties using the <property> tag, and you can pass system properties to Java applications using the <sysproperty> tag nested within the <java> element.

Discussion

Example 3-3 shows an Ant buildfile that demonstrates system properties. It echoes the property name/value pairs to the console, and then invokes a Java application that echoes the same properties.

Example 3-3. Buildfile demonstrating system properties

```xml
<?xml version="1.0"?>
<project name="sysprops" default="run" basedir=".">
  <!-- define two properties -->
  <property name="prop1" value="Property 1 from Buildfile"/>
  <property name="prop2" value="Property 2 from Buildfile"/>

  <target name="clean">
    <delete dir="com"/>
  </target>

  <target name="compile">
    <javac srcdir="." destdir=".">
      <classpath path="."/>
    </javac>
  </target>

  <target name="run" depends="compile">
    <!-- echo each of the properties to the console -->
    <echo message="Now in buildfile..."/>
    <echo message="prop1    = ${prop1}"/>
    <echo message="prop2    = ${prop2}"/>
    <!-- The 'prop3' property must be defined on the command
         line or it shows up like '${prop3}' -->
```

Example 3-3. Buildfile demonstrating system properties (continued)

```
<echo message="prop3    = ${prop3}"/>
<echo message="user.home = ${user.home}"/>

<!-- execute the main() method in a Java class -->
<java classname="com.oreilly.javaxp.ShowProps">
  <classpath path="."/>
  <!-- pass one of the properties -->
  <sysproperty key="prop1" value="${prop1}"/>
</java>
</target>

</project>
```

Our buildfile defines two properties. Regardless of where properties are defined, they are globally visible:

```
<property name="prop1" value="Property 1 from Buildfile"/>
<property name="prop2" value="Property 2 from Buildfile"/>
```

Properties are always name/value pairs, and can be overridden from the command line (shown shortly). They are referenced later in the buildfile using the ${prop1} and ${prop2} syntax. The run target echoes these property name/value pairs, and you can override them from the command-line:

```
<echo message="prop1    = ${prop1}"/>
<echo message="prop2    = ${prop2}"/>
<!-- The 'prop3' property must be defined on the command
     line or it shows up like '${prop3}' -->
<echo message="prop3    = ${prop3}"/>
<echo message="user.home = ${user.home}"/>
```

As you can see, the buildfile tries to echo prop3 and user.home, even though they were not defined earlier. As the comment indicates, the value for prop3 must be specified on the command-line or it will be undefined. The user.home property is a standard Java system property, so it will have a default value.

Finally, the buildfile invokes a Java application, but passes only one of the properties:

```
<!-- pass one of the properties -->
<sysproperty key="prop1" value="${prop1}"/>
```

Now let's look at a little Java program that displays the same properties. Example 3-4 shows how you use System.getProperty() to retrieve system properties.

Example 3-4. Java application to print properties

```
package com.oreilly.javaxp;

public class ShowProps {
    public static void main(String[] args) {
        System.out.println("Now in ShowProps class...");
        System.out.println("prop1    = " + System.getProperty("prop1"));
```

Example 3-4. Java application to print properties (continued)

```
        System.out.println("prop2     = " + System.getProperty("prop2"));
        System.out.println("prop3     = " + System.getProperty("prop3"));
        System.out.println("user.home = " +
                System.getProperty("user.home"));
    }
}
```

To tie this all together, let's look at some sample output. When the user types **ant**, they see the output shown next. This is the result of the default target, run, being executed.

```
[echo] Now in buildfile...
[echo] prop1     = Property 1 from Buildfile
[echo] prop2     = Property 2 from Buildfile
[echo] prop3     = ${prop3}
[echo] user.home = C:\Documents and Settings\ericb
[java] Now in ShowProps class...
[java] prop1     = Property 1 from Buildfile
[java] prop2     = null
[java] prop3     = null
[java] user.home = C:\Documents and Settings\ericb
```

As you can see, prop3 is undefined in the buildfile because it was not specified on the command line. The user.home property is available because the Java runtime sets it for us. Once the demonstration enters the ShowProps class, we see that properties are not automatically propagated from the Ant buildfile to Java applications. The value for prop1 is available to the ShowProps application because it was explicitly passed using <sysproperty>.

Here is the output when you type **ant -Dprop1="First Prop" -Dprop3="Third Prop"** on the command line:

```
[echo] Now in buildfile...
[echo] prop1     = First Prop
[echo] prop2     = Property 2 from Buildfile
[echo] prop3     = Third Prop
[echo] user.home = C:\Documents and Settings\ericb
[java] Now in ShowProps class...
[java] prop1     = First Prop
[java] prop2     = null
[java] prop3     = null
[java] user.home = C:\Documents and Settings\ericb
```

To summarize, this shows how we can pass system properties from the command line to the Ant buildfile. Once inside the buildfile, we can use <sysproperty> to pass the properties to Java applications. This is a useful technique because we can use properties to avoid hardcoded values in buildfiles and Java programs.

See Also

See the JavaDoc for `java.lang.System` for a list of standard system properties. Use Ant's echoproperties task to list all properties in the current project.

3.6   Checking for the Existence of Properties

Problem

You want to check for the existence of several properties and/or environment variables before you perform a build.

Solution

Define a "checkProperties" target that uses the `fail` task to abort the build if any properties are undefined.

Discussion

Suppose that various parts of your buildfile require several environment variables. First, specify a target that checks those properties:

```
<target name="checkProperties">
  <fail unless="env.TOMCAT_HOME">TOMCAT_HOME must be set</fail>
  <fail unless="env.JUNIT_HOME">JUNIT_HOME must be set</fail>
  <fail unless="env.JBOSS_HOME">JBOSS_HOME must be set</fail>
</target>
```

This causes the build to fail if any one of these environment variables is not set. To execute this target, list it as a dependency from some other target:

```
<target name="compile" depends="checkProperties">
  ...
</target>
```

The dependency ensures that the `checkProperties` target executes before Ant attempts to compile your code.

See Also

The previous two recipes showed how to define environment variables and Ant properties.

3.7   Defining a Classpath

Problem

You want to define a classpath and reuse it throughout a buildfile.

Solution

Use the <path> element to define the classpath along with a unique ID. Then refer to the classpath using the ID.

Discussion

Example 3-5 shows how to define a classpath and refer to it later from the javac task.

Example 3-5. Reusing a classpath

```xml
<?xml version="1.0" encoding="UTF-8"?>
<project name="Classpath Sample" default="compile" basedir=".">
  <!-- get an environment variable -->
  <property environment="env"/>
  <property name="tomcatHome" value="${env.TOMCAT_HOME}"/>

  <!-- define some directories -->
  <property name="dir.src" value="src"/>
  <property name="dir.build" value="build"/>
  <property name="dir.lib" value="lib"/>

  <!-- Define a classpath for use throughout the buildfile -->
  <path id="project.classpath">
    <pathelement location="${dir.src}"/>
    <!-- include Tomcat libraries -->
    <fileset dir="${tomcatHome}/common/lib">
      <include name="*.jar"/>
    </fileset>
    <!-- include our own libraries -->
    <fileset dir="${dir.lib}">
      <include name="*.jar"/>
    </fileset>
  </path>

  <target name="clean">
    <delete dir="${dir.build}"/>
  </target>

  <target name="prepare">
    <mkdir dir="${dir.build}"/>
  </target>

  <target name="compile" depends="prepare">
    <!-- use <pathconvert> to convert the path into a property -->
```

Example 3-5. Reusing a classpath (continued)

```
<pathconvert targetos="windows" property="windowsPath"
             refid="project.classpath"/>
<!-- now echo the path to the console -->
<echo>Windows path = ${windowsPath}</echo>

<!-- Here is how to use the classpath for compiling -->
<javac destdir="${dir.build}">
  <src path="${dir.src}"/>
  <classpath refid="project.classpath"/>
</javac>
  </target>
</project>
```

Several aspects of this buildfile are worthy of discussion. We define our classpath using the `<path>` element, giving it a unique ID so it can be referenced and reused more than once:

```
<path id="project.classpath">
```

You can construct a path consisting of many different files using a combination of nested `<pathelement>` and `<fileset>` elements. The first nested `<pathelement>` in our example adds the source directory to our path:

```
<pathelement location="${dir.src}"/>
```

We then use two `<fileset>`s to add numerous JAR files to our path:

```
<fileset dir="${tomcatHome}/common/lib">
  <include name="*.jar"/>
</fileset>
<!-- include our own libraries -->
<fileset dir="${dir.lib}">
  <include name="*.jar"/>
</fileset>
```

All of these items are added in the order listed in the buildfile. Later, we use `<pathconvert>` to store our path in a property named `windowsPath`:

```
<pathconvert targetos="windows" property="windowsPath"
             refid="project.classpath"/>
```

This does not affect the path in any way. Instead, it creates the `windowsPath` property, which might contain something like:

```
C:\myproj\src;C:\tomcat\common\lib\servlet.jar;etc...
```

This property is useful for debugging purposes because you can echo it to the console for inspection.

Our buildfile concludes by using the classpath with the `javac` task:

```
<javac destdir="${dir.build}">
  <src path="${dir.src}"/>
  <classpath refid="project.classpath"/>
</javac>
```

Since the classpath has an ID, you can refer to it from other targets throughout the buildfile as shown.

 We almost always create a *lib* directory in source control and put all the JARs we depend on there. This makes it easy to find the JAR files and update them in a controlled manner.

See Also

The next two recipes provide additional information about setting up paths.

3.8   Defining Platform-Independent Paths

Problem

You want to define paths that work on Windows, Unix, and other operating systems.

Solution

Define your paths, as shown in Recipe 3.7. Ant takes care of converting the paths to whatever platform you are running on. Use forward-slashes (/) between directories. Use either semi-colons (;) or colons (:) between paths; Ant handles both.

Discussion

Ant determines what operating system you are running on and converts paths accordingly. You should avoid Windows-style drive letters whenever possible; they will not work on Unix. If you must refer to a drive letter, use a system property as outlined in Recipe 3.5 to avoid hardcoding the path.

Use the pathconvert task to convert an Ant path to native format and store it in a property. Here is how you define a path and then convert it to Unix format:

```
<path id="path.test">
  <!-- find all unit tests under the build directory -->
  <fileset dir="${dir.build}">
    <include name="**/Test*.class"/>
  </fileset>
</path>

<!-- convert the path to UNIX format, storing it in a property -->
<pathconvert targetos="unix" property="unixPath" refid="path.test"/>
```

See Also

See the Ant user manual for more examples of the pathconvert task.

3.9   Including and Excluding Files

Problem

You want to include and/or exclude certain files and directories from a build.

Solution

Use Ant patterns along with <include> and <exclude> tags, or includes and excludes attributes.

Discussion

Ant uses a simple pattern syntax for selecting files, which you have undoubtedly seen in other examples throughout this chapter. Here is how you can use this syntax to include all *.java* files in a particular directory:

```
includes="src/com/oreilly/util/*.java"
```

Because Java projects are typically divided into numerous packages and subdirectories, you frequently use the ** wildcard to scan all subdirectories:

```
includes="src/**/*.java"
```

This tells Ant to locate all files ending with *.java* in the *src* directory and any subdirectories.

In the Ant pattern language, "*" matches any number of characters and "?" matches one character. So you can locate *Test1.java* and *Test2.java* as follows:

```
includes="Test?.java"
```

Because "?" matches a single character, *TestABC.java* is not matched by the preceding pattern.

Patterns can be combined. Table 3-2 shows some additional pattern examples.

Table 3-2. Ant pattern-matching examples

Pattern	Matches	Does not match
*.java	Person.java	Person.class
Person*.java	Person.java, PersonA.java, PersonBoss.java	P.java, BossPerson.java
Test?.java	TestA.java	Test.java, TestOne.java
**/*.txt	a.txt, src/a.txt, src/com/oreilly/b.txt	Files not ending in .txt

Table 3-2. Ant pattern-matching examples (continued)

Pattern	Matches	Does not match
src/**/*.java	src/A.java, src/com/oreilly/File.java	B.java, src/com/oreilly/C.class
/a/	a (if 'a' is a filename), build/File.txt, src/a/File.txt	a.java, src/b/C.class

See Also

Search for "Directory Based Tasks" in the Ant user manual for a discussion of Ant's pattern matching syntax.

3.10   Implementing Conditional Logic

Problem

You want to selectively execute portions of a build based on conditional logic.

Solution

Use target dependencies, properties, and the if and unless attributes of the <target> tag.

Discussion

Ant does not support true conditional logic, such as if/then/else. You can, however, execute targets depending on the state of properties. This target only executes if the xalanInstalled property is set:

```
<target name="compile" if="xalanInstalled">
  ...
</target>
```

If the property is not set, the target is ignored. You can also specify that a target should execute unless a property is set:

```
<target name="installXalan" unless="xalanInstalled">
  ...
</target>
```

See Also

Recipe 3.14 shows how to abort the build if a property is not set. This is a form of conditional logic that is specific to the fail task. See the Ant documentation for the condition task to learn how to set properties based upon existence of files, classes, or other resources.

3.11   Defining a Consistent Environment

Problem

You want to ensure that all developers on a team are building the project with identical configurations.

Solution

Ant buildfiles should be as self-contained as possible. Any reliance on external resources, such as the CLASSPATH environment variable, opens the door for different developers to have different settings.

Discussion

Without tools like Ant, different developers probably use different tools to compile their code. Some might prefer to work in text editors like Emacs, while others may use IDEs like IntelliJ IDEA or Borland JBuilder. Each developer probably has her own unique configuration in such an environment.

Regardless of which tools individuals use, every member of a project should be able to compile her code in a controlled manner before committing changes to a shared repository. Nothing is wrong with letting developers use the tools they are most comfortable with, but you should use a tool like Ant for a common baseline.

Here are some specific tips for setting up an Ant buildfile to ensure a consistent build by all developers:

- The buildfile should not rely on any external CLASSPATH.
- If the build requires third party JAR files, put the correct versions in a shared directory so each developer builds with the same versions.*
- The buildfile itself should be kept under version control.
- Provide a "clean" target that destroys all generated code.

The clean target is essential because it ensures everything will be compiled during the next build. Ant relies on file timestamps to determine when class files are out of date with respect to source files. Although this catches most dependencies, it does not handle many semantic dependencies. For example, you might remove a method from a base class; the base class will recompile, but any derived classes will not. The compile may succeed (incorrectly) until you perform a clean build and find the problem.

---

* We highly recommend you keep JAR files under version control.

See Also

Recipe 3.7 shows how to define a classpath.

3.12   Preventing Build Breaks

Problem

You are concerned because developers keep "breaking the build" by checking in broken code to your version control tool.[*]

Solution

Adopt a policy in which developers must perform a clean build using Ant before checking in changes to the source repository. Ask them to run all unit tests, as well.

Discussion

This is largely a project management issue. If your team has an Ant buildfile along with a suite of unit tests, the build should not be breaking on a routine basis. Understand that people do make mistakes, such as forgetting to commit some changes to CVS despite having tested their changes.

Each developer should follow these suggestions in order to minimize integration problems:

- Work in pairs. Your partner should encourage you to follow the full testing procedure before checking in code.
- Work on one problem at a time. Keeping track of dozens of changes for days at a time is a good way to get out of sync with the rest of the team and introduce build problems.
- Perform a clean build before testing changes.
- Run the entire suite of unit tests before committing changes to the version control tool.

See Also

Chapters 1 and 2 discuss XP practices such as continuous integration and pair programming.

---

[*] A version control tool is something like CVS or Microsoft Visual SourceSafe.

3.13 Building JAR Files

Problem

You want to build a JAR file.

Solution

Use Ant's jar task.

Discussion

The jar task creates JAR files, as expected. In its simplest form, you specify the name of the new JAR file along with the directory containing files to add to the archive. All files in the directory specified by basedir along with subdirectories and files are added:

```
<jar jarfile="${dir.dist}/oreilly.jar"
     basedir="${dir.build}"/>
```

The jar task tries to be as efficient as possible. Before creating a new JAR, it checks for an existing archive and compares file timestamps. In our example, *oreilly.jar* is only created if it does not exist, or if any of the files in ${dir.build} are newer than *oreilly.jar*.

This next example refines our operation by only including *.class* files, unless they are unit tests matching the *Test*.class* pattern:

```
<jar jarfile="${dir.dist}/oreilly.jar"
     basedir="${dir.build}"
     includes="**/*.class"
     excludes="**/Test*.class"/>
```

The includes and excludes attributes use the ** pattern to represent any subdirectory. Use nested <fileset> tags for more sophisticated selections:

```
<jar jarfile="${dir.dist}/oreilly.jar">
  <fileset dir="${dir.build}"
           includes="**/*.class"
           excludes="**/Test*.class"/>
  <fileset dir="${dir.src}"
           includes="**/*.properties"/>
</jar>
```

This JAR file consists of all *.class* files (except for *Test*.class*) in the build directory tree. It also contains all *.properties* files under the source directory tree.

Ant makes it completely trivial to exclude test cases from a production JAR file—literally, less than one line of text in the build file. Some teams make their lives quite hard by having a separate source tree for their test classes, enduring all kinds of IDE gymnastics because they are mortified they might inflate their production JARs with test cases.

See Also

Recipe 3.9 covers Ant's pattern-matching syntax.

3.14 Installing JUnit

Problem

You need to configure JUnit so you can run your tests using Ant. Although you have added *junit.jar* to your classpath, you still see errors.

Solution

You have three possible solutions:

1. Install Ant's *optional.jar* as well as JUnit's *junit.jar* in the ANT_HOME/*lib* directory.

2. Ensure that neither *optional.jar* nor *junit.jar* is in the ANT_HOME/*lib* directory. Then set up a classpath in your buildfile that includes both JAR files.

3. Ensure that neither *optional.jar* nor *junit.jar* is in the ANT_HOME/*lib* directory. Then set your CLASSPATH environment variable to include both JAR files.

Discussion

Ant's junit task is implemented by a class named JUnitTask, which is found in the *optional.jar* file that ships with the Ant distribution. Ant includes many so-called "optional" tasks, which generally depend on external libraries in order to function. In the case of the junit task, *junit.jar* is required. It is your responsibility to download JUnit and properly configure it to work with Ant.

Class loading problems are common in cases where optional Ant tasks depend on external libraries such as *junit.jar*. The Java ClassLoader instance that loads the JUnitTask class must also be able to load various JUnit classes. For the proper classes to be visible, you must follow one of the three solutions that were just mentioned.

You generally install Ant's *optional.jar* in the ANT_HOME/*lib* directory, so the easiest way to configure JUnit is to also install *junit.jar* in ANT_HOME/*lib*. Example 3-6 shows an Ant buildfile with an "install.junit" target that automatically installs *junit.jar* for you. This target can be added to any of your buildfiles, thus ensuring that JUnit is properly configured to work with Ant.

Example 3-6. Installing JUnit

```
<project name="Java XP Cookbook" default="compile" basedir=".">
  <property name="dir.build" value="build"/>
  <property name="dir.src" value="src"/>
  <property environment="env"/>

  <path id="classpath.project">
    <pathelement path="${dir.build}"/>
  </path>

  <target name="install.junit">
    <fail unless="env.JUNIT_HOME">
      The JUNIT_HOME environment variable must be set.
    </fail>

    <available property="junit.already.installed"
               file="${ant.home}/lib/junit.jar"/>

    <copy file="${env.JUNIT_HOME}/junit.jar"
          todir="${ant.home}/lib"
          failonerror="true"/>

    <fail unless="junit.already.installed">
      junit.jar was not found in ANT_HOME/lib prior to this
      build, so it was copied for you. Please try your build again.
    </fail>
  </target>

  <target name="prepare" depends="install.junit">
    <mkdir dir="${dir.build}"/>
  </target>

...remainder of buildfile omitted
```

Our target first ensures that the JUNIT_HOME environment variable is set. If it isn't, the build fails with an error message. Next, it sets an Ant property junit.already.installed if it finds that *junit.jar* is already present under ANT_HOME/*lib*.

After setting the property, our buildfile goes ahead and copies *junit.jar* from the JUnit directory to the Ant directory. If the file already exists, the copy operation does not do anything. If the copy fails, the build fails. The copy might fail, for example, if your JUNIT_HOME environment variable is set to some invalid directory.

Finally, our target fails the build if it finds that JUnit was not already installed before it performed the copy operation:

```
<fail unless="junit.already.installed">
  junit.jar was not found in ANT_HOME/lib prior to this
  build, so it was copied for you. Please try your build again.
</fail>
```

You may wonder why we fail the build even though we just finished copying *junit.jar* to the ANT_HOME/*lib* directory. We have to abort the build because when the build first started, JUnit was not already installed. By this time the Ant class loader has already located all of the JAR files in ANT_HOME/*lib*, so we must start a new build in order for it to see *junit.jar*.

Another Technique

Here's another idea for configuring Ant and JUnit. Put *ant.jar*, *optional.jar*, and *junit.jar* in your project's *lib* directory, which is under version control so all developers see the same JAR files. Write your own *ant.bat* script and place it next to your buildfile. This custom *ant.bat* puts just the desired few jars on the classpath, does not include the user's environment classpath, and invokes Ant. Thus, there is no need to install Ant or JUnit on the development machine at all.

See Also

Recipe 3.7 shows how to define a classpath.

3.15   Running Unit Tests

Problem

You want to run all of the unit tests in your project using Ant.

Solution

Follow a consistent naming convention for all of your test classes, and then use Ant's junit and batchtest tasks to locate and run the tests.

Discussion

Writing unit tests is a key XP practice, and Ant makes it easy to run those tests. A well-written buildfile should provide a target for running all tests in the project with a single command. In Example 3-7, programmers type **ant junit** to compile everything and then run all of the unit tests.

Example 3-7. Running unit tests

```
<?xml version="1.0"?>
<project name="Java XP Cookbook" default="compile" basedir=".">
  <property name="dir.build" value="build"/>
  <property name="dir.src" value="src"/>
  <property environment="env"/>
```

Example 3-7. Running unit tests (continued)

```
<path id="classpath.project">
  <pathelement path="${dir.build}"/>
</path>

<target name="install.junit">
  <fail unless="env.JUNIT_HOME">
    The JUNIT_HOME environment variable must be set.
  </fail>

  <available property="junit.already.installed"
             file="${ant.home}/lib/junit.jar"/>

  <copy file="${env.JUNIT_HOME}/junit.jar"
        todir="${ant.home}/lib"
        failonerror="true"/>

  <fail unless="junit.already.installed">
    junit.jar was not found in ANT_HOME/lib prior to this
    build, so it was copied for you. Please try your build again.
  </fail>
</target>

<target name="prepare" depends="install.junit">
  <mkdir dir="${dir.build}"/>
</target>

<target name="clean"
        description="Remove all generated files.">
  <delete dir="${dir.build}"/>
</target>

<target name="compile" depends="prepare"
        description="Compile all source code.">
  <javac srcdir="${dir.src}" destdir="${dir.build}">
    <classpath refid="classpath.project"/>
  </javac>
</target>

<target name="junit" depends="compile">
  <junit printsummary="on"
         fork="false"
         haltonfailure="false"
         failureproperty="tests.failed"
         showoutput="true">

    <classpath refid="classpath.project"/>
    <formatter type="brief" usefile="false"/>

    <batchtest>
      <fileset dir="${dir.src}">
        <include name="**/Test*.java"/>
      </fileset>
```

Example 3-7. Running unit tests (continued)

```
    </batchtest>
  </junit>

  <fail if="tests.failed">
  ********************************************************
  ********************************************************
  One or more tests failed. Check the output...
  ********************************************************
  ********************************************************
  </fail>
 </target>
</project>
```

This buildfile includes logic presented earlier in Recipe 3.14 that automatically installs *junit.jar* to the ANT_HOME/*lib* directory. Once this succeeds, we can proceed with the tests.

We use several attributes on the junit task to configure how Ant runs our tests. Table 3-3 outlines what each of the shown junit attributes means. This is only a subset of the available attributes; refer to the Ant documentation for a complete list of attributes.

Table 3-3. junit task attributes

Attribute	Description
printsummary="on"	Instructs Ant to print a one-line summary for each test as it runs. We recommend this setting so you get some sense of progress as your tests run.
fork="false"	Run the tests in the same JVM as Ant. This is the most efficient way to run your tests.
haltonfailure="false"	Do not abort the build if a test failure or error occurs.
failureproperty="test.failed"	If a test fails, set the "test.failed" Ant property. We will use this later to display a big error message that grabs the user's attention.
showoutput="true"	Print output from each test to the console.

In addition to XML attributes, the junit task contains several nested elements. The classpath element, as you might expect, defines where the classes for your tests are found. In this case, we reference the project-wide classpath defined earlier in the buildfile.

The formatter element defines how test results are formatted:

```
<formatter type="brief" usefile="false"/>
```

The available formatter types are brief, plain, and xml. By specifying usefile="false", we indicate that output should go to the console rather than a file. The brief formatter is the most concise, providing information about tests that fail. The plain formatter shows statistics for every test in text format, and the xml formatter is useful for converting test output to other forms such as HTML. We will see how to use xml output in Recipe 3.17.

Finally, we use a nested batchtest element to select which tests are actually executed:

```
<batchtest>
  <fileset dir="${dir.src}">
    <include name="**/Test*.java"/>
  </fileset>
</batchtest>
```

The batchtest element selects a set of files using a specified naming convention. In our case, we include all files named Test*.java found under the source directory. Once these files are located, batchtest converts the filenames into Java classnames, passing those to the junit task where they are executed.

See Also

The next recipe shows how to run a single test, rather than all tests. Ant and JUnit may also be used for other kinds of tests. For instance, you may provide targets for customer acceptance tests that also use the JUnit framework.

3.16 Running Specific Tests

Problem

You want to use Ant to run a single test case.

Solution

Use the junit task with a nested test element.

Discussion

Recipe 3.15 showed how to use junit in conjunction with batchtest to run every test in one or more paths. There may be times, however, when you want to selectively run a single test. For instance, you might be working on a specific class and don't want to run hundreds of tests for each change you make. To run a single test using Ant, use the test element instead of batchtest. Example 3-8 shows how to define a target that runs a specific test.

Example 3-8. Running a single test

```
<target name="junit2" depends="compile">
  <!-- you may override this on the command line:
       ant -Dtestcase=com/oreilly/javaxp/junit/TestGame junit2 -->
  <property name="testcase"
            value="com/oreilly/javaxp/junit/TestPerson"/>
```

Example 3-8. Running a single test (continued)

```
  <junit fork="false">
    <classpath refid="classpath.project"/>
    <formatter type="plain" usefile="false"/>

    <test name="${testcase}"/>
  </junit>
</target>
```

Rather than hardcode the name of the test, our example allows the user to specify the test name on the Ant command line. This takes advantage of Ant's ability to obtain properties from the command line using the -D syntax.

See Also

The previous recipe showed how to run all tests.

3.17   Generating a Test Report

Problem

You want to produce a nicely formatted HTML report that summarizes results from all of your tests.

Solution

Use batchtest along with junitreport.

Discussion

In earlier examples, we sent test results directly to the console. In order to format our results as HTML, we need to first write the test results to a series of XML files. We do this with the following line:

```
  <formatter type="xml"/>
```

This causes test results to go to a series of XML files, one per test. The XML files are written to the directory named by the todir attribute of the junit task or the nested batchtest element.

Once the files are created, junitreport uses XSLT stylesheets to convert the XML files into a nice HTML report. The complete Ant target is shown in Example 3-9.

Example 3-9. Generating a test report

```
<target name="junit" depends="compile">
  <junit printsummary="on" fork="false" haltonfailure="false">
```

Example 3-9. Generating a test report (continued)

```
    <classpath refid="classpath.project"/>
    <formatter type="xml"/>

    <batchtest todir="${dir.build}">
      <fileset dir="${dir.src}">
        <include name="**/Test*.java"/>
      </fileset>
    </batchtest>

  </junit>

  <junitreport todir="${dir.build}">
    <fileset dir="${dir.build}">
      <include name="TEST-*.xml"/>
    </fileset>
    <report format="frames" todir="${dir.build}"/>
  </junitreport>

  <!-- convert an Ant path to a fully-qualified platform specific path -->
  <pathconvert dirsep="/" property="reportUrl">
    <path>
      <pathelement location="${dir.build}/index.html"/>
    </path>
  </pathconvert>

  <!-- launch a web browser to view the results -->
  <exec executable="cmd" os="Windows XP">
    <arg value="/C"/>
    <arg value="${reportUrl}"/> <!-- the full path to the report -->
  </exec>
</target>
```

Our buildfile runs all tests in the *src* directory tree and then sends XML results to the build directory, which was specified in the todir attribute of junitreport. After junitreport runs, we launch a web browser to view the test results. This last portion of the example only works on Microsoft Windows. If you are on a different plat-form, simply change the exec task to point to your browser.

See Also

The previous two recipes show other ways to run tests.

3.18   Checking Out Code from CVS

Problem

You want your Ant buildfile to check out code from CVS before compiling.

Solution

Use Ant's cvs task.

Discussion

You can use the cvs Ant task to execute any CVS command. In order for this to work, you must have installed the *cvs* executable on your system path. If Ant does not find *cvs*, it issues an error and the build fails.

By default, the cvs task executes a checkout command. Here is the syntax to check-out the cookbook module from CVS:

```
<cvs cvsroot="${cvsroot}"
     package="cookbook"/>
```

You can also execute any other CVS command, such as update as shown here:

```
<cvs command="update -dP"
     cvsroot="${cvsroot}"
     dest="cookbook"/>
```

This tells CVS to update the most recent files in the *cookbook* directory, creating missing directories and pruning empty directories.

 If cvsroot is not specified, the already-defined CVS root from the checked out project is used.

See Also

See the CVS documentation for information about all of the CVS commands.

3.19   Bootstrapping a Build

Problem

You want to use Ant to kick off a nightly build process.

Solution

Create a "bootstrap" buildfile that checks out a clean copy of all sources from revision control. Then, pass off control to the main buildfile that was one of the files just checked out.

Discussion

Many projects set up a build server that performs complete, clean builds at scheduled times. A clean build ensures that every file in the system compiles. If you do not start with a clean slate, you may end up with a successful build just because some obsolete source or class files are lingering in your directory structure.

A clean build consists of the following high-level steps:

1. Start the build with a scheduling mechanism of some sort. This is generally platform-specific and is not covered here.

2. Use a script to checkout all files into a clean directory. This is what we are covering in this recipe.

3. Once all files are checked out, including the main project buildfile, invoke Ant on the main buildfile.

Example 3-10 shows the complete Ant buildfile for performing a bootstrap build. The buildfile uses the cvs task as shown in Recipe 3.18 to checkout or update the entire *cookbook* directory. Once the latest files are obtained, we invoke Ant on *cookbook/build.xml* to perform the clean build.

Example 3-10. Bootstrap buildfile

```xml
<?xml version="1.0"?>
<project name="Java XP Cookbook" default="build" basedir=".">

  <target name="prepare">
    <!-- convert the CVS repository directory into
         a fully-qualitied Windows directory -->
    <pathconvert targetos="windows" property="cvsrepository.path">
      <path>
        <pathelement location="repository"/>
      </path>
    </pathconvert>
    <!-- store the CVS root in a property -->
    <property name="cvsroot" value=":local:${cvsrepository.path}"/>

    <!-- determine if the files have been checked out -->
    <available file="cookbook" type="dir" property="already.checked.out"/>
  </target>

  <target name="clean"
          description="Remove the entire cookbook directory.">
    <delete dir="cookbook"/>
  </target>

  <target name="cvscheckout" depends="prepare"
          unless="already.checked.out">
    <cvs cvsroot="${cvsroot}"
         package="cookbook"/>
  </target>
```

Example 3-10. Bootstrap buildfile (continued)

```
  <target name="cvsupdate" depends="prepare" if="already.checked.out">
    <cvs command="update -dP"
         cvsroot="${cvsroot}"
         dest="cookbook"/>
  </target>

  <target name="build" depends="cvscheckout,cvsupdate">
    <ant dir="cookbook" target="all" inheritAll="false"/>
  </target>
</project>
```

See Also

Windows users can use "Scheduled Tasks" under the Control Panel to schedule builds for certain times of day. The CruiseControl tool is designed to help with continuous integration, and is available at *http://cruisecontrol.sourceforge.net*.

CHAPTER 4

JUnit

4.0 Introduction

Unit testing is at the heart of XP, and it is a central theme of this book. JUnit,* available from *http://www.junit.org,* is the de facto standard for Java unit testing. It is a simple framework for creating automated unit tests. JUnit test cases are Java classes that contain one or more unit test methods, and these tests are grouped into test suites. You can run tests individually, or you can run entire test suites.

 Ant includes the junit task for running JUnit tests. We show how to run JUnit tests using Ant in Chapter 3.

Each JUnit test method should execute quickly. Speed is important because as more tests are written and integrated into the build process, it takes longer to run the entire test suite. Programmers do not want to be interrupted for long periods of times while tests run—so the longer the tests take to execute the greater the likelihood programmers will skip this critical phase.

You can also increase the likelihood that programmers will run the tests by making it extremely easy, preferably with a single command. The ability to run all tests with a single command or button click is nearly a requirement to claim that your project is doing XP. We showed how to run tests with Ant in the previous chapter, and many IDEs now make it possible to run tests by clicking on a menu item.

JUnit tests are pass/fail tests explicitly designed to run without human intervention. Because of this design, you can (and should) add your test suite to your continuous integration build process so the tests run automatically.

---

* We cover JUnit Version 3.8.1 in this chapter.

4.1 Getting Started

Problem

You want to write unit tests with JUnit.

Solution

Create a subclass of junit.framework.TestCase. Each unit test is represented by a testXXX( ) method within the TestCase subclass.

Discussion

Example 4-1 shows an extremely simple test case. A *test case* is a subclass of TestCase and contains a collection of unit tests. Instances of TestCase are sometimes referred to as test *fixtures*, although we prefer to say "test case" since that matches the class name. Each unit test is a public, no-argument method beginning with "test". If you do not follow this naming convention, JUnit will not be able to locate your test methods automatically. Instead, you would have to write a suite( ) method and construct instances of your test case, passing the test method name to the constructor.

Example 4-1. Simple test case

```
package com.oreilly.javaxp.common;

import junit.framework.TestCase;

/**
 * Sample unit tests for the {@link Person} class.
 */
public class TestPerson extends TestCase {

    /**
     * This constructor is only required in JUnit 3.7 and earlier.
     * @param testMethodName the name of the test method to execute.
     */
    public TestPerson(String testMethodName) {
        super(testMethodName);
    }

    /**
     * A unit test to verify the name is formatted correctly.
     */
    public void testGetFullName( ) {
        Person p = new Person("Aidan", "Burke");
        assertEquals("Aidan Burke", p.getFullName( ));
    }

    /**
     * A unit test to verify that nulls are handled properly.
     */
```

Example 4-1. Simple test case (continued)

```
    public void testNullsInName( ) {
        Person p = new Person(null, "Burke");
        assertEquals("? Burke", p.getFullName( ));

        // this code is only executed if the previous assertEquals passed!
        p = new Person("Tanner", null);
        assertEquals("Tanner ?", p.getFullName( ));
    }
}
```

In JUnit 3.7 and earlier, the constructor is required and must have the signature shown in the TestPerson class. JUnit uses this constructor to create a new instance of the test case as it runs each of the unit test methods. The name argument matches the current unit test's method name, allowing JUnit to use reflection to invoke the corresponding method. JUnit 3.8 removed the need for this constructor, so we will not include it in the remaining examples in this chapter.

The "test" methods are the actual unit tests. You must have at least one unit test in each test case or JUnit reports an error. Our TestPerson class has two unit tests, each of which checks different aspects of the Person class's getFullName( ) method. Test methods should* follow this signature:

```
    public void test<something>( ) [throws SomeException]
```

This naming convention allows JUnit to locate unit tests by reflection. Tests may throw any subclass of java.lang.Throwable. When this happens, JUnit catches the exception and reports a test error. It continues to execute any additional test methods.

Each unit test uses various assertXXX( ) methods to do the actual testing:

```
    assertEquals("Aidan Burke", p.getFullName( ));
```

This method confirms that its two arguments are equal. If the arguments are equal, the test passes. Otherwise, a test failure is reported and the remainder of the current test method is skipped. JUnit does proceed to execute other test methods, however. In the case of Object arguments (such as two Strings), the .equals( ) method is used for checking equality.

To compile TestPerson, include *junit.jar* in your classpath. The next recipe shows how to run the tests.

See Also

Recipe 4.2 shows how to run your tests. Recipe 4.3 explains the assert( ) methods. Recipe 4.4 describes how fine-grained your tests should be.

---

* You could adopt a different naming convention; however, JUnit would not automatically find your test methods. You would have to build your test suite manually by constructing instances of your test case, passing your method names to the constructor.

4.2   Running JUnit

Problem

You want to run your tests.

Solution

We have already demonstrated how to run JUnit using Ant, back in Chapter 3. In order to run tests from a script or in an IDE, include *junit.jar* in your classpath and then use the junit.textui.TestRunner class to run your tests in text mode. Use junit.swingui.TestRunner to run the tests in a Swing GUI.*

Discussion

JUnit can run tests in text or graphical mode. Text mode is faster, and is excellent for running tests as part of an automated build process. Graphical tests are more interesting to run, and can make it easier to analyze output from a large number of tests.

Text testing

Here's an example session using the text-based TestRunner. The first line is typed at the prompt; the rest is output. The TestPerson class is the test case from the previous recipe.

```
java junit.textui.TestRunner com.oreilly.javaxp.junit.TestPerson

.F.F
Time: 0.02
There were 2 failures:
1) testGetFullName(com.oreilly.javaxp.junit.TestPerson)junit.framework.
AssertionFailedError: expected:<Aidan Burke> but was:<AidanBurke>
        at com.oreilly.javaxp.junit.TestPerson.testGetFullName(C:/cvsdata/java_xp_
cookbook/examples/src/com/oreilly/javaxp/junit/TestPerson.java:24)
2) testNullsInName(com.oreilly.javaxp.junit.TestPerson)junit.framework.
AssertionFailedError: expected:<? Burke> but was:<?Burke>
        at com.oreilly.javaxp.junit.TestPerson.testNullsInName(C:/cvsdata/java_xp_
cookbook/examples/src/com/oreilly/javaxp/junit/TestPerson.java:29)

FAILURES!!!
Tests run: 2,  Failures: 2,  Errors: 0
```

The first line of output shows a dot (.) as each test runs. Once you have dozens or hundreds of tests, the dots allow you to see that tests are progressing. JUnit also shows "F" for each failure:

```
.F.F
```

JUnit displays the cumulative time (in seconds), followed by a summary report of failures and errors. Both unit tests failed. The expected text didn't match the existing text:

```
expected:<Aidan Burke> but was:<AidanBurke>
```

---

* Use junit.awtui.TestRunner for an older, AWT-based test runner.

Either our test is incorrect, or the `Person` class failed to insert a space between the first and last names. It's the latter.. The final line shows cumulative totals from the unit tests:

```
Tests run: 2,  Failures: 2,  Errors: 0
```

This indicates that a total of two tests ran, and both had failures. No tests had errors.

 A test *failure* occurs when an `assertXXX( )` statement fails. A test *error* occurs when a unit test throws an exception.

After fixing the `Person` class, we can run the tests again. We see the following output:

```
java junit.textui.TestRunner com.oreilly.javaxp.junit.TestPerson

..
Time: 0.01

OK (2 tests)
```

Graphical testing

While text-mode testing is great for automated testing, it can be more interesting to watch your tests graphically, as in Figure 4-1. Here is the command to run the GUI:

```
java junit.swingui.TestRunner com.oreilly.javaxp.junit.TestPerson
```

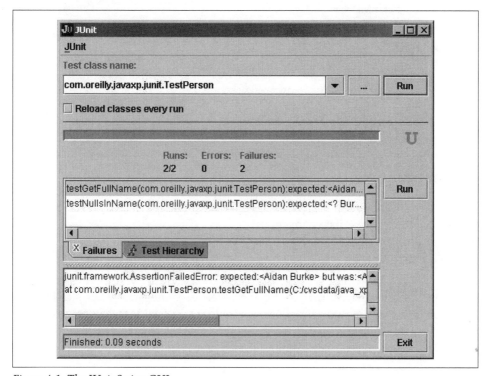

Figure 4-1. The JUnit Swing GUI

The black-and-white figure does not illustrate the fact that the progress bar near the top of the screen is red, indicating one or more errors or failures. As the tests run, the progress bar fills from left to right.

The output is essentially the same as JUnit's text UI; however, you can click on lines to see the message associated with each problem. This is a particular advantage of the graphical TestRunner when you have to sift through large numbers of problems.

Figure 4-2 shows the Test Hierarchy tab. This tab allows you to see which of the unit tests passed or failed, and allows you to re-run individual tests.

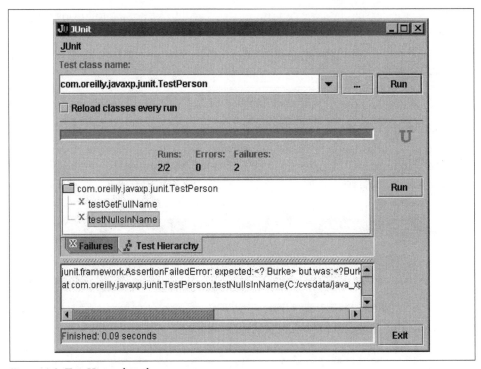

Figure 4-2. Test Hierarchy tab

Figure 4-3 shows the output once all bugs are fixed and every test passes. You cannot tell, but the progress bar is now green.

Reload classes every run

On a final note, the JUnit GUI provides a checkbox allowing you to "Reload classes every run." When checked, the JUnit ClassLoader reads the latest *.class* files for your tests each time they are run. This allows you to leave the GUI up while you recompile your source code. The new classes are loaded the next time you click the Run button.

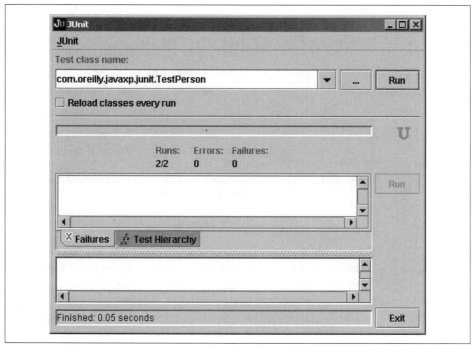

Figure 4-3. All tests pass

See Also

Most Java IDEs are integrated with JUnit. Read your IDE documentation to learn how to run tests directly within the IDE. See Recipe 4.3 to learn how to provide more descriptive error messages. Chapter 3 shows how to run JUnit using Ant.

4.3   assertXXX( ) Methods

Problem

You want to use the various assertXXX( ) methods to test different conditions.

Solution

junit.framework.TestCase, the base class for all test cases, extends from junit.framework.Assert, which defines numerous overloaded assertXXX( ) methods. Your tests function by calling these methods.

Discussion

Table 4-1 summarizes the various assertXXX() methods that can be found in junit.framework.Assert. Although you could get by with using assertTrue() for nearly every test, using one of the more specific assertXXX() methods often makes your tests more understandable and provides good failure messages. This table is only a summary; each of the methods is overloaded as described shortly.

Table 4-1. Assert method summary

Method	Description
assert()	This was deprecated in JUnit 3.7 because it interferes with the J2SE 1.4 assert keyword. You should use assertTrue() instead. This method was completely removed in JUnit 3.8.
assertEquals()	Compares two values for equality. The test passes if the values are equal.
assertFalse()	Evaluates a boolean expression. The test passes if the expression is false.
assertNotNull()	Compares an object reference to null. The test passes if the reference is not null.
assertNotSame()	Compares the memory address of two object references using the == operator. The test passes if both refer to different objects.
assertNull()	Compares an object reference to null. The test passes if the reference is null.
assertSame()	Compares the memory address of two object references using the == operator. The test passes if both refer to the same object.
assertTrue()	Evaluates a boolean expression. The test passes if the expression is true.
fail()	Causes the current test to fail. This is commonly used with exception handling, as shown in Recipe 4.12.

Optional first argument

All of the methods in Table 4-1 are overloaded to accept an optional String as the first argument. When specified, this argument provides a descriptive message should the test fail. Here is an example that shows two assert statements, one with the description and one without:

```
assertEquals(employeeA, employeeB);
assertEquals("Employees should be equal after the clone() operation.",
        employeeA, employeeB);
```

The second version is preferable because it describes why the test failed, making it easier to fix problems down the road.

 The message should describe what is asserted to be true, rather than what went wrong.

Equality comparison

The assertSame( ) method compares two object references, ensuring that they both refer to the same memory address. assertSame( ) uses the == operator for its comparison. The following two tests are functionally identical:

```
assertSame("Expected the two parts to be identical.", part1, part2);
assertTrue("Expected the two parts to be identical.", part1 == part2);
```

While assertSame( ) compares memory addresses, assertEquals( ) compares contents. For objects, this means the .equals( ) method is used instead of ==. assertEquals( ) has numerous overloaded implementations that compare objects to other objects, or primitives to other primitives. Regardless of what you are comparing, the expected value is always listed before the actual value you are testing against. Here are a few examples:

```
// compare two objects (not using the description argument)
assertEquals(expectedBirthDate, son.getBirthDate( ));
assertEquals("Garrett", son.getMiddleName( ));

// compare primitives
assertEquals(50, race.getNumLaps( ));
assertEquals('a', car.getIdentifier( ));
assertEquals(expectedByte, customer.getCategory( ));
```

JUnit provides special assertEquals( ) methods comparing doubles and floats. These methods accept a delta argument, allowing for rounding off errors. Here is how you can verify that the temperature is 97.1 degrees, accurate to within 0.001 degrees:

```
assertEquals("Temperature", expectedTemp, actualTemp, 0.001);
```

Additional examples

Here is how you check for a Boolean condition:

```
assertTrue("Expected the temperature to be non-negative.", actualTemp >= 0);
```

Prior to JUnit 3.8, you had to adjust your tests slightly to check for false conditions:

```
assertTrue("The car should not be running.", !car.isRunning( ));
```

JUnit 3.8 added the assertFalse( ) method, making the test more clear:

```
assertFalse("The car should not be running.", car.isRunning( ));
```

Checking for null is easy:

```
assertNull("Did not expect to find an employee.",
        database.getEmployee("someInvalidEmployeeId"));
```

You can also check for non-null values:

```
assertNotNull("Expected to find an employee with id=" + id,
        database.getEmployee(id));
```

And finally, you can explicitly cause a test failure using the fail( ) method:

```
fail("Unable to configure database.");
```

See Also

See the JavaDocs for `junit.framework.Assert`. The methods in `Assert` are all static, and can be called from other classes. See Recipe 6.2 for an example.

4.4   Unit Test Granularity

Problem

You want to know how fine-grained your unit tests should be.

Solution

Each unit test should check one specific piece of functionality. Do not combine multiple, unrelated tests into a single `testXXX()` method.

Discussion

Each test method can have as many `assertXXX()` calls as you like, but they can lead to problems:

```
public void testGame() throws BadGameException {
    Game game = new Game();
    Ship fighter = game.createFighter("001");
    assertEquals("Fighter did not have the correct identifier",
        "001", fighter.getId());
    Ship fighter2 = game.createFighter("001");
    assertSame("createFighter with same id should return same object",
        fighter, fighter2);
    assertFalse("A new game should not be started yet", game.isPlaying());
}
```

This is a bad design because each `assertXXX()` method is testing an unrelated piece of functionality. If the first `assertEquals()` fails, the remainder of the test is not executed. When this happens, you won't know if the other tests are functional.

Example 4-2 shows a refactored test case that tests various aspects of our game independently. We will see how to remove the duplicated code in Recipe 4.5 when we talk about `setUp()` and `tearDown()`.

Example 4-2. Refactored tests

```
public void testCreateFighter() throws BadGameException {
    Game game = new Game();
    Ship fighter = game.createFighter("001");
    assertEquals("Fighter did not have the correct identifier",
        "001", fighter.getId());
    game.shutdown();
}
```

Example 4-2. Refactored tests (continued)

```
public void testSameFighters( ) throws BadGameException {
    Game game = new Game( );
    Ship fighter = game.createFighter("001");
    Ship fighter2 = game.createFighter("001");
    assertSame("createFighter with same id should return same object",
        fighter, fighter2);
    game.shutdown( );
}

public void testGameInitialState( ) throws BadGameException {
    Game game = new Game( );
    assertFalse("A new game should not be started yet", game.isPlaying( ));
    game.shutdown( );
}
```

With this approach, one test failure will not cause the remaining assertXXX( ) statements to be skipped.

This issue raises the question: should a test method ever contain more than one assertXXX( )? The answer is a definite yes! If you are testing a series of conditions in which subsequent tests will always fail when the first fails, you may as well combine all of the asserts in one test.

See Also

See Recipe 4.5 to learn how to create the Game object in the setUp( ) method and shutdown the game in the tearDown( ) method.

4.5   Set Up and Tear Down

Problem

You want to avoid duplicated code when several tests share the same initialization and cleanup code.

Solution

Use the setUp( ) and tearDown( ) methods. Both of these methods are part of the junit.framework.TestCase class.

Discussion

JUnit follows a very specific sequence of events when invoking tests. First, it constructs a new instance of the test case for each test method. Thus, if you have five test methods, JUnit constructs five instances of your test case. For this reason, instance variables cannot be used to share state between test methods. After constructing all of the test case objects, JUnit follows these steps for each test method:

- Calls the test case's setUp( ) method
- Calls the test method
- Calls the test case's tearDown( ) method

This process repeats for each of the test methods in the test case. Example 4-3 shows how you can take advantage of setUp( ) and tearDown( ) to avoid duplicated code.

Example 4-3. setUp() and tearDown()

```java
package com.oreilly.javaxp.junit;

import com.oreilly.javaxp.common.BadGameException;
import com.oreilly.javaxp.common.Game;
import com.oreilly.javaxp.common.Ship;
import junit.framework.TestCase;

/**
 * Sample unit tests for the {@link Game} class.
 */
public class TestGame extends TestCase {
    private Game game;
    private Ship fighter;

    public void setUp() throws BadGameException {
        this.game = new Game();
        this.fighter = this.game.createFighter("001");
    }

    public void tearDown() {
        this.game.shutdown();
    }

    public void testCreateFighter() {
        assertEquals("Fighter did not have the correct identifier",
                "001", this.fighter.getId());
    }

    public void testSameFighters() {
        Ship fighter2 = this.game.createFighter("001");
        assertSame("createFighter with same id should return same object",
                this.fighter, fighter2);
    }

    public void testGameInitialState() {
        assertTrue("A new game should not be started yet",
                !this.game.isPlaying());
    }
}
```

You can often ignore the tearDown( ) method because individual unit tests are not long-running processes, and objects are garbage-collected as soon as the JVM exits. tearDown( ) can be useful, however, if your tests do things like open database connections, show GUI frames, or consume other sorts of system resources that you would like to clean up immediately. If you are running a large suite of unit tests, setting references to null in your tearDown( ) methods may help the garbage collector reclaim memory as other tests run.

You may be wondering why you should write a setUp( ) method instead of simply initializing fields in a test case's constructor. After all, since a new instance of the test case is created for each of its test methods, the constructor is always called before setUp( ). In a vast majority of cases, you can use the constructor instead of setUp( ) without any side effects.

In cases where your test case is part of a deeper inheritance hierarchy, you may wish to postpone object initialization until instances of derived classes are fully constructed. This is a good technical reason why you might want to use setUp( ) instead of a constructor for initialization. Using setUp( ) and tearDown( ) is also good for documentation purposes, simply because it may make the code easier to read.

See Also

Recipe 4.6 shows how to set up data once for a whole series of tests.

4.6   One-Time Set Up and Tear Down

Problem

You want to run some setup code one time and then run several tests. You only want to run your cleanup code after all of the tests are finished.

Solution

Use the junit.extensions.TestSetup class.

Discussion

As outlined in Recipe 4.5, JUnit calls setUp( ) before each test, and tearDown( ) after each test. In some cases you might want to call a special setup method once before a series of tests, and then call a teardown method once after all tests are complete. The junit.extensions.TestSetup class supports this requirement. Example 4-4 shows how to use this technique.

Example 4-4. One-time set up and tear down

```
package com.oreilly.javaxp.junit;

import com.oreilly.javaxp.common.Person;
import junit.extensions.TestSetup;
import junit.framework.Test;
import junit.framework.TestCase;
import junit.framework.TestSuite;

public class TestPerson extends TestCase {

    public void testGetFullName() { ... }

    public void testNullsInName() { ... }

    public static Test suite() {
        TestSetup setup = new TestSetup(new TestSuite(TestPerson.class)) {
            protected void setUp() throws Exception {
                // do your one-time setup here!
            }

            protected void tearDown() throws Exception {
                // do your one-time tear down here!
            }
        };
        return setup;
    }
}
```

TestSetup is a subclass of junit.extensions.TestDecorator, which is a base class for defining custom tests. The main reason for extending TestDecorator is to gain the ability to execute code before or after a test is run.* The setUp( ) and tearDown( ) methods of TestSetup are called before and after whatever Test is passed to its constructor. In our example we pass a TestSuite to the TestSetup constructor:

```
        TestSetup setup = new TestSetup(new TestSuite(TestPerson.class)) {
```

This means that TestSetup's setUp( ) method is called once before the entire suite, and tearDown( ) is called once afterwards. It is important to note that the setUp( ) and tearDown( ) methods within TestPerson are still executed before and after each individual unit test method within TestPerson.

See Also

Recipe 4.5 describes setUp( ) and tearDown( ).

---

* JUnit includes source code. Check out the code for TestSetup to learn how to create your own extension of TestDecorator.

4.7 Organizing Tests into Test Suites

Problem

You want to organize multiple tests into a suite of tests, all of which run at once.

Solution

JUnit does this automatically for each test case. You can construct an instance of `junit.framework.TestSuite` to create your own suites manually.

Discussion

When you use the text or graphical test runner, JUnit looks for the following method in your test case:[*]

```
public static Test suite() { ... }
```

If the method is not found, JUnit uses reflection to automatically locate all testXXX( ) methods in your test case, adding them to a suite of tests. It then runs all tests in this suite. You can duplicate the default suite( ) behavior as follows:

```
public class TestGame extends TestCase {
    ...
    public static Test suite() {
        return new TestSuite(TestGame.class);
    }
}
```

By passing the TestGame.class object to the TestSuite constructor, you are telling JUnit to locate all of the testXXX( ) methods in that class and add them to the suite. This code does not do anything above and beyond what JUnit does automatically, but there are more interesting ways to use the TestSuite class. For instance, you can add individual tests to only run certain tests, or you can control the order in which they are executed:

```
public static Test suite() {
    TestSuite suite = new TestSuite();
    // To use this idiom, you must define the String constructor in your
    // TestGame class. Remember that JUnit 3.8 made that constructor optional.
    suite.addTest(new TestGame("testCreateFighter"));
    suite.addTest(new TestGame("testSameFighters"));
    return suite;
}
```

---

[*] The Ant junit task also looks for the suite() method.

Or, even better, you can compose multiple suites into other suites. You might recognize this as the Composite design pattern.[*] For example:

```
public static Test suite() {
    TestSuite suite = new TestSuite(TestGame.class);
    suite.addTest(new TestSuite(TestPerson.class));
    return suite;
}
```

Now, when you run this test case, you will run all tests from both `TestGame` and `TestPerson`.

See Also

Recipe 4.11 provides suggestions for organizing test suites.

4.8   Running a Test Class Directly

Problem

You don't want to invoke one of the JUnit test runners. Instead, you would like to run your test directly.

Solution

Add a `main()` method to your test case. Or, use Ant to run your tests as discussed in Chapter 3.

Discussion

Adding a `main()` method can make a class easier to run. Most IDEs allow you to click on a class and select some sort of "run" option from a popup menu, provided the class has a `main()` method. Here is a sample `main()` method for our `TestGame` class:

```
public class TestGame extends TestCase {
    ...
    public static void main(String[] args) {
        junit.textui.TestRunner.run(new TestSuite(TestGame.class));
    }
}
```

When executed, this method runs the test suite in text mode. Output is sent to the console.

---

[*] See Gamma et al., *Design Patterns: Elements of Reusable Object-Oriented Software* (Addison-Wesley).

See Also

Recipe 4.2 shows how to run unit tests. Chapter 3 shows how to run tests using Ant.

4.9   Repeating Tests

Problem

You want to run certain tests repeatedly.

Solution

Use the `junit.extensions.RepeatedTest` class.

Discussion

You may want to run certain tests repeatedly to measure performance or to diagnose intermittent problems.* The `RepeatedTest` class makes this easy:

```
public static Test suite( ) {
    // run the entire test suite ten times
    return new RepeatedTest(new TestSuite(TestGame.class), 10);
}
```

`RepeatedTest`'s first argument is another `Test` to run; the second argument is the number of iterations. Since `TestSuite` implements the `Test` interface, we can repeat the entire test as just shown. Here is how you can build a test suite where different tests are repeated differently:

```
TestSuite suite = new TestSuite( );
// repeat the testCreateFighter test 100 times
suite.addTest(new RepeatedTest(new TestGame("testCreateFighter"), 100));
// run testSameFighters once
suite.addTest(new TestGame("testSameFighters"));
// repeat the testGameInitialState test 20 times
suite.addTest(new RepeatedTest(new TestGame("testGameInitialState"), 20));
```

See Also

Recipe 4.13 shows more examples of `RepeatedTest`.

---

* Threading bugs are often intermittent.

4.10   Test Naming Conventions

Problem

You want to define a naming convention for your tests.

Solution

Prefix each test case classname with a consistent word, such as "Test" or "Unit-Test". Put test cases in the same directory as the classes they are testing.

Discussion

Consistent naming conventions serve two purposes. First, they make your code more maintainable. Second, consistency facilitates automation. The tests in this chapter are prefixed with "Test", resulting in names like `TestGame`, `TestPerson`, and `TestAccount`. These correspond to the `Game`, `Person`, and `Account` classes, respectively.

Writing one test case per class makes it very easy to glance at a directory and see which tests are available. Putting "Test" at the beginning of the filenames makes sorting easier, in our opinion, particularly when your IDE provides some sort of jump-to functionality.* All tests will be grouped together and easy to identify. On the other hand, putting "Test" at the end of the filenames does make it easier to identify which classes do not have tests.

 Another popular convention is to place all test classes in a parallel directory structure. This allows you to use the same Java package names for your tests, while keeping the source files separate. To be honest, we do not like this approach because you must look in two different directories to find files. Ant can easily exclude tests from your build even if they reside in the same source directory.

Finally, a consistent naming convention makes it easier to locate tests when using Ant for your builds. You might want to exclude all of your tests when you create a production build of your software. You can do this in Ant as follows:

```
<javac destdir="${dir.build}">
  <src path="${dir.src}"/>
  <!-- see how easy it is to exclude the tests from a build! -->
  <exclude name="**/Test*.java"/>
</javac>
```

---

* IntelliJ IDEA (*http://www.intellij.com*) allows you to hit Ctrl-N and then begin typing a classname. If you follow the prefix convention, you immediately see a list of all tests as soon as you type `Test`.

See Also

Recipe 3.15 shows how to run tests using Ant based on naming conventions. Recipe 3.13 shows how to exclude test classes from a build.

4.11 Unit Test Organization

Problem

You want to organize all of your tests consistently.

Solution

Create a test case that runs all tests in the current package and subpackages. Duplicate this pattern for all packages in your application.

 Some Java IDEs allow you to automatically run all tests in your project or in a specific package, negating the need for this recipe.

Discussion

Example 4-5 shows an example of the technique outlined in the solution just presented. It runs all of the test suites in the current package as well as delegating to each AllTests class in immediate subpackages.

Example 4-5. AllTests example

```
package com.oreilly.javaxp.junit;

import junit.framework.Test;
import junit.framework.TestCase;
import junit.framework.TestSuite;
```

Example 4-5. AllTests example (continued)

```
/**
 * Runs all test suites in the current package and sub-packages.
 */
public class AllTests extends TestCase {
    /**
     * @return a suite containing all tests in this package
     *         and subpackages.
     */
    public static Test suite( ) {
        TestSuite suite = new TestSuite( );

        // add tests from the current directory. This requires manual
        // updates, which is the main weakness of this technique
        suite.addTest(new TestSuite(TestGame.class));
        suite.addTest(new TestSuite(TestPerson.class));

        // add AllTests from any sub-packages
        suite.addTest(com.oreilly.javaxp.junit.sub.AllTests.suite( ));
        // suite.addTest(...) // continue for other sub-packages

        return suite;
    }
}
```

This technique can be useful when using an IDE* because you can select any
AllTests class and run tests for a subset of your project. Assuming that you follow
this pattern consistently, you can run the AllTests in your root directory to run every
test in your application.

 AllTests intentionally avoids the TestXXX naming convention outlined in Recipe 4.10. This prevents the AllTests from being executed
when you tell Ant to find and run all TestXXX classes.

Human fallibility is the main weakness of this technique. If you are not diligent, you
will forget to add some tests to one of the AllTests classes. This can be overcome by
writing a utility to automatically generate the AllTests classes. Yet another technique is to do the same thing dynamically: to write a class that sifts through a direc-
tory/package looking for TestXXXX classes and including them in the suite.

You might also want to consider whether the AllTests classes should run tests in
subpackages, or just the current package. Here is a modification that allows you to
choose the behavior you want based on a system property:

```
public static Test suite( ) {
    TestSuite suite = new TestSuite( );
```

---

* IntelliJ IDEA allows you to right-click on any directory and run all tests in that package, thus eliminating the
need to manually create an AllTests class.

```
// add tests from the current directory
suite.addTest(new TestSuite(TestGame.class));
suite.addTest(new TestSuite(TestPerson.class));

// only test subdirectories if a system property is true
if ("true".equals(System.getProperty("test.subdirs"))) {
    // add AllTests from any sub-packages
    suite.addTest(com.oreilly.javaxp.junit.sub.AllTests.suite());
    // suite.addTest(...) // continue for other sub-packages
}

return suite;
}
```

See Also

Recipe 3.15 shows an example of Ant's batchtest element.

4.12   Exception Handling

Problem

You want to test for exceptions.

Solution

Use a try/catch block to catch the expected exception. Call the fail( ) method if the exception does not occur.

Discussion

In the following example, the Person constructor should throw an IllegalArgumentException if both of its arguments are null. The test fails if it does not throw this exception.

```
public void testPassNullsToConstructor( ) {
    try {
        Person p = new Person(null, null);
        fail("Expected IllegalArgumentException when both args are null");
    } catch (IllegalArgumentException expected) {
        // ignore this because it means the test passed!
    }
}
```

Only use this technique when you are expecting an exception. For other error conditions, let the exception propagate to JUnit. It will catch the exception and report a test error. Here is something you do not want to do:

```
// don't do this!
public void testBadStyle( ) {
```

```
    try {
        SomeClass c = new SomeClass( );
        c.doSomething( );
        ...
    } catch (IOException ioe) {
        fail("Caught an IOException");
    } catch (NullPointerException npe) {
        fail("Caught a NullPointerException");
    }
}
```

The main problem is that JUnit already catches unhandled errors, so you are doing unnecessary work. The extra try/catch code adds complexity to your tests, making them harder to maintain. The previous example is much simpler when written like this:

```
// must declare IOException because it is not a RuntimeException
public void testGoodStyle( ) throws IOException {
    SomeClass c = new SomeClass( );
    c.doSomething( );
    ...
}
```

4.13   Running Tests Concurrently

Problem

You want to run several tests concurrently using threads.

Solution

Use the junit.extensions.ActiveTestSuite class to build a suite of tests that run concurrently.

Discussion

The ActiveTestSuite class runs each of its tests in a separate thread. The suite does not finish until all of the test threads are complete. Example 4-6 shows how to run three different test methods in three different threads.

Example 4-6. Running tests in different threads

```
public static Test suite( ) {
    TestSuite suite = new ActiveTestSuite( );
    suite.addTest(new TestGame("testCreateFighter"));
    suite.addTest(new TestGame("testGameInitialState"));
    suite.addTest(new TestGame("testSameFighters"));
    return suite;
}
```

While you probably won't use this technique often, running tests in threads can serve as a rudimentary stress tester. You might also use ActiveTestSuite to help identify threading problems in your code. By combining ActiveTestSuite with RepeatedTest, you can uncover threading problems that only show up intermittently.

Example 4-7 shows how you can combine repeated tests and other test suites into an ActiveTestSuite. Each of the repeated tests runs in a different thread; therefore, you end up with four threads. If you are experiencing occasional threading glitches, you might want to increase the number of iterations and run a similar test suite overnight.

Example 4-7. A more advanced test suite

```
public static Test suite( ) {
    TestSuite suite = new ActiveTestSuite( );

    // run one test in a thread
    suite.addTest(new TestGame("testCreateFighter"));

    // run this test 100 times in a second thread
    suite.addTest(new RepeatedTest(
        new TestGame("testGameInitialState"), 100));

    // run this test 200 times in a third thread
    suite.addTest(new RepeatedTest(
        new TestGame("testSameFighters"), 200));

    // run some other test suite in a fourth thread
    suite.addTest(TestPerson.suite( ));
    return suite;
}
```

See Also

Recipe 4.9 explains the RepeatedTest class.

4.14   Testing Asynchronous Methods

Problem

You want to test asynchronous methods.

Solution

Use a mock listener to wait for the asynchronous method to complete.

Discussion

An asynchronous method executes in its own thread, notifying some listener when it is complete. Code that calls an asynchronous method does not block, meaning that you cannot write a test like this:

```
public void testSomething() {
    someAsynchronousMethod();
    assertXXX(...);
}
```

The problem with this code lies in the fact that the assertXXX() is almost certainly executed before the thread started by someAsynchronousMethod() has a chance to do its work. We really need to do something like this:

1. Call an asynchronous method.

2. Wait until the method is complete.

3. Get the results.

    - If the method times out, fail.

    - Otherwise, check the results.

To illustrate, let's look at a simple interface for searching. We assume that searching occurs in its own thread, notifying a SearchModelListener whenever the search is complete. Example 4-8 shows the API.

Example 4-8. SearchModel interface

```
public interface SearchModel {
    void search(Object searchCriteria, SearchModelListener listener);
}
```

The search() method is asynchronous, notifying the SearchModelListener when it is complete. Example 4-9 shows the code for the SearchModelListener interface.

Example 4-9. SearchModelListener interface

```
public interface SearchModelListener extends EventListener {
    void searchFinished(SearchModelEvent evt);
}
```

In order to test the search model, we must write a mock listener that waits for the search to complete. Once the mock listener receives its result, we can verify that the data is correct. Example 4-10 shows the code for a mock listener.

Example 4-10. MockSearchModelListener class

```
class MockSearchModelListener implements SearchModelListener {
    private SearchModelEvent evt;

    public void searchFinished(SearchModelEvent evt) {
        this.evt = evt;
```

Example 4-10. MockSearchModelListener class (continued)

```
        synchronized (this) {
            notifyAll( );
        }
    }

    public SearchModelEvent getSearchModelEvent( ) {
        return this.evt;
    }
}
```

The key to our mock listener is the synchronized block. This listener assumes that some other thread (our unit test) is waiting for the search to complete. By calling notifyAll( ), the mock listener allows the unit test to "wake up" and continue.* Example 4-11 shows the unit test, which ties everything together.

Example 4-11. Asynchronous unit test

```
public void testAsynchronousSearch( ) throws InterruptedException {
    MockSearchModelListener mockListener = new MockSearchModelListener( );
    SearchModel sm = new PersonSearchModel( );
    // 1. Execute the search
    sm.search("eric", mockListener);

    // 2. Wait for the search to complete
    synchronized (mockListener) {
        mockListener.wait(2000);
    }

    // 3. Get the results
    SearchModelEvent evt = mockListener.getSearchModelEvent( );

    // 3a) if the method times out, fail
    assertNotNull("Search timed out", evt);

    // 3b) otherwise, check the results
    List results = evt.getSearchResult( );
    assertEquals("Number of results", 1, results.size( ));
    Person p = (Person) results.get(0);
    assertEquals("Result", "Eric", p.getFirstName( ));
}
```

The unit test first creates a mock listener, passing that listener to the search model. It then uses a synchronized block to wait until the listener calls notifyAll( ). Calling wait(2000) indicates that the test will wait for at least two seconds before it stops waiting and continues. If this happens, the mock listener's event object is null because it was never notified by the search model.

---

* notifyAll( ) can only be called within synchronized code.

Having a timeout period is critical; otherwise, your test will wait indefinitely if the asynchronous method fails and never notifies the caller.

Assuming the search completed within two seconds, the test goes on to check the results for correctness.

See Also

Mock objects are described in Chapter 6.

4.15   Writing a Base Class for Your Tests

Problem

You want to reuse the same behavior in all of your tests without duplicating code.

Solution

Define common behavior in a subclass of `junit.framework.TestCase` and extend from your class, rather than directly extending `TestCase`.

Discussion

JUnit does not require that your tests directly extend `TestCase`. Instead, you can introduce new `TestCase` extensions for common behavior. You might want to ensure that some common initialization code is always executed before each of your tests. In that case, you might write something like this:

```
public abstract class MyAbstractTestCase extends TestCase {
    public MyAbstractTestCase() {
        initializeApplicationProperties();
    }

    public MyAbstractTestCase(String testName) {
        super(testName);
        initializeApplicationProperties();
    }

    // initialize some custom application framework. Leave this method
    // protected so subclasses can customize.
    protected void initializeApplicationProperties() {
        MyFramework.initialize("common/myappconfig.properties");
    }
}
```

Tests in your application can now extend `MyAbstractTestCase` and your framework initialization code will always be executed before the tests run.

Providing convenience methods is another reason why you might want to extend `TestCase`. We show this in the next recipe when we define a method to retrieve a Swing `JFrame` for graphical testing.

4.16 Testing Swing Code

Problem

You want to write unit tests for Swing portions of your application.

Solution

Keep application logic separate from GUI layout, thus minimizing the need to test graphical code directly. Also, design your user interface in terms of discrete components that are testable without complex setup and configuration.

Discussion

Graphical code presents many testing challenges. For instance, many Swing functions only work when the components are visible on screen. In these cases, your tests have to create dummy frames and show the components before the tests can succeed. In other cases, Swing schedules events on the AWT event queue rather than updating component states immediately. We show how to tackle this issue in the next recipe.

Ideally, you should strive to minimize the need to test Swing code in the first place. Application logic, such as computing the monthly payment amount for a loan, should not be intertwined with the `JTable` that displays the payment history. Instead, you might want to define three separate classes:

Loan
> A utility class that keeps track of payments, interest rates, and other attributes. This class can be tested independently of Swing.

LoanPaymentTableModel
> A Swing table model for a history of loan payments. Because table models are nongraphical, you can test them just like any other Java class.

JTable
> Displays the `LoanPaymentTableModel`. Because `JTable` is provided with Swing, you don't have to test it.

There are more complex scenarios where you cannot avoid Swing testing. Let's suppose you need a panel to display information about a person and would like to test it. The Person class is easily testable on its own, and probably contains methods to retrieve a name, address, SSN, and other key pieces of information. But the PersonEditorPanel is graphical and a little more challenging to test. You might start with the code shown in Example 4-12.

Example 4-12. First draft of PersonEditorPanel.java

```java
public class PersonEditorPanel extends JPanel {
    private JTextField firstNameField = new JTextField(20);
    private JTextField lastNameField = new JTextField(20);
    // @todo - add more fields later

    private Person person;

    public PersonEditorPanel() {
        layoutGui();
        updateDataDisplay();
    }

    public void setPerson(Person p) {
        this.person = person;
        updateDataDisplay();
    }

    public Person getPerson() {
        // @todo - update the person with new information from the fields
        return this.person;
    }

    private void layoutGui() {
        // @todo - define the layout
    }

    private void updateDataDisplay() {
        // @todo - ensure the fields are properly enabled, also set
        //          data on the fields.
    }
}
```

Our PersonEditorPanel does not function yet, but it is far enough along to begin writing unit tests. Before delving into the actual tests, let's look at a base class for Swing tests. Example 4-13 shows a class that provides access to a JFrame for testing purposes. Our unit test for PersonEditorPanel will extend from SwingTestCase.

Example 4-13. SwingTestCase.java

```java
package com.oreilly.javaxp.junit;

import junit.framework.TestCase;

import javax.swing.*;
import java.lang.reflect.InvocationTargetException;
```

Example 4-13. SwingTestCase.java (continued)

```java
public class SwingTestCase extends TestCase {
    private JFrame testFrame;

    protected void tearDown( ) throws Exception {
        if (this.testFrame != null) {
            this.testFrame.dispose( );
            this.testFrame = null;
        }
    }

    public JFrame getTestFrame( ) {
        if (this.testFrame == null) {
            this.testFrame = new JFrame("Test");
        }
        return this.testFrame;
    }
}
```

SwingTestCase provides access to a JFrame and takes care of disposing the frame in its tearDown( ) method. As you write more Swing tests, you can place additional functionality in SwingTestCase.

Example 4-14 shows the first few tests for PersonEditorPanel. In these tests, we check to see if the fields in the panel are enabled and disabled properly.

Example 4-14. The first PersonEditorPanel tests

```java
public class TestPersonEditorPanel extends SwingTestCase {
    private PersonEditorPanel emptyPanel;
    private PersonEditorPanel tannerPanel;
    private Person tanner;

    protected void setUp( ) throws Exception {
        // create a panel without a Person
        this.emptyPanel = new PersonEditorPanel( );

        // create a panel with a Person
        this.tanner = new Person("Tanner", "Burke");
        this.tannerPanel = new PersonEditorPanel( );
        this.tannerPanel.setPerson(this.tanner);
    }

    public void testTextFieldsAreInitiallyDisabled( ) {
        assertTrue("First name field should be disabled",
                !this.emptyPanel.getFirstNameField().isEnabled( ));
        assertTrue("Last name field should be disabled",
                !this.emptyPanel.getLastNameField().isEnabled( ));
    }

    public void testEnabledStateAfterSettingPerson( ) {
        assertTrue("First name field should be enabled",
                this.tannerPanel.getFirstNameField().isEnabled( ));
```

Example 4-14. The first PersonEditorPanel tests (continued)

```
    assertTrue("Last name field should be enabled",
            this.tannerPanel.getLastNameField().isEnabled());
}
```

You might notice that our tests have to get to the first and last name fields, so we need to introduce the getFirstNameField( ) and getLastNameField( ) methods in our panel:

```
JTextField getFirstNameField() {
    return this.firstNameField;
}

JTextField getLastNameField() {
    return this.lastNameField;
}
```

These methods are package-scope because we only need them for testing purposes. When you first run the unit tests, they will fail because we did not write any logic to enable and disable the fields. This method can be added to PersonEditorPanel in order to make the tests pass:

```
private void updateEnabledStates() {
    this.firstNameField.setEnabled(person != null);
    this.lastNameField.setEnabled(person != null);
}
```

Once you get these tests working, you can test for the actual values of the two fields:

```
public void testFirstName() {
    assertEquals("First name", "",
            this.emptyPanel.getFirstNameField().getText());
    assertEquals("First name", this.tanner.getFirstName(),
            this.tannerPanel.getFirstNameField().getText());
}

public void testLastName() {
    assertEquals("Last name", "",
            this.emptyPanel.getLastNameField().getText());
    assertEquals("Last name", this.tanner.getLastName(),
            this.tannerPanel.getLastNameField().getText());
}
```

These will also fail until you add some more logic to PersonEditorPanel to set data on the two text fields:

```
private void updateDataDisplay() {
    if (this.person == null) {
        this.firstNameField.setText("");
        this.lastNameField.setText("");
    } else {
        this.firstNameField.setText(this.person.getFirstName());
        this.lastNameField.setText(this.person.getLastName());
    }
    updateEnabledStates();
}
```

When complete, your tests should confirm that you can create an empty panel, set a person object on it, and retrieve person object after it has been edited. You should also write tests for unusual conditions, such as a null person reference or null data within the person. This is a data-oriented test, ensuring that the panel properly displays and updates its data. We did not try to verify the graphical positioning of the actual components, nor have we tried to test user interaction with the GUI.

See Also

Recipe 4.18 discusses problems with java.awt.Robot. Chapter 11 provides some references to Swing-specific testing tools. Recipe 11.5 discusses some pros and cons of making methods package-scope for the sole purpose of testing them.

4.17   Avoiding Swing Threading Problems

Problem

You want to test Swing functions that dispatch to the AWT event queue, such as focus traversal.

Solution

Write a utility method to wait until pending AWT event queue messages are processed.

Discussion

Suppose you want to test the focus traversal order of the PersonEditorPanel introduced in the previous recipe. You want to ensure that focus travels from component to component in the correct order as the user hits the tab key. To do this, you write the following test:

```
public void testTabOrder( ) {
    JTextField firstNameField = this.tannerPanel.getFirstNameField( );

    firstNameField.requestFocusInWindow( );

    // simulate the user hitting tab
    firstNameField.transferFocus( );

    // ensure that the last name field now has focus
    JTextField lastNameField = this.tannerPanel.getLastNameField( );
    assertTrue("Expected last name field to have focus",
            lastNameField.hasFocus( ));
}
```

As written, this test fails. First and foremost, the components must be visible on screen before they can obtain focus. So you try modifying your setUp( ) method as follows:

```
protected void setUp( ) throws Exception {
    this.emptyPanel = new PersonEditorPanel( );

    this.tanner = new Person("Tanner", "Burke");
    this.tannerPanel = new PersonEditorPanel( );
    this.tannerPanel.setPerson(this.tanner);

    getTestFrame().getContentPane( ).add(this.tannerPanel,
        BorderLayout.CENTER);
    getTestFrame().pack( );
    getTestFrame().show( );
}
```

This takes advantage of the JFrame provided by our base class, SwingTestCase. When you run your test again, it still fails! The initial focus never made it to the first name field. Here is a partial solution:

```
public void testTabOrder( ) {
    JTextField firstNameField = this.tannerPanel.getFirstNameField( );

    // make sure the first name field has focus
    while (!firstNameField.hasFocus( )) {
        getTestFrame().toFront( );
        firstNameField.requestFocusInWindow( );
    }

    // simulate the user hitting tab
    firstNameField.transferFocus( );

    // ensure that the last name field now has focus
    JTextField lastNameField = this.tannerPanel.getLastNameField( );
    assertTrue("Expected last name field to have focus",
            lastNameField.hasFocus( ));
}
```

This approach keeps trying until the first name field eventually gains focus. It also brings the test frame to the front of other windows because, during testing, we found that the frame sometimes gets buried if the user clicks on any other window while the test is running. We discovered this by repeating our tests and clicking on other applications while the tests ran:

```
public static Test suite( ) {
    return new RepeatedTest(
            new TestSuite(TestPersonEditorPanel.class), 1000);
}
```

We still have one more problem. When the test runs repeatedly, you will notice that the test fails intermittently. This is because the transferFocus( ) method does not occur immediately. Instead, the request to transfer focus is scheduled on the AWT event queue. In order to pass consistently, the test must wait until the event has a chance to be processed by the queue. Example 4-15 lists the final version of our test.

Example 4-15. Final tab order test

```
public void testTabOrder( ) {
    JTextField firstNameField = this.tannerPanel.getFirstNameField( );

    // make sure the first name field has focus
    while (!firstNameField.hasFocus( )) {
        getTestFrame( ).toFront( );
        firstNameField.requestFocusInWindow( );
    }

    // simulate the user hitting tab
    firstNameField.transferFocus( );

    // wait until the transferFocus( ) method is processed
    waitForSwing( );

    // ensure that the last name field now has focus
    JTextField lastNameField = this.tannerPanel.getLastNameField( );
    assertTrue("Expected last name field to have focus",
            lastNameField.hasFocus( ));
}
```

The waitForSwing( ) method is a new feature of our base class, SwingTestCase, that blocks until pending AWT events like transferFocus( ) are processed:

```
public void waitForSwing( ) {
    if (!SwingUtilities.isEventDispatchThread( )) {
        try {
            SwingUtilities.invokeAndWait(new Runnable( ) {
                public void run( ) {
                }
            });
        } catch (InterruptedException e) {
        } catch (InvocationTargetException e) {
        }
    }
}
```

Now, our test runs almost 100% of the time. When repeating the test thousands of times, you can make the test fail every once in a while by randomly clicking on other applications. This is because you take away focus just before the test asks the last name field if it has focus. This sort of problem is unavoidable, and illustrates one of the reasons why you should minimize your dependency on Swing tests.

The most valuable lesson of this recipe is the technique of repeating your graphical tests many thousands of times until all of the quirky Swing threading issues are resolved. Once your tests run as consistently as possible, remove the repeated test.

Also, while your tests are running, avoid clicking on other running applications so you don't interfere with focus events.

See Also

Chapter 11 provides some references to Swing-specific testing tools.

4.18   Testing with the Robot

Problem

You want to simulate the user clicking on the mouse or typing with the keyboard using java.awt.Robot.

Solution

We do not recommend this technique.

Discussion

java.awt.Robot allows Java applications to take command of native system input events, such as moving the mouse pointer or simulating keystrokes. At first glance, this seems to be a great way to test your GUIs. Your tests can do exactly what the user might do and then verify that your components are displaying the correct information.

We have found that this approach is dangerous.

- Robot tests are very fragile, breaking any time the GUI layout changes.
- If the user moves the mouse while the tests are running, the Robot continues clicking, sometimes on the wrong application.*
- Since the tests run so quickly, it can be impossible to stop the tests once the Robot gets confused and starts clicking on other apps and typing characters that show up in other windows.

If you really feel that you could use some Robot tests, consider naming them differently than other tests. You might have a collection of *RobotTest*.java* tests. You can then run them independently of other tests, if you are extremely careful to avoid touching the mouse while the tests run.

---

* One programmer reported that the Robot sent a partially completed email because it clicked on the send button of the mail client instead of a button in the application being tested.

See Also

Chapter 11 provides some references to Swing-specific testing tools.

4.19   Testing Database Logic

Problem

You want to test database logic using JUnit.

Solution

Write scripts to generate a stable testing database and test against that data.

Discussion

Testing against a database is challenging in many organizations because you have to define predictable data.* The only truly reliable approach is to create the test data in a private database automatically for each set of tests. When the tests are finished, you should destroy the test data. If you create the test database manually, you run the risk of corruption over time as people modify data that your tests assume is present.

> For very large databases, you may have to settle for either creating clean test data daily or weekly, or loading a subset of the database with well-known testing records.

We recommend that you follow the technique outlined in Recipe 4.6 to perform one-time setup and tear down before and after a group of tests. You can create the test data in the one-time setup, and remove it in the one-time tear down. Once you have control of the data, you can test against that data:

```
public void testDeleteEmployee( ) throws SQLException {
    EmployeeDAO dao = new EmployeeDAO( );
    assertNotNull("Employee 'ericBurke' should be present",
            dao.getEmployee("ericBurke"));
    dao.deleteEmployee("ericBurke");
    assertNull("Employee 'ericBurke' should not be present",
            dao.getEmployee("ericBurke"));
}
```

---

* This is a political battle in many companies, because the database administrators might not give programmers the permission to create new tables or perform other functions necessary to create test data.

Another challenge is the fact that early tests might modify data in ways that interfere with later tests. In these cases, you can either write functions to clean up data after the earlier tests run, or you can build your test suites manually. By building the suites manually, you can control the order in which the tests run:

```
public static Test suite( ) {
    TestSuite suite = new TestSuite( );
    suite.addTest(new TestEmployeeDB("testCreateEmployee"));
    suite.addTest(new TestEmployeeDB("testUpdateEmployee"));
    suite.addTest(new TestEmployeeDB("testDeleteEmployee"));
    return suite;
}
```

 Database-specific copy, backup, and restore mechanisms are sometimes tremendously faster than reinitializing the database with a series of SQL statements. For example, if your database is MS SQL Server, you can copy over a known testing database *.mdf/.ldf* file to get your database to a known state very quickly.

See Also

Recipe 4.6 shows how to implement `oneTimeSetUp( )` and `oneTimeTearDown( )`.

4.20   Repeatedly Testing the Same Method

Problem

You want to test a method with a wide range of input data. You are not sure if you should write a different test for each combination of input data, or one huge test that checks every possible combination.

Solution

Write a `suite( )` method that iterates through all of your input data, creating a unique instance of your test case for each unique input. The data is passed to the test cases through the constructor, which stores the data in instance fields so it is available to the test methods.

Discussion

You often want to test some piece of functionality with many different combinations of input data. Your first impulse might be to write a different test method for each possible combination of data; however, this is tedious and results in a lot of mundane coding. A second option is to write a single, big test method that checks every possible combination of input data. For example:

```
public void testSomething( ) {
    Foo foo = new Foo( );
    // test every possible combination of input data
    assertTrue(foo.doSomething(false, false, false);
    assertFalse(foo.doSomething(false, false, true);
    assertFalse(foo.doSomething(false, true, false);
    assertTrue(foo.doSomething(false, true, true);
    ...etc
}
```

This approach suffers from a fatal flaw. The problem is that the test stops executing as soon as the first assertion fails, so you won't see all of the errors at once. Ideally, you want to easily set up a large number of test cases and run them all as independent tests. One failure should not prevent the remaining tests from running.

To illustrate this technique, Example 4-16 contains a utility for determining the background color of a component. The getFieldBackground( ) method calculates a different background color based on numerous parameters—for example, whether a record is available and whether the current data is valid.

Example 4-16. UtilComponent

```
public class UtilComponent {
    public static final int ADD_MODE = 1;
    public static final int RECORD_AVAILABLE_MODE = 2;
    public static final int NO_RECORD_AVAILABLE_MODE = 3;

    public static final int KEY_FIELD = 100;
    public static final int REQUIRED_FIELD = 101;
    public static final int READONLY_FIELD = 102;
    public static final int NORMAL_FIELD = 103;

    public static final Color FIELD_NORMAL_BACKGROUND = Color.WHITE;
    public static final Color FIELD_ERROR_BACKGROUND = Color.PINK;
    public static final Color FIELD_REQUIRED_BACKGROUND = Color.CYAN;
    public static final Color FIELD_DISABLED_BACKGROUND = Color.GRAY;

    public static Color getFieldBackground(
            int screenMode,
            int fieldType,
            boolean valid,
            boolean requiredConditionMet) {
        if (fieldType == READONLY_FIELD
                || screenMode == NO_RECORD_AVAILABLE_MODE
                || (fieldType == KEY_FIELD && screenMode != ADD_MODE)) {
            return FIELD_DISABLED_BACKGROUND;
        }

        if (!valid) {
            return FIELD_ERROR_BACKGROUND;
        }
        if ((fieldType == KEY_FIELD || fieldType == REQUIRED_FIELD)
                && !requiredConditionMet) {
```

Example 4-16. UtilComponent (continued)

```
            return FIELD_REQUIRED_BACKGROUND;
        }
        return FIELD_NORMAL_BACKGROUND;
    }

    public static String colorToString(Color color) {
        if (color == null) {
            return "null";
        }
        if (color.equals(FIELD_DISABLED_BACKGROUND)) {
            return "FIELD_DISABLED_BACKGROUND";
        }
        if (color.equals(FIELD_ERROR_BACKGROUND)) {
            return "FIELD_ERROR_BACKGROUND";
        }
        if (color.equals(FIELD_REQUIRED_BACKGROUND)) {
            return "FIELD_REQUIRED_BACKGROUND";
        }
        if (color.equals(FIELD_NORMAL_BACKGROUND)) {
            return "FIELD_NORMAL_BACKGROUND";
        }
        return color.toString();
    }
}
```

There are 48 possible combinations of inputs to the getFieldBackground( ) method, and 4 possible return values. The test case defines a helper class that encapsulates one combination of inputs along with an expected result. It then builds an array of 48 instances of this class, 1 per combination of input data. Example 4-17 shows this portion of our test.

Example 4-17. Defining the test data

```
public class TestUtilComponent extends TestCase {

    private int testNumber;

    static class TestData {
        int screenMode;
        int fieldType;
        boolean valid;
        boolean requiredConditionMet;
        Color expectedColor;

        public TestData(int screenMode, int fieldType, boolean valid,
                        boolean requiredConditionMet, Color expectedColor) {
            this.screenMode = screenMode;
            this.fieldType = fieldType;
            this.valid = valid;
            this.requiredConditionMet = requiredConditionMet;
            this.expectedColor = expectedColor;
```

Example 4-17. Defining the test data (continued)

```
        }
    }

    private static final TestData[] TESTS = new TestData[] {
        new TestData(UtilComponent.ADD_MODE, // 0
                    UtilComponent.KEY_FIELD,
                    false, false,
                    UtilComponent.FIELD_ERROR_BACKGROUND),
        new TestData(UtilComponent.ADD_MODE, // 1
                    UtilComponent.KEY_FIELD,
                    false, true,
                    UtilComponent.FIELD_ERROR_BACKGROUND),
        new TestData(UtilComponent.ADD_MODE, // 2
                    UtilComponent.KEY_FIELD,
                    true, false,
                    UtilComponent.FIELD_REQUIRED_BACKGROUND),

    ...continue defining TestData for every possible input
```

The test extends from the normal JUnit TestCase base class, and defines a single private field called testNumber. This field keeps track of which instance of TestData to test. Remember that for each unit test, a new instance of TestUtilComponent is created. Thus, each instance has its own copy of the testNumber field, which contains an index into the TESTS array.

The TESTS array contains every possible combination of TestData. As you can see, we include comments containing the index in the array:

```
    new TestData(UtilComponent.ADD_MODE, // 0
```

This index allows us to track down which test cases are not working when we encounter failures. Example 4-18 shows the remainder of our test case, illustrating how the tests are executed.

Example 4-18. Remainder of TestUtilComponent

```
    public TestUtilComponent(String testMethodName, int testNumber) {
        super(testMethodName);
        this.testNumber = testNumber;
    }

    public void testFieldBackgroundColor( ) {
        TestData td = TESTS[this.testNumber];

        Color actualColor = UtilComponent.getFieldBackground(td.screenMode,
                td.fieldType, td.valid, td.requiredConditionMet);

        assertEquals("Test number " + this.testNumber + ": ",
                UtilComponent.colorToString(td.expectedColor),
                UtilComponent.colorToString(actualColor));
    }
```

Example 4-18. Remainder of TestUtilComponent (continued)

```
    public static Test suite( ) {
        TestSuite suite = new TestSuite( );
        for (int i=0; i<TESTS.length; i++) {
            suite.addTest(new TestUtilComponent("testFieldBackgroundColor", i));
        }
        return suite;
    }
}
```

Our constructor does not follow the usual JUnit pattern. In addition to the test method name, we accept the test number. This is assigned to the `testNumber` field, and indicates which data to test.

The `testFieldBackgroundColor( )` method is our actual unit test. It uses the correct `TestData` object to run `UtilComponent.getFieldBackground( )`, using `assertEquals( )` to check the color. We also use `UtilComponent` to convert the color to a text string before doing the comparison. Although this is not required, it results in much more readable error messages when the test fails.

The final portion of our test is the `suite( )` method. JUnit uses reflection to search for this method. If found, JUnit runs the tests returned from `suite( )` rather than using reflection to locate `testXXX( )` methods. In our case, we loop through our array of test data, creating a new instance of `TestUtilComponent` for each entry. Each test instance has a different test number, and is added to the `TestSuite`. This is how we create 48 different tests from our array of test data.

Although we have a hardcoded array of test data, there are other instances where you want to make your tests more customizable. In those cases, you should use the same technique outlined in this recipe. Instead of hardcoding the test data, however, you can put your test data into an XML file. Your `suite( )` method would parse the XML file and then create a `TestSuite` containing the test data defined in your XML.

See Also

Recipe 4.5 explains how JUnit normally instantiates and runs test cases.

CHAPTER 5

HttpUnit

5.0 Introduction

HttpUnit, available from *http://www.httpunit.org*, is an open source Java library for programmatically interacting with HTTP servers. With HttpUnit, your Java programs can access servers directly, without the need for a browser. HttpUnit provides an API for parsing HTML, submitting forms, following hyperlinks, setting cookies, and performing many other tasks normally associated with web browsers. It also includes a class library for direct manipulation of servlets, sometimes bypassing the need to start a web server.

Despite its name, HttpUnit is not a testing tool. Instead, it provides an API for interacting with HTML and HTTP servers. You normally think of HttpUnit as a testing tool, however, because you use HttpUnit in conjunction with JUnit to write tests. JUnit defines the testing framework and your testXXX( ) methods use the HttpUnit API to access and test web pages.

 Tests written with HttpUnit are usually more like "integration" tests than "unit" tests. A unit test normally tests a single method or class in isolation, while HttpUnit tests invoke HTTP servers across a network connection.

Using HttpUnit in combination with JUnit is the focus of the recipes in this chapter. The recipes are presented in order as portions of a simple web application developed using a test-first approach. If the web application were complete, it would allow users to subscribe and unsubscribe from a newsletter. It would also allow administrators to view the complete list of newsletter subscribers, but only after providing a username and password.

HttpUnit cannot test JavaScript. You might consider JsUnit, available at *http://sourceforge.net/projects/jsunit/*.

5.1 Installing HttpUnit

Problem

You want to install HttpUnit.

Solution

Add *httpunit.jar* and *Tidy.jar*, both included with HttpUnit, to your classpath. Also ensure that an XML parser is installed.

Discussion

httpunit.jar contains the class files for the HttpUnit application. Its API allows you to send requests to web servers, obtain responses, and test the content of the resulting web pages. It also contains the `com.meterware.servletunit` package for testing servlets directly, without going through a web server.

Tidy.jar, also included in the HttpUnit distribution, contains the Java port of HTML Tidy, an open source tool for checking the syntax of HTML. HTML Tidy also includes an API for parsing HTML, which is the part used by HttpUnit. You can learn more about the Java port of HTML Tidy at *http://sourceforge.net/projects/jtidy*.

If you are running under JDK 1.4, add *httpunit.jar* and *Tidy.jar* to your classpath. If you are running an older version of Java, you must also include a JAXP-compliant XML parser in your classpath. The next recipe shows how to do this.

See Also

Recipe 5.2 shows how to configure HttpUnit with Ant.

5.2 Preparing for Test-First Development

Problem

You want to configure your development environment to support test-first development with HttpUnit, JUnit, Tomcat, and Ant.

Solution

Create an Ant buildfile to automatically build and deploy your web application. The buildfile allows you to quickly redeploy and test after each change to your code.

Discussion

The example shown in this recipe relies on Tomcat 4.0 or later, as well as Ant Version 1.5. It uses Tomcat's *manager* application to deploy and redeploy the web application while Tomcat is running. The ability to redeploy a modified web application while the server is running is critical for test-first development because it takes too long to restart most servers. A successful XP approach depends on your ability to make lots of small code changes quickly.

In order to test using Ant's junit task, you should copy *servlet.jar*, *httpunit.jar*, *junit.jar*, and *Tidy.jar* to Ant's *lib* directory. This makes it easy to ensure that all of the required JAR files are loaded using the same Java ClassLoader when you are running your tests. Ant class loading issues were discussed in Recipe 3.14.

The first part of your buildfile should define a classpath:

```
<path id="classpath.project">
  <pathelement path="${dir.build}"/>
</path>
```

This path picks up all class files from your build directory. Ant also includes all of the JAR files from the *ANT_HOME/lib* directory. This allows you to compile the code with this target:

```
<target name="compile" depends="prepare"
        description="Compile all source code.">
  <javac srcdir="${dir.src}" destdir="${dir.build}">
    <classpath refid="classpath.project"/>
  </javac>
</target>
```

And next, your buildfile should have a target to generate the WAR file:

```
<target name="war" depends="compile">
  <!-- build the newsletter example from the HttpUnit chapter -->
  <war warfile="${dir.build}/news.war"
      webxml="httpunit_chapter/web.xml">
    <fileset dir="httpunit_chapter">
      <exclude name="web.xml"/>
    </fileset>
    <classes dir="${dir.build}">
      <include name="com/oreilly/javaxp/httpunit/**/*.class"/>
    </classes>
  </war>
</target>
```

This target assumes that your development environment has a directory named *httpunit_chapter* containing any HTML files comprising your web application. The deployment descriptor, *web.xml*, is also found in this directory. Finally, the <classes> element specifies where to find the *.class* files for the web application. Although your environment will likely be quite different, you will want targets similar to this in order to quickly generate your own WAR file.

Once you have figured out how to generate your WAR file, turn your attention to deployment. Tomcat's *manager* application uses an HTTP interface for its functionality. To deploy, use the following command:

```
http://localhost:8080/manager/install?path=/news&war=jar:file:/path/to/news.war!/
```

If you need to redeploy, you must first undeploy the application. Here is the command to undeploy the application:

```
http://localhost:8080/manager/remove?path=/news
```

The *manager* application fails unless you first configure a username and password, so you must edit the *tomcat-users.xml* file in Tomcat's *conf* directory. Simply add a user with the manager role:

```
<tomcat-users>
  <!-- add this user to access the manager application -->
  <user name="eric"    password="secret" roles="manager" />
  <user name="tomcat"  password="tomcat" roles="tomcat" />
  <user name="role1"   password="tomcat" roles="role1"  />
  <user name="both"    password="tomcat" roles="tomcat,role1" />
</tomcat-users>
```

We are almost finished! Now that the user is configured and you know how to run the manager application, you can write some Ant targets to deploy and undeploy the application.

This example requires Ant Version 1.5 or later because prior to Ant 1.5, there was no standard way to pass the required username and password to a web server from an Ant task. Ant 1.5 adds HTTP BASIC authentication support to its get task, thus supporting the username and password.

The following code example shows how to use Ant's get task to undeploy and deploy a web application to Tomcat.

```
<target name="undeploy">
  <!-- use the manager app to undeploy -->
  <get src="${url.manager}/remove?path=/news"
       dest="${dir.build}/undeployOutput.txt"
       username="eric"
       password="secret"
       verbose="true"/>

  <!-- the manager app does not delete the directory for us -->
  <delete dir="${env.TOMCAT_HOME}/webapps/news"/>
```

```xml
<!-- echo the results to the console -->
<!-- NOTE: This reports an error when you first run it,
     because the app is not initially deployed -->
<concat>
  <filelist dir="${dir.build}" files="undeployOutput.txt" />
</concat>
</target>


<target name="deploy" depends="war,undeploy">
  <!--
    Convert the project-relative path, such as "build/news.war",
    into a fully-qualitifed path like "C:/dev/news/build/news.war"
    -->
  <pathconvert dirsep="/" property="fullWarDir">
    <path>
      <pathelement location="${dir.build}/news.war"/>
    </path>
  </pathconvert>

  <!-- Use the manager app to deploy -->
  <get src="${url.manager}/install
            ?path=/news&amp;war=jar:file:${fullWarDir}!/"
       dest="${dir.build}/deployOutput.txt"
       username="eric"
       password="secret"
       verbose="true"/>
  <!-- echo the results to the console -->
  <concat>
    <filelist dir="${dir.build}" files="deployOutput.txt" />
  </concat>
</target>
```

For the icing on the cake, you should define a target that executes your unit tests.

```xml
<target name="junit" depends="deploy">
  <junit printsummary="on" fork="false" haltonfailure="false">

    <classpath refid="classpath.project"/>

    <formatter type="plain"/>

    <batchtest fork="false" todir="${dir.build}">
      <fileset dir="${dir.src}">
        <include name="**/Test*.java"/>
        <exclude name="**/AllTests.java"/>
      </fileset>
    </batchtest>
  </junit>
</target>
```

Notice the dependencies. When you type **ant junit**, the deploy target is executed. This, in turn, causes the WAR file to be built, which causes the code to be compiled.

Setting up an efficient development environment is well worth the effort. After you write each new unit test and small piece of functionality, you can type **ant junit** to compile, build the WAR file, deploy, and run all tests.

See Also

Recipe 3.14 discusses Ant class loading issues. Chapter 10 contains a much more sophisticated buildfile that handles all sorts of deployment and server startup issues.

5.3   Checking a Static Web Page

Problem

You want to test for the existence of a static web page.

Solution

Write a JUnit test fixture, and then use classes in the com.meterware.httpunit package to connect to the web page.

Discussion

When starting a brand new web application, verify that you can connect to the home page before doing anything else. This is the simplest test that you can write, and only takes a few lines of code. Example 5-1 shows how to do it.

Example 5-1. Testing for a static web page

```
package com.oreilly.javaxp.httpunit;

import com.meterware.httpunit.*;
import junit.framework.TestCase;

public class TestNewsletter extends TestCase {
    public TestNewsletter(String name) {
        super(name);
    }

    public void testIndexPageExists() throws Exception {
        WebConversation webConversation = new WebConversation();
        WebRequest request =
                new GetMethodWebRequest("http://localhost:8080/news");

        WebResponse response =
                webConversation.getResponse(request);
    }
}
```

The WebConversation class is described as HttpUnit's replacement for the web browser. WebConversation is the client, allowing you to send requests and obtain responses from a web server.

Use the GetMethodWebRequest class to issue an HTTP GET request, specifying a URL in the constructor. This mimics a user typing in a URL in their web browser. Then call the getResponse( ) method to actually issue the request and retrieve the web page. If getResponse( ) cannot find the web page, it throws a new instance of HttpNotFoundException. As customary in JUnit, you should not catch this exception. Instead, let the JUnit framework catch the exception and treat it as a test error.

Since requesting a page is such a common operation, HttpUnit offers a simplified syntax that achieves the same results:

```
WebConversation webConversation = new WebConversation( );
WebResponse response =
        webConversation.getResponse("http://localhost:8080/news");
```

We do not care about the content of the response. Instead, we are merely checking for the existence of the home page. Because of this, we can simplify the example even further. First, we get rid of the response object because we never refer to it:

```
WebConversation webConversation = new WebConversation( );
webConversation.getResponse("http://localhost:8080/news");
```

And finally, we can inline the code into a single statement. In this case, we feel that inlining makes the code easier to read, particularly because the name of our test method explains what we are trying to test. Clarity is almost always more important than brevity, so you should avoid inlining if it makes the code harder to understand. Here is the final unit test:

```
public void testIndexPageExists( ) throws Exception {
    // this throws HttpNotFoundException if the home page is not found
    new WebConversation( ).getResponse("http://localhost:8080/news");
}
```

If you set up your Ant buildfile and Tomcat as explained in Recipe 5.2, you can type **ant junit** to run this test.

See Also

Recipe 5.2 shows how to set up the build environment. Recipe 4.12 shows how to handle exceptions using JUnit.

5.4   Following Hyperlinks

Problem

You want to obtain hyperlinks, simulate clicking on them, and test that the correct response is returned.

Solution

Use the `WebResponse.getLinkWith()` method to obtain a `WebLink` object, then call `WebLink.getRequest()` to get a new `WebRequest` that you can execute. Executing this second request simulates the user clicking on the link.

Discussion

The HTTP protocol is a series of requests and responses. Following a hyperlink is merely a case of issuing an HTTP GET request and checking the response. As you are adding new links to your web application, you should attempt to write a test first. The first time you run the test, it fails because the link does not exist. Here is a test that obtains a hyperlink and then attempts to follow it:

```
public void testFollowLinkToSubscriptionPage() throws Exception {
    // get the home page
    WebConversation webConversation = new WebConversation();
    WebResponse response = webConversation.getResponse(
            "http://localhost:8080/news");

    WebLink subscriptionLink = response.getLinkWith("subscription");

    // get a request to simulate clicking on the link
    WebRequest clickRequest = subscriptionLink.getRequest();

    // throws HttpNotFoundException if the link is broken
    WebResponse subscriptionPage =
            webConversation.getResponse(clickRequest);
}
```

The `WebResponse.getLinkWith()` method searches for the first hyperlink in the web page that contains some piece of text. In our example, we are searching for a link like this:

```
<a href="someUrl">subscription</a>
```

This illustrates how HttpUnit uses the JTidy library to parse the HTML. You call the `getLinkWith()` convenience method, and HttpUnit uses JTidy to search the DOM tree for the first matching hyperlink. If one is not found, the `WebLink` object will be null.

Once you have the `WebLink` object, you get a new `WebRequest` and ask it for a new `WebResponse`:

```
// get a request to simulate clicking on the link
WebRequest clickRequest = subscriptionLink.getRequest();

// throws HttpNotFoundException if the link is broken
WebResponse subscriptionPage =
        webConversation.getResponse(clickRequest);
```

If you are following a test-first approach, the link will not be valid. It is a good idea to run the faulty test first, just to prove to yourself that your test catches the problem should the link actually fail sometime in the future. Now you can write your servlet to generate the subscription page:

```
public class NewsletterServlet extends HttpServlet {
    protected void doGet(HttpServletRequest req,
                         HttpServletResponse res)
        throws ServletException, IOException {
        res.setContentType("text/html");
        PrintWriter pw = res.getWriter();
        pw.println("<html>");
        pw.println("<body>");
        pw.println("<h1>NewsletterServlet</h1>");
        pw.println("</body>");
        pw.println("</html>");
    }
}
```

Notice how, in the test-first approach, you don't write the complete servlet. Instead, you create a stubbed-out page that generates a minimal response. You can now run your test suite again, and should see that the link is valid and the test passes. This is also a good time to go back to your web browser and bring up the web page and try out the hyperlink interactively.

See Also

The WebLink class also provides a click( ) method that returns a WebResponse object.

5.5   Writing Testable HTML

Problem

You want to use HttpUnit to test your web application, but it can't parse your HTML.

Solution

Write well-formed HTML, ensuring the tags are properly nested and attributes are quoted. For best results, write XHTML.

Discussion

Web browsers like Internet Explorer and Mozilla are extremely tolerant of bad HTML. Since so many web pages on the Internet are written using sloppy HTML, browsers have to compensate for all sorts of HTML markup errors. While browsers may be able to display sloppy HTML reasonably well, writing unit tests against HTML requires more precision.

Writing clean HTML serves two purposes. First, it makes your HTML more portable to a wide variety of browsers. Second, it makes your pages easier to test with tools like HttpUnit.

HttpUnit uses the HTML Tidy library to parse through your HTML, searching for hyperlinks, tables, form elements, and other objects. Although HTML Tidy attempts to parse poorly-formed HTML, it can only do so with limited success. In order to make your HTML more easily parsed, you should nest your tags properly and follow the HTML standard. You should not encounter any problems if you edit your web pages using a validating XML parser and adhere to one of the XHTML DTDs.

If you are encountering problems, call this method to turn on HTML Tidy warnings:

```
HttpUnitOptions.setParserWarningsEnabled(true);
```

This causes HTML Tidy to print warning messages to the console, letting you know which lines of your HTML pages are incorrect.

While printing error messages may help you diagnose problems, it is not automatic. Remember that creating automated tests is a key goal of XP. If XHTML compliance is your goal, write a unit test for each web page that passes your XHTML through an XML parser. The test will fail whenever a page is not valid XHTML. This becomes part of your normal testing suite and fails immediately as soon as someone introduces sloppy HTML.

See Also

See the HTML and XHTML specifications at the Worldwide Web Consortium *http://www.w3.org*. Also see O'Reilly's *HTML & XHTML: The Definitive Guide* by Chuck Musciano and Bill Kennedy. Chapter 11 briefly mentions XMLUnit, which can simplify validating against the XHTML DTDs.

5.6   Testing HTML Tables

Problem

You want to test the contents of one or more HTML tables.

Solution

Use `com.meterware.httpunit.WebTable` and `com.meterware.httpunit.TableCell` to analyze the content of tables in your HTML pages.

Discussion

HttpUnit provides a simple API for parsing HTML and obtaining tables, cells, and cell content. Figure 5-1 shows a sample web page for the code shown in this recipe.

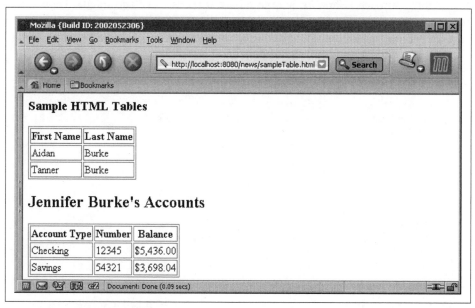

Figure 5-1. Sample HTML tables

Example 5-2 demonstrates how you can test the content of the top table. In this example, the table is located based on the text found within its first cell using the `WebResponse.getTableStartingWith( )` method.

Example 5-2. Simple table testing

```
public void testPersonTable( ) throws Exception {
    WebConversation webConversation = new WebConversation( );
    WebResponse response = webConversation.getResponse(
            "http://localhost:8080/news/sampleTable.html");

    // get the HTML table with 'First Name' as the text of its
    // first non-blank cell
    WebTable table = response.getTableStartingWith("First Name");
    assertEquals("column count", 2, table.getColumnCount( ));
    assertEquals("row count", 3, table.getRowCount( ));
```

Example 5-2. Simple table testing (continued)

```
    // get the cell at row 2, column 0
    TableCell cell = table.getTableCell(2, 0);
    assertEquals("cell text", "Tanner", cell.asText());
}
```

Once the `WebTable` object is located, the test uses various methods on the `WebTable` class to obtain the number of rows and columns, as well as to locate a `TableCell` at a particular position.

While this approach is fine for simple tables, it tends to be too fragile. People may redesign page layout frequently, and this sort of test is sensitive to things like exact row and column positions. A better approach, shown in Example 5-3, is to assign identifiers to critical portions of your tables.

Example 5-3. Testing a table with identifiers

```
public void testAccountTable() throws Exception {
    WebConversation webConversation = new WebConversation();
    WebResponse response = webConversation.getResponse(
            "http://localhost:8080/news/sampleTable.html");

    WebTable accountTable = response.getTableWithID("accountInfoTbl");
    assertNotNull("account table", accountTable);

    // get the checking account number
    TableCell checkingCell =
            accountTable.getTableCellWithID("checkingAcctNbr");
    assertEquals("Checking account number",
            "12345", checkingCell.asText());
}
```

Now, by locating identifiers, you can rearrange your table layout as you see fit. Unless you change the identifiers, your tests continue functioning. Example 5-4 shows the HTML for the table being tested here, so you can see what the id tag looks like.

Example 5-4. HTML for table using identifiers

```
<table id="accountInfoTbl" border="1">
  <tr id="headingRow">
    <th>Account Type</th><th>Number</th><th>Balance</th>
  </tr>

  <tr>
    <td>Checking</td>
    <td id="checkingAcctNbr">12345</td>
    <td id="checkingAcctBal">$5,436.00</td>
  </tr>

  <tr>
    <td>Savings</td>
```

Example 5-4. HTML for table using identifiers (continued)

```
    <td id="savingsAcctNbr">54321</td>
    <td id="savingsAcctBal">$3,698.04</td>
  </tr>
</table>
```

 If you are concerned about the larger HTML pages required by the ID attributes, consider writing a script to strip out all of the identifiers after your tests have all passed.

See Also

Recipe 5.5 discusses testable HTML.

5.7   Testing a Form Tag and Refactoring Your Tests

Problem

You want to test for the existence of an HTML form.

Solution

Use the `com.meterware.httpunit.WebForm` class to test the form method and action.

Discussion

Adding HTML forms to a web application implies that the application is beginning to take on dynamic behavior. As your application gets more complex, you should continually refactor your tests in order to keep them as simple as possible. The solution outlined here shows how to test for an HTML form, as well as showing a refactored test fixture. Example 5-5 opens with a test for a basic HTML form.

Example 5-5. Refactored unit test

```
package com.oreilly.javaxp.httpunit;

import com.meterware.httpunit.*;
import junit.framework.TestCase;

public class TestNewsletter extends TestCase {
    private WebConversation webConversation;

    public TestNewsletter(String name) {
        super(name);
    }
```

Example 5-5. Refactored unit test (continued)

```
    public void setUp( ) throws Exception {
        this.webConversation = new WebConversation( );
    }

    ...tests from earlier recipes are not shown here

    public void testSubscriptionForm( ) throws Exception {
        WebForm form = getBlankSubscriptionForm( );

        assertEquals("subscription form action",
                "subscription", form.getAction( ));
        assertEquals("subscription form method",
                "post", form.getMethod().toLowerCase( ));
    }

    private WebForm getBlankSubscriptionForm( ) throws Exception {
        WebResponse response = getBlankSubscriptionPage( );
        return response.getFormWithID("subscriptionForm");
    }

    private WebResponse getBlankSubscriptionPage( ) throws Exception {
        return this.webConversation.getResponse(
                "http://localhost:8080/news/subscription");
    }
}
```

The HTML form we are testing will eventually allow the user to enter their name and email address to subscribe or unsubscribe from a newsletter. For now, it is sufficient to test that the form exists. Once the form is tested, you can move on to testing the content within the form as shown in the next recipe.

The test fixture shown in Example 5-5 is designed to make it easy to get to the WebForm object using the getBlankSubscriptionForm( ) method. As you write more and more tests, you should look for repeated functionality and refactor it into helper methods as shown here. Since most of the tests in this chapter require an instance of the WebConversation class, its initialization has been moved to the setUp( ) method.

Example 5-6 shows a refactored version of the servlet that was originally presented in Recipe 5.4. As you can see, the println( ) statements have been removed. Instead, the servlet uses RequestDispatcher to delegate page rendering to a JSP.

Example 5-6. Servlet that dispatches to a JSP

```
package com.oreilly.javaxp.httpunit;

import javax.servlet.*;
import javax.servlet.http.*;
import java.io.IOException;

public class NewsletterServlet extends HttpServlet {
    protected void doGet(HttpServletRequest req,
```

Example 5-6. Servlet that dispatches to a JSP (continued)

```
                        HttpServletResponse res)
        throws ServletException, IOException {

    RequestDispatcher dispatcher =
            req.getRequestDispatcher("subscription.jsp");

    dispatcher.forward(req, res);
    }
}
```

Using servlets in combination with JSPs is a much more realistic way to implement a complex web application. From the perspective of HttpUnit, the server-side architecture rarely matters. HttpUnit is simulating a web browser, so it does not need to know that the servlet is dispatching to a JSP.

 Unit tests from earlier recipes tested NewsletterServlet when it was written using println( ) statements. After refactoring the servlet to use RequestDispatcher, the tests still pass. These tests provide reassurance that the servlet implementation change did not break things that used to work.

The final piece of the refactored web application is the JSP, shown in Example 5-7. Since the test only checks to see if the form exists, the JSP is simple, only generating the form.

Example 5-7. subscription.jsp

```
<html>
  <head>
    <title>Newsletter Subscription</title>
  </head>

  <body>
    <h1>Newsletter Subscription</h1>
    <form method="post" action="subscription" id="subscriptionForm">
    </form>
  </body>
</html>
```

5.8   Testing for Elements on HTML Forms

Problem

You want to test for the existence of various elements in your HTML forms, such as buttons and fields.

Solution

Use JUnit's WebForm class to parse the HTML form. WebForm provides numerous methods to check that buttons, fields, radio buttons, and other elements exist on the page.

Discussion

Building on the example from the previous recipe, you might start by writing a test to check for the existence of buttons on the HTML page as shown here.

```java
public void testButtonsOnSubscriptionForm( ) throws Exception {
    WebForm form = getBlankSubscriptionForm( );
    SubmitButton subscribeBtn = form.getSubmitButton("subscribeBtn");
    SubmitButton unsubscribeBtn = form.getSubmitButton("unsubscribeBtn");

    assertNotNull("subscribeBtn should not be null", subscribeBtn);
    assertNotNull("unsubscribeBtn should not be null", unsubscribeBtn);
}
```

The getBlankSubscriptionForm( ) method is shown back in Example 5-5. When you first write this test, it fails because the buttons do not exist yet. After observing the test failure, you can update the JSP from Example 5-7 to include the two buttons.

```html
<form method="post" action="subscription" id="subscriptionForm">
    <input type="submit" name="subscribeBtn" value="Subscribe"/>
    <input type="submit" name="unsubscribeBtn" value="Unsubscribe"/>
</form>
```

Now, the testButtonsOnSubscriptionForm( ) test should pass. Next, you might want to test for fields that allow the user to enter their name and email address. Here is that test code:

```
public void testFieldsOnSubscriptionForm( ) throws Exception {
    WebForm form = getBlankSubscriptionForm( );

    // get the values of the two text fields
    // HttpUnit treats most HTML form elements the same way
    String nameFieldValue = form.getParameterValue("nameField");
    String emailFieldValue = form.getParameterValue("emailField");

    // the empty fields should contain empty strings. If they are
    // null, this indicates they are not present on the page.
    assertEquals("nameField", "", nameFieldValue);
    assertEquals("emailFieldValue", "", emailFieldValue);
}
```

The getParameterValue( ) method checks to see if the HTML form contains elements with a given name. We are looking for input fields with certain names. You can also use the getParameterValue( ) method to check for other HTML form elements, such as lists and multiline text areas.

Example 5-8 shows the JSP, containing all of the form elements that our tests are checking for.

Example 5-8. JSP containing the HTML form

```
<html>
  <head>
    <title>Newsletter Subscription</title>
  </head>

  <body>
    <h1>Newsletter Subscription</h1>
    <form method="post" action="subscription" id="subscriptionForm">
        <table>
          <tr>
            <td>Name:</td>
            <td><input type="text" name="nameField"></td>
          </tr>
          <tr>
            <td>Email:</td>
            <td><input type="text" name="emailField"> (required)</td>
          </tr>
        </table>
        <input type="submit" name="subscribeBtn" value="Subscribe"/>
        <input type="submit" name="unsubscribeBtn" value="Unsubscribe"/>
    </form>
  </body>
</html>
```

Figure 5-2 shows what the JSP looks like when rendered in Mozilla. This is a simple page layout, but you can add fancy layout and graphics later. Again, having the unit tests in place allows you to make page layout changes later without fear of accidentally breaking the web application functionality that currently works.

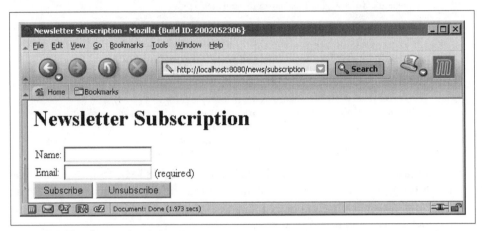

Figure 5-2. Newsletter subscription page

It is important to note that the HttpUnit tests are not verifying every aspect of page layout. While they do a good job of testing the page's functionality, you must still manually inspect the actual web application to ensure the page layout is visually appealing and correct.

See Also

Recipe 5.7 shows how to check for the existence of a form.

5.9   Submitting Form Data

Problem

You want to write a test that submits your HTML forms and verifies the forms functionality.

Solution

Set parameters on the WebForm using its setParameter( ) method. Then simulate clicking a button by asking for one of the form's buttons and submitting it using the WebConversation instance.

Discussion

You fill in form field values using the setParameter( ) method on a WebForm instance. This simulates what the user would do if he was filling out a form in a web browser. You then ask the form for a WebRequest object, passing in the name of one of the submit buttons. All of this is shown in Example 5-9.

Example 5-9. Submitting a form

```
public void testSubmitSubscriptionWithoutRequiredField( )
        throws Exception {
    WebForm form = getBlankSubscriptionForm( );
    form.setParameter("nameField", "Eric Burke");
    WebRequest request = form.getRequest("subscribeBtn");

    // Submit the page. The web app should return us right back to
    // the subscription page because the Email address is not specified
    WebResponse response = this.webConversation.getResponse(request);

    // make sure the user is warned about the missing field
    String pageText = response.getText( );
    assertTrue("Required fields warning is not present",
            pageText.indexOf("Email address is required") > -1);

    // make sure the nameField has the original text
    form = response.getFormWithID("subscriptionForm");
    assertEquals("Name field should be pre-filled",
            "Eric Burke", form.getParameterValue("nameField"));
}
```

The comments in Example 5-9 explain what is expected at each step. The overall goal is to ensure that the form treats the email address as a required field. If the field is missing, the form should be redisplayed with an error message. When the form is redisplayed, the name field should be pre-filled with the previously entered value.

Example 5-10 shows the updated servlet. As is typical in a web application, the validation logic is contained within the servlet, rather than the JSP. Even better, you might want to refactor the validation logic into a helper class rather than the servlet itself. This step would allow you to write standalone tests against the validation logic without invoking the servlet. Once the request is fully validated, the servlet dispatches to the JSP for rendering.

Example 5-10. Servlet with validation logic

```
public class NewsletterServlet extends HttpServlet {
    protected void doGet(HttpServletRequest req,
            HttpServletResponse res) throws ServletException, IOException {
        dispatchToSubscriptionPage(req, res);
    }

    protected void doPost(HttpServletRequest req, HttpServletResponse res)
            throws ServletException, IOException {
```

Example 5-10. Servlet with validation logic (continued)

```
    if (req.getParameter("subscribeBtn") != null) {
        handleSubscribeButton(req, res);
    } else if (req.getParameter("unsubscribeBtn") != null) {
        // @todo - handle this later, but only after writing more tests
    }
    dispatchToSubscriptionPage(req, res);

}

private void dispatchToSubscriptionPage(HttpServletRequest req,
        HttpServletResponse res) throws ServletException, IOException {
    RequestDispatcher dispatcher =
            req.getRequestDispatcher("subscription.jsp");

    dispatcher.forward(req, res);
}

private void handleSubscribeButton(HttpServletRequest req,
        HttpServletResponse res) throws ServletException, IOException {
    String name = req.getParameter("nameField");
    String email = req.getParameter("emailField");

    // email is required
    if (email == null || email.trim().length() == 0) {
        req.setAttribute("errorMessage",
                "Email address is required");
        dispatchToSubscriptionPage(req, res);
    } else {
        // @todo - subscribe the user!
    }
  }
}
}
```

The `NewsletterServlet` is nearly at its final form. A `doPost( )` method was added to handle the form submission, and the logic formerly found in `doGet( )` has been refactored into the `dispatchToSubscriptionPage( )` method. This refactoring avoids code duplication and is easily tested with the existing suite of unit tests.

Pay particular attention to the `@todo` comments. These indicate that portions of the code are not complete. With the test-first approach taken in this chapter, these pieces of functionality should not be written until the corresponding unit tests are written. You might also consider putting your `@todo` comments in your test cases, rather than in the code itself. This strategy provides stronger encouragement to focus on test-driven development when those features are eventually added.

Avoid the urge to write all of the functionality at once. Instead, work on tiny pieces of functionality with each new test. This process reduces the likelihood that you will procrastinate and skip some of the tests.

Finally, Example 5-11 shows the revised JSP. The JSP now contains logic to display the error message attribute, which is sometimes provided by the servlet. It also pre-fills the value of the name field if necessary.

Example 5-11. Revised JSP with some dynamic display

```
<html>
  <% String errorMsg = (String) request.getAttribute("errorMessage");
     String name = request.getParameter("nameField");
     if (name == null) {
         name = "";
     }
  %>

  <head>
    <title>Newsletter Subscription</title>
  </head>

  <body>
    <h1>Newsletter Subscription</h1>
    <% if (errorMsg != null) { %>
        <font color="red"><%= errorMsg %></font>
    <% } %>

    <form method="post" action="subscription" id="subscriptionForm">
        <table>
          <tr>
            <td>Name:</td>
            <td><input type="text" name="nameField"
                    value="<%= name %>"></td>
          </tr>
          <tr>
            <td>Email:</td>
            <td><input type="text" name="emailField"> (required)</td>
          </tr>
        </table>
        <input type="submit" name="subscribeBtn" value="Subscribe"/>
        <input type="submit" name="unsubscribeBtn" value="Unsubscribe"/>
    </form>
  </body>
</html>
```

At this point, the tests (including all of the old tests) should pass. It is also a good idea to try out the web app inside of a web browser to see if you forgot to test anything. The test-first process can continue until all of the functionality is implemented.

See Also

Recipes 5.7 and 5.8 show how to test other aspects of HTML forms.

5.10   Testing Through a Firewall

Problem

You want to test a remote web site, but your development machines are behind a firewall.

Solution

Set the proxySet, proxyHost, and proxyPort system properties.

Discussion

HttpUnit uses java.net.HttpURLConnection, which checks the proxySet system property to determine if it should operate through a proxy server. If this property is set, the proxyHost and proxyPort properties specify the server name and port.

You can set these properties in your unit test method using this code:

```
System.getProperties().put("proxySet", "true");
System.getProperties().put("proxyHost", "myProxyHostName");
System.getProperties().put("proxyPort", "10000");
```

See Also

Recipe 3.5 shows how to set system properties using Ant.

5.11   Testing Cookies

Problem

You want to create cookies and test for the existence of cookies.

Solution

Use WebConversation's addCookie() method to create new cookies, and its getCookieValue() method to retrieve cookie values.

Discussion

Cookies are little pieces of information that web applications store on the client browser's machine. Cookies allow web sites to maintain state information as you view different web pages. HttpUnit creates cookies and retrieve cookies using methods on the WebConversation class.

For the sake of an example, let's look at a simple JSP that uses cookies. Example 5-12 shows a JSP that creates a new cookie and then displays the array of cookies from the client.

Example 5-12. A JSP that generates and displays cookies

```
<%-- generate a cookie --%>
<%
   Cookie cookie = new Cookie("customerId", "12345");
   response.addCookie(cookie);
%>

<html>
  <head><title>Cookie Demo</title></head>

  <body>
    <h1>Cookies in this request</h1>
    <table>
      <tr>
        <th>Cookie Name</th>
        <th>Value</th>
      </tr>

    <%-- print all of the cookies for this request --%>
    <% Cookie[] cookies = request.getCookies();
      int numCookies = (cookies != null) ? cookies.length : 0;
      for (int i=0; i<numCookies; i++) { %>
        <tr>
          <td><%= cookies[i].getName() %></td>
          <td><%= cookies[i].getValue() %></td>
        </tr>
    <% } %>

    </table>
  </body>
</html>
```

The unit test, shown in Example 5-13, works with the JSP shown in Example 5-12. The unit test accomplishes two tasks. First, it shows how you can create new cookies from your own unit tests. In this case, it creates a cookie named "shopping-CartId". Creating a new cookie mimics a real web application in which the shopping cart cookie was created on a prior page.

Example 5-13. A unit test that uses cookies

```
public void testCookies() throws Exception {
    this.webConversation.addCookie("shoppingCartId", "98765");
    WebRequest req = new GetMethodWebRequest(
            "http://localhost:8080/news/cookieDemo.jsp");
    WebResponse cookieDemoPage = this.webConversation.getResponse(req);

    // the JSP should have created the customerId cookie
```

Example 5-13. A unit test that uses cookies (continued)

```
    assertEquals("customer ID cookie", "12345",
            this.webConversation.getCookieValue("customerId"));

    // make sure the cookie we generated on the client was found
    // somewhere in the HTML page
    String pageSource = cookieDemoPage.getText();
    assertTrue("shoppingCardId cookie was not found",
            pageSource.indexOf("shoppingCartId") > -1);
}
```

The testCookies( ) method also verifies that the JSP was able to create a new cookie, named "customerId". We use the getCookieValue( ) method to retrieve the cookie. If the JSP failed to create the cookie, its value will be null.

Finally, the unit test verifies that the JSP displays the cookie that was generated from the test. It does this using a very primitive technique, but one that works. It converts the entire page into a string using the getText( ) method. The test then searches for "shoppingCartId" as a substring of the page's text. If the text is found, it means the JSP was able to receive the cookie from the unit test. This is not something you would normally test. Instead, it is used here to show that HttpUnit's cookie functionality works.

See Also

See O'Reilly's *Java Servlet Programming* by Jason Hunter to learn more about cookies.

5.12   Testing Secure Pages

Problem

You want to test a page that requires a username and password for login.

Solution

Simulate HTTP BASIC authentication using WebConversation's setAuthorization( ) method.

Discussion

If your web application is configured to use HTTP BASIC authentication, you can use HttpUnit to simulate what happens when users enter a username and password in their browser. Our first unit test, shown next, verifies that the web application prevents unauthorized users from entering a secured web page.

```
public void testViewSubscribersWithoutLogin( ) throws Exception {
    try {
        this.webConversation.getResponse(
                "http://localhost:8080/news/viewSubscribers");
        fail("viewSubscribers should require a login");
    } catch (AuthorizationRequiredException expected) {
        // ignored
    }
}
```

If the web app prompts for a username and password, HttpUnit throws an
AuthorizationRequiredException. Since this is the expected behavior, we catch the
exception and ignore it. If the exception is not thrown, the test fails because the page
is not secure.

The next test shows how to enter a username and password within a unit test.
Behind the scenes, this simulates what happens when the user types in this information in the browser's login dialog.

```
public void testViewSubscribersWithLogin( ) throws Exception {
    this.webConversation.setAuthorization("eric", "secret");
    this.webConversation.getResponse(
            "http://localhost:8080/news/viewSubscribers");
}
```

J2EE web applications support numerous types of authentication; this recipe shows
how to use HttpUnit along with HTTP BASIC authentication. If you are using form-
based authentication, you write your test just like you are testing any other HTML form.

See Also

See O'Reilly's *Java Servlet Programming* by Jason Hunter to learn more about servlet
security.

CHAPTER 6

Mock Objects

6.0 Introduction

Writing tests for simple, standalone Java classes is easy. Just create an instance of your class and run tests against its methods. But testing gets a whole lot more interesting for classes with complex dependencies on other parts of your application. When testing becomes difficult, consider refactoring your code in order to minimize dependencies. But there will always be cases where classes cannot be tested in isolation.

Suppose that a class named Automobile only runs in the context of a class named Engine. In order to test all aspects of the Automobile class, you find that you have to create many different kinds of Engines. Rather than create real Engine objects, which may require a lot of setup logic, you can write a dummy Engine implementation. This dummy implementation is known as a mock object and it provides a simple way to set up fake testing data.

The mock Engine can even include assertions to ensure that instances of Automobile use the Engine correctly. For example, the Engine may verify that Automobile only calls the Engine.startup() method one time. This ability to verify that objects use their environment correctly is a key advantage of mock objects when compared to other testing techniques that only check to see if classes react to method calls correctly.

A mock object is a "fake" implementation of a class or interface, almost always written for the specific purpose of supporting unit tests. When writing JDBC unit tests, you might create mock implementations of interfaces such as Connection, ResultSet, and Statement. In the case of Swing code, you might create a mock implementation of the TableModelListener interface. You create mock objects that always return well-known data and your unit tests use these to exercise your application logic without relying on real objects or databases.

Mock objects should be simple, and should not have dependencies on other mock objects or too many other parts of your application. If your mock objects require a lot of complex setup before they are useful, you probably made them too complex and should look for ways to refactor your code. Additionally, mock objects can provide a self-validation mechanism whereby you can set up an expected set of conditions. As soon as an expectation is violated, the mock object fails the current test. Self-validation helps you locate problems as soon as they occur. If you reuse the same mock object in many different tests, this ability to perform some types of self-validation ensures that you do not have to duplicate the same validation logic in all of your tests.

The recipes in this chapter show a few different ways to implement and use the concept of mock objects. In the simplest form, a mock object is a dummy implementation of a Java interface. You implement specific methods that only return data pertinent to your unit tests. We also show how to use Mock Objects, an open source project containing mock implementations of many well-known Java interfaces and abstract classes. Finally, we introduce MockMaker, another open source tool for automatically generating new mock objects.

What Is a Mock Object?

There are two widely accepted interpretations of the term *mock object*:

- The generic definition states that a mock object is any dummy object that stands in for a real object that is not available, or is difficult to use in a test case.
- A more rigid interpretation states that a mock object must have the ability to set up expectations and provide a self-validation mechanism.

Recipe 6.2 shows an example of a mock object that supports expectations and self-validation. This is also the approach taken by tools like MockMaker when they generate mock objects for you. We believe that this is a useful approach because it provides a standard, well-understood way to support these features.

On the other hand, if your tests do not require sophisticated mock objects, there is nothing wrong with the first definition listed above. In our opinion, you should write mock objects to support your tests, only adding features that you currently need.

6.1   Event Listener Testing

Problem

You want to create a mock implementation of an event listener interface.

Solution

Write a class that implements the interface, but only define behavior for the methods you need for your current test.

Discussion

Java Swing user interfaces rely heavily on models and views. In the case of tables, for instance, the TableModel interface is the model and JTable is one possible view. The table model communicates with its view(s) by sending TableModelEvents whenever its data changes. Since numerous views may observe a single model, it is imperative that the model only sends the minimum number of events. Poorly written models commonly send too many events, often causing severe performance problems.

Let's look at how we can use mock objects to test the events fired by a custom table model. Our table model displays a collection of Account objects. A mock table model listener verifies that the correct event is delivered whenever a new account is added to the model. We'll start with the Account class, as shown in Example 6-1.

Example 6-1. The Account class

```
package com.oreilly.mock;

public class Account {
    public static final int CHECKING = 0;
    public static final int SAVINGS = 1;

    private int acctType;
    private String acctNumber;
    private double balance;

    public Account(int acctType, String acctNumber, double balance) {
        this.acctType = acctType;
        this.acctNumber = acctNumber;
        this.balance = balance;
    }

    public int getAccountType() {
        return this.acctType;
    }

    public String getAccountNumber() {
        return this.acctNumber;
    }

    public double getBalance() {
        return this.balance;
    }
}
```

Our table model consists of three columns of data, for the account type, number, and balance. Each row in the table represents a different account. With this knowledge, we can write a basic table model as shown next in Example 6-2.

Example 6-2. Account table model

```
package com.oreilly.mock;

import javax.swing.table.AbstractTableModel;
import java.util.ArrayList;
import java.util.List;

public class AccountTableModel extends AbstractTableModel {
    public static final int ACCT_TYPE_COL = 0;
    public static final int ACCT_BALANCE_COL = 1;
    public static final int ACCT_NUMBER_COL = 2;

    private List accounts = new ArrayList();

    public int getRowCount() {
        return this.accounts.size();
    }

    public int getColumnCount() {
        return 3;
    }

    public Object getValueAt(int rowIndex, int columnIndex) {
        Account acct = (Account) this.accounts.get(rowIndex);
        switch (columnIndex) {
            case ACCT_BALANCE_COL:
                return new Double(acct.getBalance());
            case ACCT_NUMBER_COL:
                return acct.getAccountNumber();
            case ACCT_TYPE_COL:
                return new Integer(acct.getAccountType());
        }
        throw new IllegalArgumentException("Illegal column: "
                + columnIndex);
    }

    public void addAccount(Account acct) {
        // @todo - implement this!
    }
}
```

Tests for the getRowCount( ), getColumnCount( ), and getValueAt( ) methods are not shown here. To test these methods, you can create an instance of the table model and call the methods, checking for the expected values. The addAccount( ) method, however, is more interesting because it requires a mock object.

The mock object is necessary because we want to verify that calling addAccount( ) fires a single TableModelEvent. The mock object implements the TableModelListener interface and keeps track of the events it receives. Example 6-3 shows such a mock object. This is a primitive mock object because it does not provide a way to set up expectations, nor does it provide a verify( ) method. We will see how to incorporate these concepts in coming recipes.

Example 6-3. Mock table model listener

```
package com.oreilly.mock;

import javax.swing.event.TableModelEvent;
import javax.swing.event.TableModelListener;
import java.util.ArrayList;
import java.util.List;

public class MockTableModelListener implements TableModelListener {
    private List events = new ArrayList( );

    public void tableChanged(TableModelEvent e) {
        this.events.add(e);
    }

    public int getEventCount( ) {
        return this.events.size( );
    }

    public List getEvents( ) {
        return this.events;
    }
}
```

The mock object implements TableModelListener and keeps a list of all events received. The unit test creates an instance of the mock object, adds it as a listener to the custom table model, and calls the addAccount( ) method. Afterwards, it asks the mock object for the event list and verifies that the correct event was delivered. The unit test is shown in Example 6-4.

Example 6-4. Account table model test case

```
package com.oreilly.mock;

import junit.framework.TestCase;

import javax.swing.event.TableModelEvent;

public class UnitTestAccount extends TestCase {
    private AccountTableModel acctTableModel;

    private Account[] accounts = new Account[]{
        new Account(Account.CHECKING, "001", 0.0),
        new Account(Account.CHECKING, "002", 1.1),
        new Account(Account.SAVINGS, "003", 2.2)
    };

    protected void setUp( ) throws Exception {
        this.acctTableModel = new AccountTableModel( );
        for (int i = 0; i < this.accounts.length; i++) {
            this.acctTableModel.addAccount(this.accounts[i]);
        }
    }
```

Example 6-4. Account table model test case (continued)

```java
    public void testAddAccountFiresCorrectEvent( ) {
        // create the mock listener
        MockTableModelListener mockListener =
                new MockTableModelListener( );

        // add the listener to the table model
        this.acctTableModel.addTableModelListener(mockListener);

        // call a method that is supposed to fire a TableModelEvent
        this.acctTableModel.addAccount(new Account(
                Account.CHECKING, "12345", 100.50));

        // verify that the correct event was fired
        assertEquals("Event count", 1, mockListener.getEventCount( ));

        TableModelEvent evt = (TableModelEvent)
                mockListener.getEvents( ).get(0);
        assertEquals("Event type",
                TableModelEvent.INSERT, evt.getType( ));
        assertEquals("Column",
                TableModelEvent.ALL_COLUMNS, evt.getColumn( ));
        assertEquals("First row",
                this.acctTableModel.getRowCount( )-1,
                evt.getFirstRow( ));
        assertEquals("Last row",
                this.acctTableModel.getRowCount( )-1,
                evt.getLastRow( ));
    }
}
```

With the test in hand (and failing), we can implement the addAccount( ) method as shown here:

```java
    public void addAccount(Account acct) {
        int row = this.accounts.size( );
        this.accounts.add(acct);
        fireTableRowsInserted(row, row);
    }
```

The method takes advantage of the fact that our table model extends from AbstractTableModel, which provides the fireTableRowsInserted( ) method. The unit test verifies that addAccount( ) calls this method rather than something like fireTableDataChanged( ) or fireTableStructureChanged( ), both common mistakes when creating custom table models. After writing the method, the test passes.

You can follow this technique as you add more functionality to the custom table model. You might add methods to remove accounts, modify accounts, and move rows around. Each of these operations should fire a specific, fine-grained table model event, which subsequent tests confirm using the mock table model listener.

See Also

The next recipe shows how to simplify the tests by using a mock object that encapsulates the validation logic.

6.2   Mock Object Self-Validation

Problem

You want to avoid duplicated validation logic in your tests.

Solution

Put the validation logic inside of the mock object. This way, every test that uses the mock object will reuse the validation logic automatically.

Discussion

The code in the previous recipe showed how to create a mock table model listener that kept track of a list of events. As you write more tests using this mock object, you will find that your tests have to repeatedly check the number of events as well as every field within the event objects. Rather than repeating this logic in each of your tests, move some of the validation logic into the mock object. Example 6-5 shows how this step simplifies your tests.

Example 6-5. Improved unit test

```
public void testAddAccountEvent() {
    MockTableModelListener mockListener = new MockTableModelListener();
    mockListener.setExpectedEventCount(1);
    TableModelEvent evt = new TableModelEvent(
            this.acctTableModel,
            this.accounts.length,
            this.accounts.length,
            TableModelEvent.ALL_COLUMNS,
            TableModelEvent.INSERT);
    mockListener.addExpectedEvent(evt);

    this.acctTableModel.addTableModelListener(mockListener);

    this.acctTableModel.addAccount(new Account(
            Account.CHECKING, "12345", 100.50));

    mockListener.verify();
}
```

The modified unit test begins by setting the expected event count on the improved mock object. The mock object will fail the test as soon as it receives too many events.

This is useful because it lets you see test failures as soon as the extra events are delivered, making diagnosis easier.

The test also registers a specific expected event. Once the account is added to the table model, the test calls verify( ), which tests against the expected event. Example 6-6 shows the new, improved mock object.

Example 6-6. Self-validating mock listener

```
package com.oreilly.mock;

import junit.framework.Assert;

import javax.swing.event.TableModelEvent;
import javax.swing.event.TableModelListener;
import javax.swing.table.TableModel;
import java.util.ArrayList;
import java.util.List;

public class MockTableModelListener implements TableModelListener {
    private static final int NONE_EXPECTED = -1;
    private List events = new ArrayList();
    private List expectedEvents = null;
    private int expectedEventCount = NONE_EXPECTED;

    public void addExpectedEvent(TableModelEvent e) {
        if (this.expectedEvents == null) {
            this.expectedEvents = new ArrayList();
        }
        this.expectedEvents.add(new ComparableTableModelEvent(e));
    }

    public void setExpectedEventCount(int n) {
        this.expectedEventCount = n;
    }

    public void tableChanged(TableModelEvent e) {
        this.events.add(e);
        if (this.expectedEventCount > NONE_EXPECTED
                && this.events.size() > this.expectedEventCount) {
            Assert.fail("Exceeded the expected event count: "
                + this.expectedEventCount);
        }
    }

    public int getEventCount() {
        return this.events.size();
    }

    public List getEvents() {
        return this.events;
    }
```

Example 6-6. Self-validating mock listener (continued)

```java
    public void verify( ) {
        if (this.expectedEventCount > NONE_EXPECTED) {
            Assert.assertEquals("Expected event count",
                    this.expectedEventCount,
                    this.events.size( ));
        }

        if (this.expectedEvents != null) {
            Assert.assertEquals("Expected events",
                    this.expectedEvents,
                    this.events);
        }
    }

    class ComparableTableModelEvent extends TableModelEvent {
        public ComparableTableModelEvent(TableModelEvent orig) {
            super((TableModel) orig.getSource(), orig.getFirstRow( ),
                    orig.getLastRow(), orig.getColumn(), orig.getType( ));
        }

        public boolean equals(Object obj) {
            TableModelEvent tm = (TableModelEvent) obj;
            return getSource() == tm.getSource( )
                    && getFirstRow() == tm.getFirstRow( )
                    && getLastRow() == tm.getLastRow( )
                    && getColumn() == tm.getColumn( )
                    && getType() == tm.getType( );
        }
    }
}
```

As you can see, the mock object is significantly more complex in this approach. Only write sophisticated mock objects when you find yourself using them in a lot of different tests. As is customary in an XP approach, start simple and then refactor the tests and mock objects as you observe duplicated code.

Our mock object illustrates an interesting point about JUnit. The methods in the junit.framework.Assert class are static, so we can call them from our mock object, which is not itself a unit test:

```java
Assert.fail("Exceeded the expected event count: "
        + this.expectedEventCount);
```

See Also

Recipe 6.6 shows how to autogenerate complex mock objects using MockMaker.

6.3   Writing Testable JDBC Code

Problem

You want to design your JDBC code so it is testable.

Solution

Modularize your code so that the JDBC connection is created independently of your database logic. This allows you to test your logic using a mock connection, statement, and result set.

 This solution illustrates a generally useful pattern. When you create an object, give it references to the objects it needs to talk to, rather than having it go somewhere and get them. This step gives you the ability to reuse the object in other applications or test it in isolation. The idea is not specific to JDBC.

Discussion

A good unit test exercises a small piece of functionality in isolation from the remainder of the system. You may want to test your JDBC logic without actually creating a real database. Testing without a database is advantageous for numerous reasons:

- The tests run faster.
- You don't have to keep a testing database in sync with your unit tests.
- You can test all sorts of error conditions without going to the trouble of creating invalid data in your database.

Testing against a real database is very important, but can be done separately from your other tests. You may end up with 25 tests that actually use a real database and another 50 tests that simulate the database using mock objects. Effective testing requires a variety of approaches (and plenty of creativity) to ensure adequate coverage and good test performance.

Let's start with a class called AccountFactory containing a method that retrieves an Account object from a database. You might write something like this:

```
public Account getAccount(String acctNumber) throws DataSourceException {
    Connection conn = null;
    PreparedStatement ps = null;
    ResultSet rs = null;
    try {
        conn = DriverManager.getConnection(this.dbUrl);

        ...lots of JDBC code here
```

```
    } catch (SQLException e) {
        throw new DataSourceException(e);
    } finally {
        DbUtil.close(rs);
        DbUtil.close(ps);
        DbUtil.close(conn);
    }
}
```

The DataSourceException is a custom exception that wraps around the underlying
SQLException, shielding the caller from the implementation details of this method.
The Connection, PreparedStatement, and ResultSet are created within this method,
which makes the method difficult to test without setting up a real database.*
Example 6-7 shows refactored code that makes the logic testable.

Example 6-7. Refactored database logic

```
public Account getAccount(String acctNumber) throws DataSourceException {
    Connection conn = null;
    try {
        conn = DriverManager.getConnection(this.dbUrl);
        return getAccount(acctNumber, conn);
    } catch (SQLException e) {
        throw new DataSourceException(e);
    } finally {
        DbUtil.close(conn);
    }
}
```

Example 6-8 shows the package-scope getAccount() method, which contains the
actual database access logic. This method also uses another helper method called
getAccountType(), which converts a database account type code into a Java constant. Both of these methods are now testable.

Example 6-8. Package-scope method designed for testing

```
// a package-scope method that makes it easier for a unit test
// to pass in a mock connection
Account getAccount(String acctNumber, Connection conn)
        throws SQLException, DataSourceException {
    PreparedStatement ps = null;
    ResultSet rs = null;
    try {
        ps = conn.prepareStatement(
                "SELECT balance, acctType " +
                "FROM Accounts " +
                "WHERE acctNumber = ?");
```

---

* You could conceivably test this method by writing a mock JDBC driver and registering it with the JDBC
DriverManager class. You would then pass a mock database URL to the DriverManager's getConnection()
method.

Example 6-8. Package-scope method designed for testing (continued)

```
        ps.setString(1, acctNumber);
        Account acct = null;
        rs = ps.executeQuery( );
        if (rs.next( )) {
            double balance = rs.getDouble("balance");
            String acctTypeStr = rs.getString("acctType");
            int acctType = getAccountType(acctTypeStr);
            acct = new Account(acctType, acctNumber, balance);
        }
        return acct;
    } finally {
        DbUtil.close(rs);
        DbUtil.close(ps);
    }
}

// convert a database account code, such as "CH", into a Java constant
int getAccountType(String acctTypeStr)
        throws SQLException, DataSourceException {
    if ("SA".equals(acctTypeStr)) {
        return Account.SAVINGS;
    }
    if ("CH".equals(acctTypeStr)) {
        return Account.CHECKING;
    }
    throw new DataSourceException("Unknown account type: " + acctTypeStr);
}
```

The getAccount( ) method can be tested because the ResultSet and Connection are both interfaces and we can provide mock implementations. The getAccountType( ) method is particularly easy to test because we do not need to setup any mock objects.

See Also

The next recipe shows how to test the code shown in this recipe. Recipe 6.7 explains the getAccountType( ) method in more detail.

6.4   Testing JDBC Code

Problem

You want to use mock objects to test JDBC code.

Solution

Use mock implementations of JDBC interfaces like Connection, PreparedStatement, and ResultSet.

Discussion

Although you could create your own implementations of the JDBC interfaces, the Mock Objects framework from *http://www.mockobjects.com* makes your work easier. This framework provides mock implementations of the key JDBC interfaces so you don't have to manually stub out every method of interfaces like java.sql. ResultSet. Your tests extend from and use these mock implementations.

 These examples work with Version 0.4rc1 of the Mock Objects framework. You will almost certainly have to alter the code when newer versions of Mock Objects are available.

Example 6-9 shows a test for the getAccount( ) method shown in the previous recipe.

Example 6-9. Testing the getAccount() method

```
public void testGetAccount( ) throws Exception {
    class MyMockResultSet extends MockResultSetJdk14 {

        public Object getObject(int columnIndex) throws SQLException {
            return null;
        }

        public Object getObject(String columnName) throws SQLException {
            if ("acctType".equals(columnName)) {
                return "CH";
            }
            if ("balance".equals(columnName)) {
                return new Double(100.0);
            }
            return null;
        }

        public boolean next( ) throws SQLException {
            super.myNextCalls.inc( );
            return true;
        }

        public int getRow( ) throws SQLException {
            return 1;
        }
    }

    MockResultSet mockRs = new MyMockResultSet( );
    mockRs.setExpectedCloseCalls(1);
    mockRs.setExpectedNextCalls(1);

    MockPreparedStatement mockPs = new MockPreparedStatement( );
    mockPs.addExpectedSetParameter(1, "0001");
    mockPs.setExpectedCloseCalls(1);
    mockPs.addResultSet(mockRs);
```

Example 6-9. Testing the getAccount() method (continued)

```
    MockConnection mockConnection = new MockConnection( );
    mockConnection.setupAddPreparedStatement(mockPs);
    mockConnection.setExpectedCloseCalls(0);
    AccountFactory acctFact = new AccountFactory( );

    // call the method that we are actually testing
    Account acct = acctFact.getAccount("0001", mockConnection);

    mockRs.verify( );
    mockPs.verify( );
    mockConnection.verify( );
}
```

MyMockResultSet is the key to this test. It extends MockResultSetJdk14 (described shortly). MyMockResultSet overrides a handful of abstract methods in order to simulate data that would normally be returned from a true database call. Our goal is to support our unit tests without relying on a real database, and we only need to stub out the actual methods that our test calls.

The remainder of the unit test should look familiar if you read through the recipes presented earlier in this chapter. Specifically, we tell the mock result set how many calls to expect. We then create and set up the mock prepared statement and connection, using them to exercise the code in AccountFactory. When finished, we ask each of the mock objects to verify themselves.

It turns out that the version of Mock Objects used in this chapter does not fully support J2SE 1.4. Specifically, many new JDBC methods are not defined in the MockResultSet class. For this reason, we created MockResultSetJdk14, as shown in Example 6-10. This class merely provides dummy implementations of the new JDBC methods so our examples compile under J2SE 1.4.

Example 6-10. Making MockResultSet work with J2SE 1.4

```
package com.oreilly.mock;

import com.mockobjects.sql.MockResultSet;

import java.net.URL;
import java.sql.*;

public abstract class MockResultSetJdk14 extends MockResultSet {
  public URL getURL(int columnIndex) throws SQLException {
      notImplemented( );
      return null;
  }

  public URL getURL(String columnName) throws SQLException {
      notImplemented( );
      return null;
  }
```

Example 6-10. Making MockResultSet work with J2SE 1.4 (continued)

```
public void updateRef(int columnIndex, Ref x) throws SQLException {
    notImplemented( );
}

public void updateRef(String columnName, Ref x) throws SQLException {
    notImplemented( );
}

// etc...
public void updateBlob(int columnIndex, Blob x) throws SQLException
public void updateBlob(String columnName, Blob x) throws SQLException
public void updateClob(int columnIndex, Clob x) throws SQLException
public void updateClob(String columnName, Clob x) throws SQLException
public void updateArray(int columnIndex, Array x) throws SQLException
public void updateArray(String columnName, Array x) throws SQLException
}
```

The fact that we had to write our own class to support J2SE 1.4 illustrates a pitfall of the mock object approach to testing. The mock objects must be kept up-to-date whenever new methods are added to the interfaces you are testing.

It is important to remember that these tests are not actually testing SQL or the database. Instead, they are testing code at the database access layer of an application by "faking out" the database.

See Also

The previous recipe shows how to modularize JDBC code so it is testable. The Mock Objects framework is available at *http://www.mockobjects.com*.

6.5   Generating Mock Objects with MockMaker

Problem

You want to automatically generate a mock object from any Java interface.

Solution

Use MockMaker, available from *http://www.mockmaker.org*.

Discussion

Writing mock objects by hand is tedious, and relying on a framework like Mock Objects is troublesome because it might not provide mock implementations for all of the interfaces you need to test against. The MockMaker project allows you to automatically generate new mock objects from any existing Java interface.

Using MockMaker is simple. Just include the MockMaker JAR files in your CLASS-PATH and invoke the tool as follows:

```
java mockmaker.MockMaker <interfaceName>
```

The generated source code is then echoed to the console. Example 6-11 shows the output from typing the following command:

```
java mockmaker.MockMaker javax.swing.event.TableModelListener
```

Example 6-11. Generated mock object

```
import mockmaker.ReturnValues;
import com.mockobjects.*;
import javax.swing.event.TableModelListener;
import javax.swing.event.TableModelEvent;
public class MockTableModelListener implements TableModelListener{
    private ExpectationCounter myTableChangedCalls = new ExpectationCounter("javax.swing.
event.TableModelListener TableChangedCalls");
    private ExpectationList myTableChangedParameter0Values = new ExpectationList("javax.
swing.event.TableModelListener TableChangedParameter0Values");
    public void setExpectedTableChangedCalls(int calls){
        myTableChangedCalls.setExpected(calls);
    }
    public void addExpectedTableChangedValues(TableModelEvent arg0){
        myTableChangedParameter0Values.addExpected(arg0);
    }
    public void tableChanged(TableModelEvent arg0){
        myTableChangedCalls.inc( );
        myTableChangedParameter0Values.addActual(arg0);
    }
    public void verify( ){
        myTableChangedCalls.verify( );
        myTableChangedParameter0Values.verify( );
    }
}
```

The generated code relies on code found in the Mock Objects framework for keeping track of expectations, such as the expected events or number of times a method was called. You use this class almost exactly like you would use the hand-coded mock object, as shown in Example 6-5 (although the method names are slightly different).

Here is how you can run MockMaker from an Ant buildfile:

```
<path id="classpath.mockmaker">
  <pathelement path="${dir.build}"/>
  <pathelement location="${env.MOCKMAKER_HOME}/mockmaker.jar"/>
  <pathelement location="${env.MOCKMAKER_HOME}/mmmockobjects.jar"/>
  <pathelement location="${env.MOCKMAKER_HOME}"/>
</path>

...
```

```
<target name="generateMockObjects" depends="prepare">
  <java fork="true" classname="mockmaker.MockMaker"
        output="${dir.generatedSrc}/MockTableModelListener.java">
    <classpath refid="classpath.mockmaker"/>
    <arg line="javax.swing.event.TableModelListener"/>
  </java>
</target>
```

See Also

Recipes 6.1 and 6.2 show how to hand-code mock objects that look similar to the code generated by MockMaker. The Mock Objects web site, *http://www.mockobjects. com*, lists URLs for several other mock object generation tools, including Easy Mock, Mock Creator, and Mock Doclet.

6.6   Breaking Up Methods to Avoid Mock Objects

Problem

You want to test a method without resorting to the complexity of mock objects.

Solution

Split the method into smaller pieces, ensuring that each piece performs one task. Small, single-purpose methods improve code quality in addition to making them testable.

Discussion

Example 6-12 shows a method that is hard to test. It is hard because you must create a mock ResultSet implementation in order to write your tests.

Example 6-12. Hard to test

```
// fetch an account type code from the database and convert it
// into one of the Account constants
int getAccountType(ResultSet rs, String acctTypeColName)
        throws SQLException, DataSourceException {
    String acctStr = rs.getString(acctTypeColName);
    if ("SA".equals(acctStr)) {
        return Account.SAVINGS;
    }
    if ("CH".equals(acctStr)) {
        return Account.CHECKING;
    }
    throw new DataSourceException("Unknown account type: " + acctStr);
}
```

The fundamental problem is that this method performs two tasks, rather than one. It is also a little messy because it throws two types of exceptions. The first task is to retrieve data from the ResultSet. The second task is to convert that data into some other form.

When confronted with a method like this, do not try to write a sophisticated unit test. Instead, first try to simplify the method. Example 6-13 shows a simplified version of this method. It is now assumed that the caller obtains the account code from the database before calling this method, whose sole purpose is converting that string into a Java constant.

Example 6-13. The same logic, now testable

```
// convert a database account code, such as "CH", into a Java constant
int getAccountType(String acctTypeStr)
            throws DataSourceException {
    if ("SA".equals(acctTypeStr)) {
        return Account.SAVINGS;
    }
    if ("CH".equals(acctTypeStr)) {
        return Account.CHECKING;
    }
    throw new DataSourceException("Unknown account type: " + acctTypeStr);
}
```

You can now test this method without resorting to mock objects. We also eliminated the extra SQLException because we no longer use JDBC in this method. Example 6-14 shows the test.

Example 6-14. Test for the getAccountType() method

```
public void testGetAccountType( ) throws Exception {
    AccountFactory acctFact = new AccountFactory( );
    assertEquals("account type", Account.CHECKING,
                acctFact.getAccountType("CH"));
    assertEquals("account type", Account.SAVINGS,
                acctFact.getAccountType("SA"));
    try {
        acctFact.getAccountType("bogus");
        fail("Expected DataSourceException");
    } catch (DataSourceException expected) {
    }
}
```

See Also

This method was taken from Example 6-8 earlier in this chapter.

6.7 Testing Server-Side Business Logic

Problem

You want to test business logic that normally depends on a database, but mocking out the low-level SQL is far too complex.

Solution

Organize your server-side code using business objects and database access objects (DAOs). Place all business logic in your business objects, and all database access in your DAOs. Use a factory to create mock implementations of your DAOs when testing your business objects.

Discussion

We showed how to write mock objects to simulate low-level SQL code earlier in this chapter. It is a useful technique for testing the data access tier of your application, but tends to be far too complex for business logic tests. For business objects, you should strive to create mock implementations of the entire data access tier, rather than mock implementations of the JDBC interfaces.

Figure 6-1 illustrates a common design pattern for server-side Java code. In this diagram, either an EJB or a servlet dispatches method calls to CustomerBO, a business object that contains server-side business logic. The business object is what we would like to test.

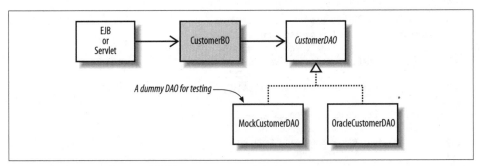

Figure 6-1. Business object and DAO pattern

The first box in Figure 6-1 shows either an EJB or a servlet. This pattern works well with either approach, although the EJB approach allows you to easily invoke many different business objects under the umbrella of a single transaction. Regarding testing, the business object pattern is fantastic because you can test CustomerBO as you would test any other standalone Java class. That is, you don't need to run your tests inside of the application server.

The second key to making business objects testable is keeping data access code separate. The `CustomerDAO` interface defines an API to a data source, and the `OracleCustomerDAO` is an Oracle-specific implementation. When using this approach, your business objects generally locate the correct DAO implementations using some sort of factory object. Example 6-15 shows what some of the methods in `CustomerDAO` might look like.

Example 6-15. CustomerDAO methods

```java
public interface CustomerDAO {
    Customer getCustomer(long customerId) throws DataSourceException;
    void deleteCustomer(long customerId) throws DataSourceException;
    CustomerSummaryInfo[] searchByFirstName(String firstName)
            throws DataSourceException;
}
```

There are no specific requirements for the DAO, other than that it should not expose JDBC implementation details to the caller. Notice that our methods all throw `DataSourceException`, which is an exception we made up for this example. If our methods throw `SQLException`, it would make them harder to implement for non-relational data sources.

 Rather than creating a mock DAO implementation, you might want to create a DAO implementation that hits a small, local database rather than the official database. This allows you to run tests against small, easily configured data without the political battles often required to make changes to the main project database.

Example 6-16 shows an imaginary test case for the business object.

Example 6-16. Imaginary test case for CustomerBO

```java
public class TestCustomerBO extends TestCase {
    public void testSomething( ) throws DataSourceException {

        // instantiate and test the business object
        CustomerBO custBo = new CustomerBO( );
        assertEquals("...", custBo.doSomething( ));
    }
}
```

The test constructs a `CustomerBO` and calls methods on it. It is within these methods that the `CustomerBO` presumably performs the business logic that we are testing. Example 6-17 shows what a method in `CustomerBO` might look like.

Example 6-17. CustomerBO method

```java
public class CustomerBO {
    public void deleteCustomer(long customerId)
            throws DataSourceException {
```

Example 6-17. CustomerBO method (continued)

```
        CustomerDAO dao = MyDAOFactory.getCustomerDAO( );
        dao.deleteCustomer(customerId);
        ...perhaps some business logic here
    }
}
```

From the perspective of CustomerBO, the actual DAO implementation is completely unknown. The MyDAOFactory class takes care of instantiating the correct DAO, whether it is a mock implementation or the real Oracle implementation. You will have to come up with a mechanism to inform the factory which DAO implementation to create. An easy approach is to set a system property in your Ant buildfile. The system property allows you to avoid hardcoding in your application, making it possible to plug in different DAO implementations in the future.

The details of the mock DAO implementations are not important. The general rule is that they should do as little as possible. Their sole purpose is to support the unit tests, so they should be implemented on an as-needed basis to support different tests. They are nothing more than hardcoded dummy classes.

See Also

Search for "J2EE Patterns Catalog" on Google. It should bring up links to Sun's Java Blueprints documentation, which explains the DAO pattern in detail. Our implementation assumes that the business object is a standalone Java class, while Sun's examples usually implement the business object as an EJB. This topic is also discussed in Chapter 11.

CHAPTER 7

Cactus

7.0 Introduction

Cactus, available from *http://jakarta.apache.org/cactus*, is an open source unit-testing framework for server side Java code. Specifically, Cactus allows you to test servlets, JSPs, and servlet filters.* Cactus extends JUnit to provide three specific junit.framework.TestCase subclasses:

```
org.apache.cactus.ServletTestCase
org.apache.cactus.JspTestCase
org.apache.cactus.FilterTestCase
```

Each Cactus test case provides a specific function and is discussed in more detail in the following recipes. Cactus tests execute on both client and server. This is a significant departure from other testing frameworks and deserves some explanation. When using Cactus, you create a single subclass of one of the previously mentioned classes. Cactus then creates and runs two instances of your test case. One instance runs on the client JVM and the other runs inside of the servlet container's JVM. The client side allows HTTP headers and HTTP parameters to be added to the outgoing request. The server side invokes your servlet's methods, performs any necessary assertions, and sends back a response to the client. The client may then assert that the response contained the expected information.

It is important to know that you have to deploy your Cactus tests to the server. Specifically, you must create a web-application WAR file containing a valid *web.xml* file, all Cactus tests, and all support classes needed for your tests to execute. This is necessary because Cactus tests are executed on both the client and server. The recipes in this chapter delve into how this is done.

---

* Cactus may also be used to test Enterprise JavaBean code. This chapter does not discuss this technique. For more information please consult the Cactus documentation.

Implicit Objects

Each Cactus test case has a set of implicit objects. Implicit objects are only valid on the test case instance running in the server. These objects are used to set up information that a servlet expects to exist before invoking any methods to test. For example, you can use the config implicit object to set up initialization parameters. Here are the implicit objects defined by each test case:

org.apache.cactus.ServletTestCase

```
HttpServletRequestWrapper request
HttpServletResponse response
HttpSession session
ServletConfigWrapper config
```

org.apache.cactus.JspTestCase

```
PageContextWrapper pageContext
JspWriter out
```

org.apache.cactus.FilterTestCase

```
HttpServletRequestWrapper request
HttpServletResponse response
FilterConfigWrapper config
FilterChain filterChain
```

How Does It Work?

Cactus executes your tests on the client and server. This means two instances of your test case are created to run the tests. Figure 7-1 shows the execution of a Cactus test.

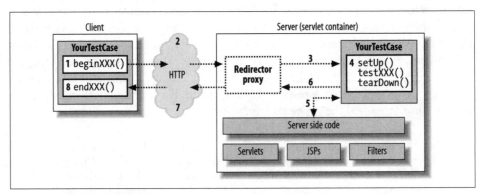

Figure 7-1. Execution of a Cactus test

First, the JUnit test runner, executing in the client JVM, creates one instance of your test case. A *redirector proxy* executing in the server JVM creates the second instance. A redirector proxy is responsible for managing the server-side execution of a test. Let's walk through an example:

1. The JUnit test runner instantiates your test case on the client and executes the runTest( ) method. For each testXXX( ) method, Cactus looks for an optional beginXXX(WebRequest) method. For example, if the test method is called testGetCustomerInformation( ), then Cactus looks for a method called beginGetCustomerInformation(WebRequest) to execute on the client.

   The beginXXX(WebRequest) allows for HTTP Parameters, HTTP Headers, Cookies, etc. to be added to the WebRequest object. This capability provides your test a chance to set up valid or invalid information for your servlet to handle.

2. An HTTP connection is made with the server and a redirector is invoked. Cactus sends the WebRequest through the open connection to the server, too. This allows for the client to pass information to the servlet just like a typical HTTP request.

3. The redirector proxy, executing on the server, takes control, instantiates a new instance of your test case, and sets up the appropriate implicit (depending on the Cactus test case). Only after the new instance is successfully constructed are the implicit objects valid.

> The implicit objects are only available on the server side instance of your test case. Accessing these objects in the client side test case causes a NullPointerException.

4. The redirector invokes the setUp( ) method, followed by the testXXX( ) method.

5. The testXXX( ) method must instantiate a new instance of your servlet and the call methods needed to execute your test.* JUnit assertion methods are used to test if the servlet's logic passed or failed. After the testXXX( ) method completes, the redirector calls the tearDown( ) method.

6. The redirector proxy collects all test results and exceptions.

7. Once all tests are complete, the information collected by the redirector proxy is sent back to the client.

8. If a test did not fail, the optional endXXX(WebResponse) method is invoked (the one that matches the testXXX( ) method). For example, if you have a method called testGetCustomerInformation( ), then Cactus looks for a method called endGetCustomerInformation(WebResponse).

   The endXXX(WebResponse) method allows for the client to perform assertions on the information sent back by a servlet or JSP.

---

* You, the unit test writer, must instantiate the servlet yourself. Cactus does not take on the role of a servlet container and therefore does not instantiate the servlet for you.

7.1 Configuring Cactus

Problem

You want to set up Cactus to test Servlets, JSPs, and Filters.

Solution

Add *junit.jar, cactus.jar, httpclient.jar, commons-logging.jar, log4j.jar*, and *aspectjrt. jar* to the client classpath. Add *junit.jar, cactus.jar, commons-logging.jar*, and *log4j. jar* to your web application's *WEB-INF/lib* directory.

Discussion

A Cactus test suite executes on both client and server, requiring both client and server classpaths to be set properly. Cactus configuration is tricky and almost all Cactus problems are related to classpath issues. This chapter assumes Cactus 1.4.1, which bundles the JAR files listed below.

 The JAR files that come bundled with Cactus 1.4 and higher include the version of the tool in the filename. For example, the JUnit JAR file used in Cactus 1.4.1 is *junit-3.7.jar*, specifying JUnit 3.7 is being used. This chapter does not assume any specific version for JAR files because you are free to use any compatible version of a third party tool.

Client-side classpath

junit.jar contains the JUnit framework that Cactus extends from, and is needed to compile and run the Cactus test suite. All Cactus framework test cases, as mentioned in the introduction, extend the `org.junit.framework.TestCase` class.

cactus.jar contains the Cactus framework, which includes three Cactus test cases (`ServletTestCase`, `JspTestCase`, `FilterTestCase`) that your test classes may extend.

httpclient.jar contains a framework supporting HTTP-based methods such as GET and POST, provides the ability to set cookies, and uses BASIC authentication.

aspectjrt.jar is used by Cactus to perform tasks such as configuration checking and logging when methods begin and end.

commons-logging.jar is the Jakarta Commons Logging facade framework. Cactus uses this framework to allow for different logging frameworks to be plugged in. For example, you may seamlessly use log4j or JDK 1.4 logging. Even if you do not want to use logging, HttpClient needs this JAR file in the classpath.

log4j.jar is an optional JAR file needed if you plan on using log4J to log client-side information during your tests.

httpunit.jar, *tidy.jar* and *xerces.jar* are optional JAR files needed if you plan to use HttpUnit in your endXXX( ) methods. HttpUnit provides these three JAR files in its distribution.

cactus.properties is a Java properties file that configures the Cactus testing environment.

Server-side classpath

The server-side test is deployed as a web application to your servlet container. This means that your web applications, including cactus tests, are deployed as self-contained WAR files. Cactus executes the testXXX( ) methods inside the servlet container's JVM and requires, at minimum, the JAR files described below, which ultimately go in your web application's *WEB-INF/lib* directory.

cactus.jar contains the core Cactus framework needed by the server to locate Cactus classes used by your Cactus test.

junit.jar contains the core JUnit framework that Cactus extends from.

aspectjrt.jar is used by Cactus to perform tasks such as configuration checking and logging when methods begin and end.

log4j.jar is an optional JAR file needed if you plan on using log4J to log server side information during your tests.

commons-logging.jar is the Jakarta Commons Logging facade framework.

 You may be tempted to put these JAR files in your servlet container's shared library path. We recommend that you include all third party JAR files in your web application's *WEB-INF/lib* directory. This guarantees that the servlet container will find and load the correct classes. Your servlet container probably has different classloaders for your web applications, and different classloaders for running the core libraries needed by your container. See your servlet container's documentation for more information.

See Also

Recipe 7.2 shows how to create an Ant buildfile to support server-side testing. Recipe 7.3 describes the *cactus.properties* file. Recipe 7.4 shows how to use Ant to automatically generate the *cactus.properties* file.

7.2   Setting Up a Stable Build Environment

Problem

You want to configure your environment to support test-first development with Cactus, Tomcat, and Ant.

Solution

Create an Ant buildfile to automatically build, start Tomcat, deploy to the server, execute your web application's test suite, and stop Tomcat.

Discussion

Setting up an Ant buildfile to properly handle Cactus tests is nontrivial and deserves some explanation A successful environment allows developers to make and test small code changes quickly, and requires a server that supports hot deploying. The ability to hot deploy a modified web application is critical for test-first development because it takes too long to restart most servers. Tomcat provides a built-in web application called *manager* that supports hot deploying. For more information on Tomcat see Chapter 10.

Figure 7-2 shows a graphical view of the Ant buildfile we are creating. Setting up a stable and easy-to-use environment is imperative for server-side testing. For example, typing **ant cactus** prepares the development environment, compiles all out-of-date files, creates a new WAR file, starts Tomcat (if it isn't already started), removes the old web application (if it exists), deploys the updated web application, and invokes the Cactus test suite. The developer does not have to worry about whether the server is started. Ant takes care of the details, allowing developers to concentrate on writing testable code. If the tests are too hard to execute, then developers will not write them.

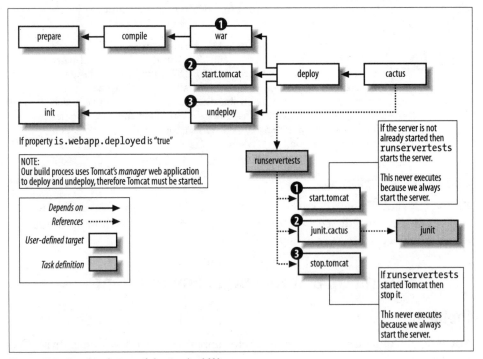

Figure 7-2. Graphical view of the Ant buildfile

The properties defined below set up information used throughout the buildfile. For example, the properties username.manager and username.password are needed to login to Tomcat's *manager* application for deploying and removing web applications while Tomcat is running, a concept known as *hot deploying*. If the username or password changes, we only have to change it here.

```
<property environment="env"/>
<property name="dir.build" value="build"/>
<property name="dir.src" value="src"/>
<property name="dir.resources" value="resources"/>
<property name="dir.lib" value="lib"/>
<property name="url.manager" value="http://localhost:8080/manager"/>
<property name="username.manager" value="javaxp"/>
<property name="password.manager" value="secret"/>
<property name="host" value="http://localhost"/>
<property name="port" value="8080"/>
<property name="webapp.context.name" value="xptest"/>
<property name="servlet.redirector" value="ServletRedirector"/>
<property name="cactus.service" value="RUN_TEST"/>
<property name="jsp.redirector" value="JspRedirector"/>
<property name="filter.redirector" value="FilterRedirector"/>
```

The classpath shown below is used to compile the web application, and is used as the client-side classpath when executing Cactus.

```
<path id="classpath.project">
  <pathelement location="${dir.build}"/>
  <pathelement location="${env.CACTUS_HOME}/lib/aspectjrt-1.0.5.jar"/>
  <pathelement location="${env.CACTUS_HOME}/lib/cactus-1.4.1.jar"/>
  <pathelement location="${env.CACTUS_HOME}/lib/commons-logging-1.0.jar"/>
  <pathelement location="${env.CACTUS_HOME}/lib/httpclient-2.0.jar"/>
  <pathelement location="${env.CACTUS_HOME}/lib/httpunit-1.4.1.jar"/>
  <pathelement location="${env.CACTUS_HOME}/lib/junit-3.7.jar"/>
  <pathelement location="${env.CACTUS_HOME}/lib/log4j-1.2.5.jar"/>
  <pathelement location="${env.CACTUS_HOME}/lib/servletapi-2.3.jar"/>*
</path>
```

The next target sets the property is.tomcat.started if Tomcat is running. The property is.webapp.deployed is set if Tomcat is started and there is an instance of our web application currently installed. The Ant http conditional subtask returns a response code, and if that response code indicates some sort of success, we can assume the application is deployed. The undeploy target uses the is.webapp.deployed property to determine if an old copy of the web application should be removed:

```
<target name="init">
  <condition property="is.tomcat.started">
    <http url="${host}:${port}"/>
  </condition>
  <condition property="is.webapp.deployed">
    <and>
```

* Cactus 1.4 and higher now ships with the Servlet 2.3 API.

```
        <isset property="is.tomcat.started"/>
        <http url="${host}:${port}/${webapp.context.name}"/>
      </and>
    </condition>
  </target>
```

The code is compiled with this target:

```
<target name="compile" depends="prepare"
        description="Compile all source code.">
  <javac srcdir="${dir.src}" destdir="${dir.build}">
    <classpath refid="classpath.project"/>
  </javac>
</target>
```

Next, your buildfile should have a target to generate the WAR file:

```
<target name="war" depends="compile">
  <war warfile="${dir.build}/${webapp.context.name}.war"
      webxml="${dir.resources}/web.xml">
    <classes dir="${dir.build}">
      <include name="com/oreilly/javaxp/cactus/**/*.class"/>
    </classes>
    <lib dir="${env.CACTUS_HOME}/lib">
      <include name="aspectjrt-1.0.5.jar"/>
      <include name="cactus-1.4.1.jar"/>
      <include name="commons-logging-1.0.jar"/>
      <include name="httpunit-1.4.1.jar"/>
      <include name="junit-3.7.jar"/>
    </lib>
    <fileset dir="${dir.resources}">
      <include name="*.jsp"/>
      <include name="*.html"/>
    </fileset>
  </war>
</target>
```

Cactus tests need a few support classes on the web application's classpath. The simplest way to ensure that these files are on the web application's classpath is to include them in the *WEB-INF/lib* directory. Using the lib subtask accomplishes this goal. Finally, if you are testing JSPs, then you need to copy the *jspRedirector.jsp** file to the root of your web application—otherwise, do not worry about it.

Since we are using Tomcat's *manager* web application to deploy, Tomcat must be started. In order to achieve test-first development, we created a new Ant task to start Tomcat. We need our build process to patiently wait until the server is started before trying to deploy.

```
<target name="start.tomcat">
  <taskdef name="starttomcat"
      classname="com.oreilly.javaxp.tomcat.tasks.StartTomcatTask">
    <classpath>
```

---

* This file is located under the *CACTUS_HOME/sample-servlet/web*. For convenience, this file has been copied to our project's *resources* directory.

```
        <path location="${dir.lib}/tomcat-tasks.jar"/>
      </classpath>
    </taskdef>

    <starttomcat
        testURL="${host}:${port}"
        catalinaHome="${env.CATALINA_HOME}"/>
</target>
```

Before deploying, the old instance of the web application must be removed, if it exists. First, the init target is called to see if the web application has been deployed. If so, then Tomcat's RemoveTask is used to remove the old instance.

The RemoveTask fails if the web application is not installed (previously deployed), causing the build to stop. Depending on your needs, this may or may not be what you expect. In our case, it's not what we expect, and is why we verify that the web application is deployed before trying to remove it.

```
<target name="undeploy" depends="init" if="is.webapp.deployed">
    <taskdef name="remove" classname="org.apache.catalina.ant.RemoveTask">
      <classpath>
        <path location="${env.CATALINA_HOME}/server/lib/catalina-ant.jar"/>
      </classpath>
    </taskdef>

    <remove
        url="${url.manager}"
        username="${username.manager}"
        password="${password.manager}"
        path="/${webapp.context.name}"/>
</target>
```

The deploy target depends on generating a new WAR file, starting Tomcat, and removing a previously-deployed instance of the web application. Tomcat's InstallTask is used to install the WAR file.

```
<target name="deploy" depends="war,start.tomcat,undeploy">
    <taskdef name="install" classname="org.apache.catalina.ant.InstallTask">
      <classpath>
        <path location="${env.CATALINA_HOME}/server/lib/catalina-ant.jar"/>
      </classpath>
    </taskdef>

    <pathconvert dirsep="/" property="fullWarDir">
      <path>
        <pathelement location="${dir.build}/${webapp.context.name}.war"/>
      </path>
    </pathconvert>

    <install
        url="${url.manager}"
        username="${username.manager}"
```

```
        password="${password.manager}"
        path="/${webapp.context.name}"
        war="jar:file:/${fullWarDir}!/"/>
    </target>
```

After the web application is successfully deployed, the Cactus test suite is executed. Cactus provides an Ant task called RunServerTestsTask to execute the tests. This task is located in the *cactus-ant-1.4.1.jar* file. Here is how to setup a target to execute Cactus tests:[*]

```
<target name="cactus " depends="deploy"
    description="Deploys and runs the Cactus Test suite on Tomcat 4.1.x">

    <taskdef name="runservertests"
        classname="org.apache.cactus.ant.RunServerTestsTask">
        <classpath>
            <path location="${env.CACTUS_HOME}/lib/cactus-ant-1.4.1.jar"/>
        </classpath>
    </taskdef>

    <runservertests
        testURL="${host}:${port}/${webapp.context.name}/${servlet.redirector}?
                 Cactus_Service=${cactus.service}"
        startTarget="start.tomcat"
        testTarget="junit.cactus"
        stopTarget="stop.tomcat"/>
</target>
```

The runservertests task defines four attributes:

- The testURL attribute checks if the specified URL is available by constantly polling the server. Cactus recommends using a specific URL to the server is ready to execute Cactus tests. This URL invokes the ServletTestRedirector servlet and passes a parameter to it, telling the servlet to check if all is well to execute tests. If the URL fails, then the server has not been started, or the web application is not properly deployed (probably classpath issues).

 If the server hangs when executing this task, you need to check the Tomcat logfiles. Typically, the web application did not start properly due to classpath issues. Almost all Cactus problems are classpath-related.

- The startTarget attribute specifies a target within the buildfile that starts the server, if the server is not already started.

- The testTarget attribute specifies a target within your buildfile that executes the Cactus tests.

- The stopTarget attribute specifies a target within your buildfile that stops the server. The server is only stopped if the startTarget started the server.

---

[*] The testURL attribute value has a line break so that the URL fits nicely on the page.

First, the startTarget starts the server, if the server is not already started. Once the server is running, the testTarget is responsible for starting the tests. A Cactus test suite is started the same way as a JUnit test suite. The next target uses the junit task to start the Cactus tests on the client. It's important to know that Cactus retains control during test execution, ensuring that the client and server tests are kept in sync.

```
<target name="junit.cactus">
  <junit printsummary="yes" haltonfailure="yes" haltonerror="yes" fork="yes">
    <classpath refid="classpath.project"/>
    <formatter type="plain" usefile="false"/>
    <batchtest fork="yes" todir="build">
      <fileset dir="src">
        <include name="**/Test*.java"/>
      </fileset>
    </batchtest>
  </junit>
</target>
```

After the tests are complete, the stopTarget is executed to stop the server (if the server was started by startTarget). Otherwise, the server is left running. In order to facilitate test-first development, we created a custom Ant task specifically to stop Tomcat. Here is the target to stop Tomcat:

```
<target name="stop.tomcat">
  <taskdef name="stoptomcat"
      classname="com.oreilly.javaxp.tomcat.tasks.StopTomcatTask">
    <classpath>
      <path location="${dir.lib}/tomcat-tasks.jar"/>
    </classpath>
  </taskdef>

  <stoptomcat
      testURL="${host}:${port}"
      catalinaHome="${env.CATALINA_HOME}"/>
</target>
```

See Also

Chapter 10 describes the custom Ant tasks to start and stop Tomcat.

7.3   Creating the cactus.properties File

Problem

You are setting up your Cactus environment and need to create the *cactus.properties* file.

Solution

Create a file called *cactus.properties* and place it on the client classpath.

Discussion

Cactus uses a Java properties file called *cactus.properties* to specify client-side attributes needed to successfully execute your tests. This file must be located on the client classpath, and simply tells Cactus the web context of your test application and the redirector values. The redirector values are URL patterns used in the deployment descriptor that point to a particular Cactus redirector proxy. Here's an example of the *cactus.properties* file:

```
cactus.contextURL=http://localhost:8080/xptest
cactus.servletRedirectorName=ServletRedirector
cactus.jspRedirectorName=JspRedirector
cactus.filterRedirectorName=FilterRedirector
```

Here's the corresponding deployment descriptor *web.xml* file:*

```
<?xml version="1.0" encoding="ISO-8859-1"?>
<!DOCTYPE web-app
    PUBLIC "-//Sun Microsystems, Inc.//DTD Web Application 2.3//EN"
    "http://java.sun.com/dtd/web-app_2_3.dtd">

<web-app>
  <filter>
    <filter-name>FilterRedirector</filter-name>
      <filter-class>
        org.apache.cactus.server.FilterTestRedirector
      </filter-class>
  </filter>
  <filter-mapping>
    <filter-name>FilterRedirector</filter-name>
    <url-pattern>/FilterRedirector</url-pattern>
  </filter-mapping>
  <servlet>
    <servlet-name>ServletRedirector</servlet-name>
    <servlet-class>
      org.apache.cactus.server.ServletTestRedirector
    </servlet-class>
  </servlet>
  <servlet>
      <servlet-name>JspRedirector</servlet-name>
      <jsp-file>/jspRedirector.jsp</jsp-file>
  </servlet>
  <servlet>
      <servlet-name>CustomerServlet</servlet-name>
      <servlet-class>
        com.oreilly.javaxp.cactus.servlet.CustomerServlet
      </servlet-class>
  </servlet>
  <servlet-mapping>
```

---

* If you are using the JSP Redirector, you must add the *jspRedirector.jsp* file to your web application. This file is located under the *CACTUS_HOME/sample-servlet/web* directory.

```
    <servlet-name>JspRedirector</servlet-name>
    <url-pattern>/JspRedirector</url-pattern>
  </servlet-mapping>
  <servlet-mapping>
    <servlet-name>ServletRedirector</servlet-name>
    <url-pattern>/ServletRedirector</url-pattern>
  </servlet-mapping>
</web-app>
```

Table 7-1 describes each property in detail.

Table 7-1. Cactus properties

Property	Description
cactus.contextURL	A URL specifying the host, port, and web context name of the Cactus test web application.
cactus.servletRedirectorName	The name of the Cactus Servlet redirector specified by the url-pattern element in the *web.xml* file. This property is needed only if your tests extend org.apache.cactus.ServletTestCase.
cactus.jspRedirectorName	The name of the Cactus JSP redirector specified by the url-pattern element in the *web.xml* file. This property is needed only if your tests extend org.apache.cactus.JspTestCase.
cactus.filterRedirectorName	The name of the Cactus Filter redirector specified by the url-pattern element in the *web.xml* file. This property is needed only if your tests extend org.apache.cactus.FilterTestCase.

See Also

Recipe 7.4 shows how to use Ant to automatically generate the *cactus.properties* file.

7.4   Generating the cactus.properties File Automatically

Problem

You want to automatically generate the *cactus.properties* file to match the current environment.

Solution

Create a target within your Ant buildfile to generate the *cactus.properties* file each time Cactus tests are run.

Discussion

Writing Cactus tests is pretty straightforward, but configuring your environment can be cumbersome, especially if your environment changes over time. Automatically generating configuration files eases the burden of keeping your testing environment in sync with your development environment.

Ant is the obvious choice for generating the *cactus.properties* file. The first step is to ensure that the following Ant properties are defined in your buildfile:[*]

```
<property name="dir.build" value="build"/>
<property name="host" value="http://localhost"/>
<property name="port" value="8080"/>
<property name="webapp.context.name" value="xptest"/>
<property name="servlet.redirector" value="ServletRedirector"/>
<property name="jsp.redirector" value="JspRedirector"/>
<property name="filter.redirector" value="FilterRedirector"/>
```

By setting up global properties, you ensure that a single change ripples through the rest of the buildfile. Next, your buildfile should execute the propertyfile task:

```
<target name="prepare">
  <mkdir dir="${dir.build}"/>

  <propertyfile file="${dir.build}/cactus.properties">
    <entry key="cactus.contextURL"
           value="${host}:${port}/${webapp.context.name}"/>
    <entry key="cactus.servletRedirectorName"
           value="${servlet.redirector}"/>
    <entry key="cactus.jspRedirectorName"
           value="${jsp.redirector}"/>
    <entry key="cactus.filterRedirectorName"
           value="${filter.redirector}"/>
  </propertyfile>
</target>
```

 The propertyfile task is an optional Ant task. If you are using Ant 1.4 then you must include the optional Ant JAR file in Ant's classpath. The simplest way to do this is to copy the optional Ant JAR file to Ant's *lib* directory. If you are using Ant 1.5 or greater you do not have to do anything.

The best place to generate the *cactus.properties* file is within a target that executes each time the Cactus test suite runs. In this recipe, the property file is generated within the prepare target, which is the first target executed when running the test suite. Each time you run the Cactus test suite the *cactus.properties* file is generated by Ant to reflect any changes to the host, port, web context name, or redirector values.

See Also

Recipe 7.3 describes the details of the *cactus.properties* file. Recipe 7.2 describes how to setup a stable build environment for server-side testing.

---

[*] Your test environment may require different property values for the host, port, web application context name, etc. than shown here.

7.5   Writing a Cactus Test

Problem

You want to use Cactus to test server-side code.

Solution

Extend the appropriate Cactus test-case class and implement one or more testXXX( ), beginXXX( ), and endXXX( ) methods.

Discussion

Cactus is a testing framework that extends JUnit to provide a way to execute tests against code running in a server. Specifically, Cactus allows for testing servlets, JSPs, and filters while running within a servlet container.

There are seven main steps to writing a Cactus test.

1. Import the JUnit and Cactus classes:

   ```
   import org.apache.cactus.*;
   import junit.framework.*;
   ```

2. Extend one of three Cactus test case classes:

   org.apache.cactus.ServletTestCase

   Extend this class when you want to write unit tests for your servlets. For example, if you need to test how a servlet handles HttpServletRequest, HttpServletResponse, HttpSession, ServletContext, or ServletConfig objects, write a ServletTestCase:

   ```
   public class TestMyServlet extends ServletTestCase {
   }
   ```

   org.apache.cactus.JspTestCase

   Extend this class when you want to write unit tests for your JSPs. For example, if you need to test a custom tag library or JspWriter, write a JspTestCase:

   ```
   public class TestMyJsp extends JspTestCase {
   }
   ```

   org.apache.cactus.FilterTestCase

   Extend this class when you want to write unit tests for your filters. For example, if you need to test that a FilterChain or FilterConfig object executes correctly, write a FilterTestCase:

   ```
   public class TestMyFilter extends FilterTestCase {
   }
   ```

3. Implement the JUnit setUp( ) and tearDown( ) methods. The setUp( ) and tearDown( ) methods are optional methods that can be overridden by your test. Unlike a normal JUnit test that executes these methods on the client, Cactus

executes these methods on the server. This allows you access to the implicit objects defined by Cactus. Here is an example of setting an attribute on the HttpSession implicit object:

```
public void setUp( ) throws Exception {
    this.session.setAttribute("BookQuantity", new Integer(45));
}

public void tearDown( ) throws Exception {
    this.session.removeAttribute("BookQuantity");
}
```

As in JUnit, the setUp( ) and tearDown( ) methods are executed for each testXXX( ) method. The only twist is that Cactus executes these methods on the server.

Using the Constructor in Place of setUp( ) May Cause Problems

An idiom for writing JUnit tests is to use the constructor instead of overriding the setUp( ) method. This works because each testXXX( ) method creates a new instantiation of the test class, so instance variables are allocated for each test. Here's an example of using the setUp( ) method:

```
public void setUp( ) {
    this.myobject = new MyObject( );
}
```

Here's how the same thing can be accomplished using the constructor:

```
public MyJUnitTest(String name) {
    super(name);
    this.myobject = new MyObject( );
}
```

This technique may cause problems with Cactus if you try to set up information on any of the implicit objects. The implicit objects are only valid on the server and are not initialized until after the constructor is executed. The following code causes a NullPointerException:

```
public MyCactusTest(String name) {
    super(name);

    // the implicit HttpSession is null
    this.session.setAttribute("name","value");
}
```

Here's the correct solution:

```
public void setUp( ) {
    // the implicit HttpSession is valid
    this.session.setAttribute("name","value");
}
```

Be careful when using JUnit idioms because extensions of the JUnit framework may behave quite differently than expected.

---

4. Implement the testXXX( ) methods. All Cactus test methods are defined exactly the same as JUnit test methods. The only difference is that Cactus test methods are executed on the server. In the testXXX( ) method you:

- Instantiate and optionally initialize the servlet to test.
- Call the method to test.
- Use the standard JUnit assertion methods to verify the expected results.

Here is an example:

```
public void testMyTest( ) throws Exception {
    MyServlet servlet = new MyServlet( );
    assertTrue(servlet.doSomethingThatEvaluatesToTrueOrFalse( ));
}
```

Notice the explicit instantiation of the servlet. This is something that servlet developers never have to do in a real web application because the servlet container is responsible for the servlet's lifecycle. In the Cactus world, you must take on the role of the servlet container and ensure that the servlet is instantiated, and if needed, initialized by invoking init(ServletConfig) method.

5. Optionally, implement the beginXXX(WebRequest) method. For each testXXX( ) method, you may define a corresponding beginXXX( ) method. This method is optional and executes on the client before the testXXX( ) method. Since this method executes on the client, the implicit objects we had access to in the setUp( ), tearDown( ), and testXXX( ) are null.

6. Here is the full signature:

```
public void beginXXX(org.apache.cactus.WebRequest) {
    // insert client side setup code here
}
```

This method can be used to initialize HTTP related information, such as HTTP parameters, cookies, and HTTP headers. The values set here become available in the testXXX( ) method through the appropriate implicit object.

7. Optionally, implement the endXXX(WebResponse) method. For each testXXX( ) method you may define a corresponding endXXX( ) method. This method is optional and executes on the client after the testXXX( ) method successfully completes. If the testXXX( ) method throws an exception this method is not executed.

Cactus provides support for two endXXX(WebResponse) signatures. Here are the valid signatures:

```
public void endXXX(org.apache.cactus.WebResponse) {
    // insert client side assertions
}

public void endXXX(com.meterware.httpunit.WebResponse) {
    // insert client side assertions
}
```

Use the first signature if you want to use the WebResponse that comes with the Cactus framework. This object provides a very simple view of the response. Use the second signature if you want to use the WebResponse object that is distributed with HttpUnit. This object provides a detailed view of the response, providing a much richer API. The Cactus framework accepts either signature in your test with absolutely no effort on your part.

8. Finally, compile, deploy the web application to the server, and execute the tests.

See Also

Recipe 7.2 describes how to set up a stable build environment for server-side testing. For more information on using HttpUnit to perform complex assertions in the endXXX(WebResponse) method, see Chapter 5.

7.6 Submitting Form Data

Problem

You want to verify that your servlet correctly handles form parameters.

Solution

Write a ServletTestCase to simulate passing valid and invalid form parameters to a servlet.

Is Cactus Too Difficult?

Cactus provides a way to test server-side code running within a servlet container. A Cactus test, commonly known as an in-container test, can sometimes be overkill, depending on what you are testing. For example, this recipe shows how to use Cactus to test form parameters passed to a servlet. You may recall that Chapter 5 also shows how to test form parameters. In our opinion, HttpUnit is a lot easier to use than Cactus. Another approach, which some would argue is even easier, is to use a mock object. Specifically, you would have a mock implementation of the HttpServletRequest interface that provides the functionality you need to test request (form) parameters. So which is better? The answer lies in what you are comfortable using. If you are using Cactus for most of your tests, it may make sense to bite the bullet and use Cactus for all tests, even if the test is harder to write. On the other hand, if you do not mind mixing different unit testing frameworks in your project, then a mock implementation is probably the easiest solution.

Discussion

Most web applications have some sort of user input. A good example is a page for new customers to create an account. The page might ask for name, address, age, and gender. In the web world, this calls for an HTML form containing one or more input elements to solicit information from a user. The information contained in the input elements is added to the HTTP request by the browser when the user submits the form. As a servlet programmer, you must process each parameter and ensure that invalid information does not cause the servlet to crash or, even worse, corrupt a data store.

Start this recipe by looking at an example HTML form that is submitted to a servlet:[*]

```
<form method="post" action="LoginServlet">
  <table border="1">
    <tr>
      <td>Username:</td>
      <td><input type="text" name="username"/></td>
    </tr>
    <tr>
      <td>Password:</td>
      <td><input type="password" name="password"/></td>
    </tr>
    <tr>
      <td colspan="2" align="center" >
        <input type="submit" name="submit" value="Login"/>
      </td>
    </tr>
  </table>
</form>
```

When forms are submitted, the browser automatically adds each form field to the outgoing request. In the example above, the form data is sent to a servlet mapped to the name LoginServlet. The LoginServlet retrieves, verifies, and processes the data, which in this case is intended to authenticate a user. Example 7-1 shows the first iteration of the servlet.

Example 7-1. First iteration of the LoginServlet

```
package com.oreilly.javaxp.cactus.servlet;

import javax.servlet.http.HttpServlet;
import javax.servlet.http.HttpServletRequest;
import javax.servlet.http.HttpServletResponse;
import javax.servlet.ServletException;
import java.io.IOException;

public class LoginServlet extends HttpServlet {
```

---

[*] The HTML form shown here is not used by any part of our test.

Example 7-1. First iteration of the LoginServlet (continued)

```
/**
 * Cactus does not automatically invoke this method. If you want to
 * test this method then your test method must explicitly invoke it.
 */
protected void doPost(HttpServletRequest req, HttpServletResponse res)
        throws IOException, ServletException {
    if (!validateParameters(req)) {
        req.setAttribute("errorMessage",
                            "Please enter your username and password");
        req.getRequestDispatcher("/login.jsp").forward(req, res);
        return;
    }

    // authenticate user
}

protected boolean validateParameters(HttpServletRequest req) {
    // @todo - implement this!
    return false;
}
}
```

Our servlet overrides the doPost( ) method and immediately calls the validateParameters( ) method, which is the method we are going to test. First, we make the test fail, and then write the code to make it pass. Example 7-2 shows the next iteration of the Cactus test.

Example 7-2. Second iteration of the LoginServlet test

```
package com.oreilly.javaxp.cactus.servlet;

import org.apache.cactus.ServletTestCase;
import org.apache.cactus.WebRequest;

public class TestLoginServlet extends ServletTestCase {

    private LoginServlet servlet;

    public TestLoginServlet(String name) {
        super(name);
    }

    public void setUp() {
        this.servlet = new LoginServlet();
    }

    public void beginValidFormParameters(WebRequest webRequest) {
        webRequest.addParameter("username", "coyner_b", WebRequest.POST_METHOD);
        webRequest.addParameter("password", "secret", WebRequest.POST_METHOD);
    }

    public void testValidFormParameters() {
```

Example 7-2. Second iteration of the LoginServlet test (continued)

```
        assertTrue("Valid Parameters.",
                    this.servlet.validateParameters(this.request));
    }
}
```

The test method testValidFormParameters( ) fails because our servlet is hardcoded to return false. Now that we have seen our test fail, let's update the validateParameters( ) method to make our test pass. Example 7-3 shows the new and improved servlet code.

Example 7-3. Updated servlet

```
protected boolean validateParameters(HttpServletRequest req) {
    String username = req.getParameter("username");
    String password = req.getParameter("password");
    if ((username == null || "".equals(username)) ||
        (password == null || "".equals(password))) {
        return false;
    } else {
        return true;
    }
}
```

Servlets must always check request parameters for null and an empty string. A parameter is null if the parameter does not exist in the request. A parameter contains an empty string when the parameter exists without a value. Example 7-4 shows how to test for these conditions.

Example 7-4. Improved unit test

```
package com.oreilly.javaxp.cactus.servlet;

import org.apache.cactus.ServletTestCase;
import org.apache.cactus.WebRequest;

public class UnitTestLoginServlet extends ServletTestCase {

    private LoginServlet servlet;

    public TestLoginServlet(String name) {
        super(name);
    }

    public void setUp( ) {
        this.servlet = new LoginServlet( );
    }

    public void beginValidFormParameters(WebRequest webRequest) {
        webRequest.addParameter("username", "coyner_b", WebRequest.POST_METHOD);
        webRequest.addParameter("password", "secret", WebRequest.POST_METHOD);
    }
```

Example 7-4. Improved unit test (continued)

```
public void testValidFormParameters() {
    assertTrue("Valid Parameters.",
               this.servlet.validateParameters(this.request));
}

public void beginUsernameParameterNull(WebRequest webRequest) {
    webRequest.addParameter("password", "secret", WebRequest.POST_METHOD);
}

public void testUsernameParameterNull() {
    assertTrue("Username form field not specified in request.",
               !this.servlet.validateParameters(this.request));
}

public void beginUsernameParameterEmptyString(WebRequest webRequest) {
    webRequest.addParameter("username", "", WebRequest.POST_METHOD);
    webRequest.addParameter("password", "secret", WebRequest.POST_METHOD);
}

public void testUsernameParameterEmptyString() {
    assertTrue("Username not entered.",
               !this.servlet.validateParameters(this.request));
}

public void beginPasswordParameterNull(WebRequest webRequest) {
    webRequest.addParameter("username", "coyner_b", WebRequest.POST_METHOD);
}

public void testPasswordParameterNull() {
    assertTrue("Passord form field not specified in request.",
               !this.servlet.validateParameters(this.request));
}

public void beginPasswordParameterEmptyString(WebRequest webRequest) {
    webRequest.addParameter("username", "coyner_b", WebRequest.POST_METHOD);
    webRequest.addParameter("password", "", WebRequest.POST_METHOD);
}

public void testPasswordParameterEmptyString() {
    assertTrue("Password not entered.",
               !this.servlet.validateParameters(this.request));
}
}
```

See Also

Chapter 5 provides an alternate tool for testing server side code. Chapter 6 provides
a discussion on mock objects.

7.7 Testing Cookies

Problem

You want to test a servlet that uses cookies.

Solution

Write a `ServletTestCase` that tests if your servlet correctly handles creating and managing cookies.

Discussion

Cookies are small pieces of information passed back and forth between the web server and the browser as a user navigates a web application. Web applications commonly use cookies for session tracking because a cookie's value uniquely identifies the client. There is a danger for a web application to rely solely on cookies for session tracking because the user may, at any time, disable cookies. For this reason, you must design your web application so that your web application still works if cookies are disabled.

Cactus Proves that Code Works

Cactus provides some comfort when a test passes, because it passed while running in a servlet container. This fact helps prove the code actually works when deployed. This type of test is very useful when testing critical aspects of a web application—for example, session tracking. Session tracking usually mixes three technologies (or concepts): URL rewriting, cookies, and the servlet-session API. Typically, web applications use all three in order to provide a robust web application. Testing this part of a web application is challenging. By writing tests that execute in a servlet container, you are helping to guarantee that your code actually works as designed when deployed.

Example 7-5 shows how to write a test for a servlet that uses cookies to keep track of how many times a user has visited the site.

Example 7-5. A simple cookie counter

```
package com.oreilly.javaxp.cactus.servlet;

import org.apache.cactus.ServletTestCase;
import org.apache.cactus.WebRequest;
import org.apache.cactus.WebResponse;
```

Example 7-5. A simple cookie counter (continued)

```java
import javax.servlet.http.Cookie;

public class TestCookieServlet extends ServletTestCase {

    private CookieServlet servlet;

    public TestCookieServlet(String name) {
        super(name);
    }

    protected void setUp( ) throws Exception {
        this.servlet = new CookieServlet( );
    }

    public void testGetInitialCookie( ) throws Exception {

        Cookie cookie = this.servlet.getCookie(this.request);
        assertNotNull("Cookie.", cookie);
        assertEquals("Cookie Name.",
                    CookieServlet.TEST_COOKIE_NAME,
                    cookie.getName( ));
        assertEquals("Cookie Value.",
                    "0",
                    cookie.getValue( ));
    }

    public void beginGetUpdatedCookie(WebRequest req) {
        req.addCookie(CookieServlet.TEST_COOKIE_NAME, "3");
    }

    public void testGetUpdatedCookie( ) throws Exception {
        this.servlet.doGet(this.request, this.response);
    }

    public void endGetUpdatedCookie(WebResponse res) throws Exception {
        org.apache.cactus.Cookie cookie =
                res.getCookie(CookieServlet.TEST_COOKIE_NAME);
        assertNotNull("Returned Cookie.", cookie);
        assertEquals("Cookie Value.", "4", cookie.getValue( ));
    }
}
```

testGetInitialCookie( )

This test simulates a user hitting the servlet for the first time. The CookieServlet tests that the getCookie( ) method returns a Cookie that is not null, has a name defined by the constant CookieServlet.TEST_COOKIE_NAME, and whose value is zero.

testGetUpdatedCookie( )

This test is a little more complicated because it requires the request to be set up properly before invoking the doGet( ) method on the CookieServlet. Remember that before Cactus invokes a testXXX( ) method, it looks for a beginXXX( ) method to execute on the client.

The code to add a cookie to the request looks like this:

```
public void beginGetUpdatedCookie(WebRequest req) {
    req.addCookie(CookieServlet.TEST_COOKIE_NAME, "3");
}
```

Now Cactus invokes the testGetUpdatedCookie( ) method on the server. This test calls the doGet( ) method on the CookieServlet to simulate an HTTP GET.

```
public void testGetUpdatedCookie( ) throws Exception {
    this.servlet.doGet(this.request, this.response);
}
```

If the testGetUpdatedCookie( ) method completes successfully, Cactus looks for a method called endGetUpdatedCookie(WebResponse). This method is invoked on the client and allows you to assert that the servlet correctly updated the cookie.

```
public void endGetUpdatedCookie(WebResponse res) throws Exception {
    org.apache.cactus.Cookie cookie =
            res.getCookie(CookieServlet.TEST_COOKIE_NAME);
    assertNotNull("Returned Cookie.", cookie);
    assertEquals("Cookie Value.", "4", cookie.getValue( ));
}
```

The returned response object should contain a non-null cookie whose name is defined by CookieServlet.TEST_COOKIE_NAME. The value of the cookie should be four, exactly one more than the value before invoking the doGet( ) method on the servlet.

Example 7-6 shows the cookie servlet.

Example 7-6. Cookie servlet

```
package com.oreilly.javaxp.cactus.servlet;

import javax.servlet.http.HttpServlet;
import javax.servlet.http.HttpServletResponse;
import javax.servlet.http.HttpServletRequest;
import javax.servlet.http.Cookie;
import java.io.IOException;

public class CookieServlet extends HttpServlet {

    public static final String TEST_COOKIE_NAME = "testCookie";

    protected void doGet(HttpServletRequest req, HttpServletResponse res)
            throws IOException {

        Cookie cookie = getCookie(req);
        int count = Integer.parseInt(cookie.getValue( ));
```

Example 7-6. Cookie servlet (continued)

```
            count++;
            cookie.setValue(String.valueOf(count));
            res.addCookie(cookie);
    }

    protected Cookie getCookie(HttpServletRequest req) {
        Cookie[] cookies = req.getCookies();
        if (cookies != null) {
            for (int i=0; i<cookies.length; i++) {
                if (TEST_COOKIE_NAME.equals(cookies[i].getName())) {
                    return cookies[i];
                }
            }
        }

        return new Cookie(TEST_COOKIE_NAME, "0");
    }
}
```

The CookieServlet looks for a cookie named testCookie defined by the constant CookieServlet.TEST_COOKIE_NAME. If the cookie does not exist—it's the first time the user has hit the servlet—then a new cookie is created and its value set to zero. The cookie's value is incremented by one and added to the HttpServletResponse to be sent back the client browser.

See Also

Recipe 7.8 shows how to test code that uses an HttpSession object.

7.8   Testing Session Tracking Using HttpSession

Problem

You want to test that your servlet properly handles session tracking when using an HttpSession.

Solution

Write a ServletTestCase to test that your servlet properly handles adding and removing objects from an HttpSession.

Discussion

Servlet developers know that session tracking is critical for any web application that needs to maintain state between user requests. Since HTTP is a stateless protocol, it provides no way for a server to recognize consecutive requests from the same client.

This causes problems with web applications that need to maintain information on behalf of the client. The solution to this problem is for the client to identify itself with each request. Luckily, there are many solutions to solving this problem. Probably the most flexible solution is the servlet session-tracking API. The session tracking API provides the constructs necessary to manage client information on the server. Every unique client of a web application is assigned a javax.servlet.http. HttpSession object on the server. The session object provides a little space on the server to hold information between requests. For each request, the server identifies the client and locates the appropriate HttpSession object.* The servlet may now add and remove items from a session depending on the user's request.

This recipe focuses on the popular "shopping cart." The shopping cart example is good because it is easy to understand. Our shopping cart is very simple: users may add and remove items. With this knowledge, we can write the first iteration of the servlet as shown in Example 7-7.

Example 7-7. First iteration of the ShoppingCartServlet

```
package com.oreilly.javaxp.cactus.servlet;

import javax.servlet.http.HttpServlet;
import javax.servlet.http.HttpServletRequest;
import javax.servlet.http.HttpServletResponse;
import javax.servlet.http.HttpSession;
import javax.servlet.ServletException;
import java.io.IOException;

public class ShoppingCartServlet extends HttpServlet {

    public static final String INSERT_ITEM = "insert";
    public static final String REMOVE_ITEM = "remove";
    public static final String REMOVE_ALL = "removeAll";
    public static final String INVALID = "invalid";
    public static final String CART = "cart";

    protected void doGet(HttpServletRequest req, HttpServletResponse res)
            throws ServletException, IOException {
        HttpSession session = req.getSession(true);
        ShoppingCart cart = (ShoppingCart) session.getAttribute(CART);
        if (cart == null) {
            cart = new ShoppingCart();
            session.setAttribute(CART, cart);
        }
        updateShoppingCart(req, cart);
    }
```

---

* An HttpSession, when first created, is assigned a unique ID by the server. Cookies and URL rewriting are two possible methods for the client and server to communicate this ID.

Example 7-7. First iteration of the ShoppingCartServlet (continued)

```
protected void updateShoppingCart(HttpServletRequest req,
                                  ShoppingCart cart)
        throws ServletException {
    String operation = getOperation(req);
    if (INSERT_ITEM.equals(operation)) {
        // @todo - implement adding item to the cart
    } else if (REMOVE_ITEM.equals(operation)) {
        // @todo - implement removing item from the cart
    } else if (REMOVE_ALL.equals(operation)) {
        // @todo - implement removing all items from the cart
    } else {
        throw new ServletException("Invalid Shopping Cart operation: " +
                                   operation);
    }
}

protected String getOperation(HttpServletRequest req) {
    String operation = req.getParameter("operation");
    if (operation == null || "".equals(operation)) {
        return INVALID;
    } else {
        if (!INSERT_ITEM.equals(operation)
                && !REMOVE_ITEM.equals(operation)
                && !REMOVE_ALL.equals(operation)) {
            return INVALID;
        }

        return operation;
    }
}

protected String getItemID(HttpServletRequest req) {
    String itemID = req.getParameter("itemID");
    if (itemID == null || "".equals(itemID)) {
        return INVALID;
    } else {
        return itemID;
    }
}
}
```

When doGet( ) is called we ask the HttpServletRequest to give us the client's session. The true flag indicates that a new session should be created if one does not exist. Once we have the session, we look to see if a shopping cart exists. If a valid shopping cart does not exist, one is created and added to the session under the name ShoppingCartServlet.CART. Next, the updateShoppingCart( ) method is executed to either add or remove items from the shopping cart. The details for adding and removing items from the shopping cart are left unimplemented, allowing the tests to fail first. After a test fails, code is added to make the test pass.

Before we continue with the test, let's take a look at the support classes. A regular Java object called ShoppingCart represents our shopping cart. A ShoppingCart holds zero or more Java objects called Item. These objects are not dependent on server code and therefore should be tested outside of a server using JUnit. Example 7-8 and Example 7-9 show these objects.

Example 7-8. Shopping cart class

```java
package com.oreilly.javaxp.cactus.servlet;

import java.io.Serializable;
import java.util.Map;
import java.util.HashMap;
import java.util.Iterator;

public class ShoppingCart implements Serializable {

    private Map cart = new HashMap( );

    public void addItem(Item item) {
        this.cart.put(item.getID( ), item);
    }

    public void removeItem(String itemID) {
        this.cart.remove(itemID);
    }

    public Item getItem(String id) {
        return (Item) this.cart.get(id);
    }

    public Iterator getAllItems( ) {
        return this.cart.values().iterator( );
    }

    public void clear( ) {
        this.cart.clear( );
    }
}
```

Example 7-9. Shopping cart item class

```java
package com.oreilly.javaxp.cactus.servlet;

import java.io.Serializable;

public class Item implements Serializable {

    private String id;
    private String description;

    public Item(String id, String description) {
        this.id = id;
```

Example 7-9. Shopping cart item class (continued)

```
        this.description = description;
    }

    public String getID( ) {
        return this.id;
    }

    public String getDescription( ) {
        return this.description;
    }
}
```

Objects used by an HttpSession should implement the java.io.Serializable interface to allow the session to be distributed in a clustered environment. The Item class is very basic, holding only an ID and description.

Now let's turn our attention to writing the Cactus tests. Example 7-10 shows how to test the addition of a new item to the shopping cart.

Example 7-10. Testing the addition of an item to a shopping cart

```
package com.oreilly.javaxp.cactus.servlet;

import org.apache.cactus.ServletTestCase;
import org.apache.cactus.WebRequest;

public class TestShoppingCartServlet extends ServletTestCase {

    private ShoppingCartServlet servlet;

    public TestShoppingCartServlet(String name) {
        super(name);
    }

    public void setUp( ) {
        this.servlet = new ShoppingCartServlet( );
    }

    /**
     * Executes on the client.
     */
    public void beginAddItemToCart(WebRequest webRequest) {
        webRequest.addParameter("operation",
                                ShoppingCartServlet.INSERT_ITEM);
        webRequest.addParameter("itemID", "12345");
    }

    /**
     * Executes on the server.
     */
    public void testAddItemToCart( ) throws Exception {
        this.servlet.doGet(this.request, this.response);
```

Example 7-10. Testing the addition of an item to a shopping cart (continued)

```
        Object obj = this.session.getAttribute(ShoppingCartServlet.CART);
        assertNotNull("Shopping Cart should exist.", obj);
        assertTrue("Object should be a ShoppingCart",
                    obj instanceof ShoppingCart);
        ShoppingCart cart = (ShoppingCart) obj;
        Item item = cart.getItem("12345");
        assertNotNull("Item should exist.", item);
    }
}
```

The test starts execution on the client. In this example, the method under test is testAddItemToCart. Cactus uses reflection to locate a method called beginAddItem-ToCart(WebRequest) to execute on the client. The beginAddItemToCart(WebRequest) method adds two parameters to the outgoing request. The parameter named operation is assigned a value telling the shopping cart servlet to add an item to the shopping cart. The itemID parameter specifies which item to look up and store in the shopping cart. Next, Cactus opens an HTTP connection with server and executes the test method testAddItemToCart( ) (remember testXXX( ) methods are executed on the server). The testAddItemToCart( ) explicitly invokes the doGet( ) method, which performs the necessary logic to add a new item to the shopping cart. The test fails because we have not yet implemented the logic to add a new item to the shopping cart. Example 7-11 shows the updated servlet adding an item to the shopping cart.

Example 7-11. Updated ShoppingCartServlet (add item to the shopping cart)

```
protected void updateShoppingCart(HttpServletRequest req,
                                  ShoppingCart cart)
        throws ServletException {
    String operation = getOperation(req);
    if (INSERT_ITEM.equals(operation)) {
        addItemToCart(getItemID(req), cart);
    } else if (REMOVE_ITEM.equals(operation)) {
        // @todo - implement removing item from the cart
    } else if (REMOVE_ALL.equals(operation)) {
        // @todo - implement removing all items from the cart.
    } else {
        throw new ServletException("Invalid Shopping Cart operation: " +
                                   operation);
    }
}

protected void addItemToCart(String itemID, ShoppingCart cart) {
    Item item = findItem(itemID);
    cart.addItem(item);
}

protected Item findItem(String itemID) {
    // a real implementation might retrieve the item from an EJB.
    return new Item(itemID, "Description " + itemID);
}
```

Executing the tests again results in the test passing. Writing the tests for removing items from the cart follows the same pattern: write the test first, watch it fail, add the logic to the servlet, redeploy the updated code, run the test again, and watch it pass.

See Also

Recipe 7.7 shows how to test cookies. Recipe 7.9 shows how to test initialization parameters.

7.9   Testing Servlet Initialization Parameters

Problem

You want to set up your servlet tests to execute with different initialization parameters without modifying the deployment descriptor (*web.xml*) file.

Solution

Use the implicit `config` object, declared by the `ServletTestCase` redirector, to set up initialization parameters before invoking methods on a servlet.

Discussion

Each registered servlet in a web application can be assigned any number of specific initialization parameters using the deployment descriptor. Initialization parameters are available to the servlet by accessing its `ServletConfig` object. The `ServletConfig` object is created by the server and given to a servlet through its `init(ServletConfig)` method. The servlet container guarantees that the `init( )` method successfully completes before allowing the servlet to handle any requests.

Creating a Cactus test for testing initialization parameters is tricky because we have to play the role of the servlet container. Specifically, we have to make sure to call the servlet's `init(ServletConfig)` method, passing the implicit `config` object. Failure to call `init(ServletConfig)` results in a `NullPointerException` when invoking methods on the servlet's `ServletConfig` object.

Is Cactus Overkill, Again?

Before writing any test, especially a server-side test, determine if the behavior of the server is needed for the test to pass. In this recipe, do we need the behavior of the servlet container to test initialization parameters? The answer is not black and white. If you are testing that valid and invalid initialization parameters are properly handled by your servlet, you may not need the behavior of a servlet container. You can get away with using JUnit. On the other hand, if you are testing that an initialization parameter causes the servlet to invoke or retrieve an external resource, a Cactus test may be what you want.

Here is an example test method that shows how to correctly set up the servlet:

```
public void testValidInitParameters() throws Exception {

    this.config.setInitParameter(ConfigParamServlet.CONFIG_PARAM,
                              ConfigParamServlet.CONFIG_VALUE);
    // critical step!
    this.servlet.init(this.config);
    assertTrue("Valid Init Parameter.",
               this.servlet.validateInitParameters());
}
```

The ServletTestCase redirector servlet provides an implicit object named config. This object is of type org.apache.cactus.server.ServletConfigWrapper and provides methods to set initialization parameters. Thus, you can add initialization parameters without having to modify the deployment descriptor, the *web.xml* file. This technique provides a flexible alternative to writing and managing different deployment descriptors for testing purposes. Now your tests can set up valid and invalid initialization parameters for each test method and verify that the servlet handles them appropriately.

See Also

See Recipe 7.6 for a discussion on alternate ways to test servlet code that may or may not depend on the behavior of an actual running server.

7.10   Testing Servlet Filters

Problem

You want to test servlet filters.

Solution

Write a FilterTestCase class and assert that the filter continues down the chain or that the filter causes the chain to break. A mock FilterChain needs to be written to simulate filter-chaining behavior, too.

Discussion

Filters were introduced in Version 2.3 of the Servlet specification, and allow for preprocessing of the request and post-processing of the response. Filters act like an interceptor, in that they are executed before and after the servlet is called. Some common uses of filters are to perform logging, ensure that a user is authenticated, add extra information to a response such as an HTML footer, etc.

Example 7-12 shows how to test a filter that ensures a user is authenticated with the server. If the user is not authenticated with the server, she is redirected to a login page. The next recipe talks about how to setup an authenticated user in Cactus.

Example 7-12. Security filter

```
package com.oreilly.javaxp.cactus.filter;

import javax.servlet.*;
import javax.servlet.http.HttpServletRequest;
import java.io.IOException;
import java.security.Principal;

public class SecurityFilter implements Filter {

    public void init(FilterConfig config) {
    }

    public void doFilter(ServletRequest req,
                         ServletResponse res,
                         FilterChain chain)
            throws IOException, ServletException {

        Principal principal = ((HttpServletRequest) req).getUserPrincipal();
        if (principal == null) {
            req.setAttribute("errorMessage", "You are not logged in!");
            req.getRequestDispatcher("/login.jsp").forward(req, res);
        } else {

            // this is an instance of our MockFilterChain
            chain.doFilter(req, res);
        }
    }

    public void destroy() {
    }
}
```

This filter is fairly simple. First we get the user principal from the request. If the principal is `null`, the user is not authenticated with the server, so we redirect the user to login screen. If a principal exists, we continue the filter chain.

Now let's write a Cactus test. Example 7-13 shows two tests. The first test ensures that if an authenticated user exists, the filter chain continues. The second test ensures that if an authenticated user does not exist, the filter chain breaks.

Example 7-13. Security filter test

```
package com.oreilly.javaxp.cactus.filter;

import org.apache.cactus.FilterTestCase;
import org.apache.cactus.WebRequest;
import org.apache.cactus.client.authentication.BasicAuthentication;
```

Example 7-13. Security filter test (continued)

```java
public class TestSecurityFilter extends FilterTestCase {

    private SecurityFilter filter;
    private MockFilterChain mockChain;

    public TestSecurityFilter(String name) {
        super(name);
    }

    public void setUp() {
        this.filter = new SecurityFilter();
        this.mockChain = new MockFilterChain();
    }

    // this method runs on the client before testAuthenticatedUser()
    public void beginAuthenticatedUser(WebRequest webRequest) {
        webRequest.setRedirectorName("SecureFilterRedirector");
        webRequest.setAuthentication(
                new BasicAuthentication("coyner_b", "secret"));
    }

    // this method runs on the server
    public void testAuthenticatedUser() throws Exception {
        this.mockChain.setExpectedInvocation(true);
        this.filter.doFilter(this.request, this.response, this.mockChain);
        this.mockChain.verify();
    }

    public void testNonAuthenticatedUser() throws Exception {
        this.mockChain.setExpectedInvocation(false);
        this.filter.doFilter(this.request, this.response, this.mockChain);
        this.mockChain.verify();
    }
}
```

Filters are typically executed in a chain; each filter in the chain has the ability to continue or break the chain. A good filter test asserts that the chain either continues or breaks according to the filter's logic. The SecurityFilter continues the chain if an authenticated user exists in the request; otherwise, the chain breaks. The simplest way to test chaining behavior is with a Mock Object. This Mock Object needs to implement the FilterChain interface and set a flag to true if the doFilter() method is invoked. Example 7-14 shows how to create the mock object.

Example 7-14. Mock FilterChain

```java
package com.oreilly.javaxp.cactus.filter;

import junit.framework.Assert;

import javax.servlet.FilterChain;
import javax.servlet.ServletRequest;
```

Example 7-14. Mock FilterChain (continued)

```java
import javax.servlet.ServletResponse;
import javax.servlet.ServletException;
import java.io.IOException;

public class MockFilterChain implements FilterChain {

    private boolean shouldBeInvoked;
    private boolean wasInvoked;

    public void doFilter(ServletRequest req, ServletResponse res)
            throws IOException, ServletException {
        this.wasInvoked = true;
    }

    public void setExpectedInvocation(boolean shouldBeInvoked) {
        this.shouldBeInvoked = shouldBeInvoked;
    }

    public void verify( ) {

        if (this.shouldBeInvoked) {
            Assert.assertTrue("Expected MockFilterChain to be invoked.",
                              this.wasInvoked);
        } else {
            Assert.assertTrue("Expected MockFilterChain filter not to be invoked.",
                              !this.wasInvoked);
        }
    }
}
```

See Also

Recipe 7.11 describes how to write a secure Cactus test. For more information on Mock Objects, see Chapter 6.

7.11 Securing Cactus Tests

Problem

You want to test a servlet that depends on an authenticated user.

Solution

Configure your web application to handle BASIC authentication and use Cactus to automatically create an authenticated user.

Discussion

Testing server-side code is challenging by itself. Throw in server-side code that relies on an authenticated user, and the challenge grows. Cactus provides a way to test server-side code that relies on an authenticated user—by creating a user for you.* If your servlet or filter uses the following methods then you need Cactus to create an authenticated user:

- `HttpServletRequest.getRemoteUser( )`
- `HttpServletRequest.getUserPrincipal( )`
- `HttpServletRequest.isUserInRole(String)`

If your web application requires an authenticated user, your web application must be secured. In the deployment descriptor, you must declare the URL patterns to secure and which logical roles are allowed. Example 7-15 shows how this is done.

Example 7-15. Securing a web application

```
<?xml version="1.0" encoding="ISO-8859-1"?>
<!DOCTYPE web-app
    PUBLIC "-//Sun Microsystems, Inc.//DTD Web Application 2.3//EN"
    "http://java.sun.com/dtd/web-app_2_3.dtd">

<web-app>

  <!-- other elements left out for brevity -->

  <!-- URL pattern not secured -->
  <filter>
      <filter-name>FilterRedirector</filter-name>
      <filter-class>
        org.apache.cactus.server.FilterTestRedirector
      </filter-class>
  </filter>

  <!-- URL pattern secured -->
  <filter>
      <filter-name>SecureFilterRedirector</filter-name>
      <filter-class>
        org.apache.cactus.server.FilterTestRedirector
      </filter-class>
  </filter>
  <filter-mapping>
    <filter-name>SecureFilterRedirector</filter-name>
    <url-pattern>/SecureFilterRedirector</url-pattern>
  </filter-mapping>

  <security-constraint>
    <web-resource-collection>
```

---

* Cactus 1.4 only supports BASIC authentication.

Example 7-15. Securing a web application (continued)

```
        <web-resource-name>SecurityRestriction</web-resource-name>
        <url-pattern>/SecureFilterRedirector</url-pattern>
        <http-method>POST</http-method>
        <http-method>GET</http-method>
    </web-resource-collection>
    <auth-constraint>
        <role-name>filterTest</role-name>
    </auth-constraint>
    </security-constraint>

    <login-config>
        <auth-method>BASIC</auth-method>
    </login-config>
    <security-role>
        <role-name>filterTest</role-name>
    </security-role>
</web-app>
```

The example above can be applied to any URL pattern, not just filters. For instance, if you want to secure access to a servlet or JSP, simply add more url-pattern elements. The role name is a logical role that is mapped to one or more users. An underlying authorization mechanism defines how role names are mapped. Tomcat, by default, uses the *TOMCAT_HOME/conf/tomcat-users.xml* file to define users and their roles. This is not a very strong authentication and authorization mechanism but does provide a convenient and easy means to run our tests. Here's an example showing how to add a new user and role to the *tomcat-users.xml* file:

```
<tomcat-users>
    <user name="javaxp" password="secret" roles="manager"/>
    <user name="coyner_b" password="secret" roles="filterTest"/>
</tomcat-users>
```

Notice that the filterTest role matches the role name in the deployment descriptor. Example 7-16 shows how to set up a test method to provide an authenticated user. The beginAuthenticatedUser(WebRequest) method is accompanied by a test method called testAuthenticatedUser( )—not shown here. The WebRequest object allows for the redirector to be specified before executing the server side test. Recall that Cactus uses a *cactus.properties* file to set up redirectors for each Cactus test case. The values in the properties file are simply the URL patterns defined in the deployment descriptor. Thus, setting the redirector name programmatically simply changes the URL pattern. This provides ultimate flexibility because multiple test methods can be tested using a secured or nonsecured URL, where a secured URL requires an authenticated user.

Example 7-16. Setting up an authenticated user

```
public void beginAuthenticatedUser(WebRequest webRequest) {
    webRequest.setRedirectorName("SecureFilterRedirector");
    webRequest.setAuthentication(
            new BasicAuthentication("coyner_b", "secret"));
}
```

See Also

Recipe 7.10 shows how to test servlet filters.

7.12 Using HttpUnit to Perform Complex Assertions

Problem

You want to use HttpUnit to perform complex assertions on the returned result.

Solution

Implement an endXXX(com.meterware.httpunit.WebResponse) method for a given testXXX( ) method.

Discussion

Cactus provides support for two endXXX(WebResponse) signatures. You, as the test writer, need to choose one of the method signatures. Cactus ensures that the correct method is invoked.

```
// write this method for the standard Cactus response
public void endXXX(org.apache.cactus.WebResponse) {
    // insert simple assertions
}

// or write this method to use HttpUnit
public void endXXX(com.meterware.httpunit.WebResponse) {
    // insert complex assertions
}
```

These methods are executed on the client side JVM after the corresponding server side testXXX( ) method completes without throwing an exception.

See Also

For more information on how to use HttpUnit to perform complex assertions, see Chapter 5.

7.13 Testing the Output of a JSP

Problem

You want to test the output of a JSP.

Solution

Write a ServletTestCase that sets up any information the JSP needs to execute and use a RequestDispatcher to forward to the JSP page. The client side endXXX(WebResponse) method can then be used to perform assertions on the content of the JSP, which may be XML, HTML, or any other format that you expect.

Discussion

Testing the output, or result, of a JSP is done using the client side endXXX(WebResponse) method. Example 7-17 shows how to write this test. The first step in writing a test like this is to write a ServletTestCase that sets up any information the JSP needs to generate the content. For example, the JSP may expect a particular object to be in the HttpSession. This information might be retrieved though JDBC or an EJB. If the JSP does not rely on an object retrieved from an external source, or that external source is easily mocked, then Cactus is probably overkill.

Example 7-17. Testing the result of a JSP

```
package com.oreilly.javaxp.cactus.jsp;

import org.apache.cactus.ServletTestCase;
import org.apache.cactus.WebResponse;

import javax.servlet.RequestDispatcher;

public class SimpleJspTest extends ServletTestCase {

    public SimpleJspTest(String methodName) {
        super(methodName);
    }

    public void testForwardingToJsp() throws Exception {
        // Perform business logic to gather information needed by the
        // JSP. This could be retrieving information from a data store
        // with JDBC or talking with an EJB.

        RequestDispatcher rd = this.config.getServletContext().
                getRequestDispatcher("/simple.jsp");
        rd.forward(this.request, this.response);
    }

    public void endForwardingToJsp(WebResponse webResponse) {
        // now assert that the given response contains the information
        // you expect.
    }
}
```

See Also

Recipe 7.12 describes how to use the endXXX(WebResponse) method with HttpUnit to perform complex assertions on a response. Recipe 7.15 provides information on designing testable JSPs.

7.14 When Not to Use Cactus

Problem

You want to test a utility class that your servlet uses.

Solution

Design most of your application logic to be independent of servlets and JSPs and then use JUnit to test standalone, non-server code.

Discussion

Cactus is a good testing framework, but testing server-side code is still a significant challenge. For this reason, you should strive to minimize the amount of code that can only be tested when running in an application server. Putting too much application logic directly into servlets and JSPs is a common mistake. Whenever possible, you should strive to write standalone helper classes that your servlets and JSPs delegate to. Provided that these classes do not have dependencies on interfaces like HttpServletRequest, HttpServletResponse, or HttpSession, they are much easier to test using JUnit.

A perfect example is Recipe 7.8, on testing session-tracking code. The ShoppingCart and Item objects are not dependent on a running server, and therefore should be tested using JUnit.

See Also

For more information on testing non-server specific code, see Chapter 4. Recipe 7.8 shows how to test the use of an HttpSession for handling user sessions. Recipe 7.15 discusses designing JSPs to use standalone helper classes.

7.15 Designing Testable JSPs

Problem

Designing JSPs to be testable outside of a running server.

Solution

Write your JSPs to use helper classes that do not depend on a running server, and then test those helper classes with JUnit.

Discussion

Testing server code is challenging, as we have seen throughout this chapter. JSPs pose a greater risk of failure because multiple technologies are intermingled. JSPs mix snippets of Java code with snippets of HTML, XML, JSTL, and JavaBeans; add the deployment of JSP and the problems of testing only get worse. A better approach to designing and testing JSPs is to write support classes that do not depend on a running server to perform logic. These support classes can then be tested outside of a running server using JUnit.

See Also

Recipe 7.14 discusses testing non-server–dependent classes.

CHAPTER 8

JUnitPerf

8.0   Introduction

Performance issues inevitably sneak into a project. Tracking down the issues is trouble-some without the proper tools. Commercial performance-monitoring tools, such as JProbe or OptimizeIt, help pinpoint performance problems. These tools excel at pro-viding performance metrics but typically require expert human intervention to run and interpret the results. These tools are not designed to execute automatically as part of a continuous integration process—which is where JUnitPerf enters the picture.

JUnitPerf, available from *http://www.clarkware.com/software/JUnitPerf.html*, is a tool for continuous performance testing. JUnitPerf transparently wraps, or *decorates* exist-ing JUnit tests without affecting the original test.* Remember that JUnit tests should execute quickly. Figure 8-1 shows the UML diagram for the JUnitPerf TimedTest.

> JUnitPerf tests can (and should) be executed separately from normal JUnit tests. This approach ensures that the overall execution of JUnit tests isn't hindered by the additional time spent executing JUnitPerf tests.

Here's a quick overview of how a JUnitPerf timed test works. The following occurs when a JUnitPerf TimedTest.run(TestCase) method is invoked:

1. Retrieve the current time (before JUnit test execution).

2. Call super.run(TestResult) to run the JUnit test, where super refers to the JUnit TestDecorator.

3. Retrieve the current time (after JUnit test execution).

4. If the elapsed time turns out to be greater than the maximum allowed time, then a junit.framework.AssertionFailedError(String) is thrown. Otherwise, the test passes.

---

* For more information on the decorator pattern refer to *Design Patterns: Elements of Reusable Object-Oriented Software* (Addison-Wesley) by Erich Gamma, et al.

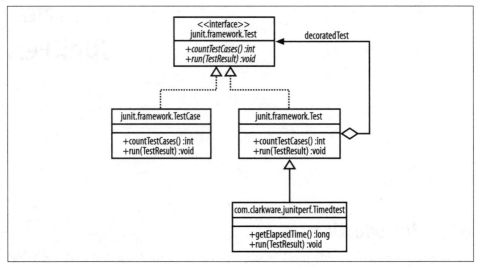

Figure 8-1. JUnitPerf UML diagram

8.1   When to Use JUnitPerf

Problem

You want to track down potential performance and scalability problems but are unsure of the tools you need.

Solution

Use a commercial profiling tool, such as JProbe or OptimizeIt, to manually inspect code and identify application bottlenecks. Use JUnitPerf to ensure that new features and refactoring do not slow down code that used to be fast enough.

Discussion

JUnitPerf is a tool for continuous performance testing. The goal of a performance test is to ensure that the code executes fast enough, even under varying load conditions. Let's take a look at a typical scenario.

You just completed a custom search algorithm, complete with a suite of JUnit tests. Next, the code is run through a profiling tool to look for any potential bottlenecks. If any performance issues are found, a new JUnit test is written to isolate the code (if one does not already exist). For example, the profiling tool reports that the search took ten seconds, but requirements dictate that it execute in less than three. The new JUnit test is wrapped around a JUnitPerf `TimedTest` to expose the performance bug. The timed test should fail; otherwise, there is no performance issue with the code you have isolated. Next, refactor the code that is causing the performance problem until the timed test passes.

If the profiling tool did not report any performance issues, you do not have to write JUnitPerf tests. If you are concerned that a new feature might slow down an important piece of code, consider adding a JUnit-Perf test to ensure that the code is always fast enough.

Here are the typical steps for writing a JUnitPerf test:

1. Write a JUnit test suite for you search algorithm.

2. Run the search algorithm through a profiling tool to find bottlenecks.

Having a test that runs just the algorithm and exercises it with a reasonable set of test data makes it easy to gather repeatable metrics. Instead of manually clicking through an application, you can run your test through the profiler.

3. If performance is an issue, write another JUnit test to isolate the code with poor performance (if one does not already exist).

4. Write a JUnitPerf `TimedTest` for the new JUnit test. The test should fail. If the test passes, there is no performance issue with the code you have isolated.

5. Tune the code until the performance test passes.

See Also

Recipe 8.2 shows how to create a JUnitPerf `TimedTest`. Recipe 8.6 shows how to use Ant to execute JUnitPerf tests.

8.2   Creating a Timed Test

Problem

You need to make sure that code executes within a given amount of time.

Solution

Decorate an existing JUnit `Test` with a JUnitPerf `TimedTest`.

Discussion

A `TimedTest` is a JUnit test decorator that measures the total elapsed time of a JUnit test and fails if the maximum time allowed is exceeded. A timed test tests time-critical code, such as a sort or search.

A `TimedTest` is constructed with an instance of a JUnit test, along with the maximum allowed execution time in milliseconds. Here is an example of a timed test that fails if the elapsed time of the `TestSearchModel.testAsynchronousSearch( )` method exceeds two seconds:

```
public static Test suite( ) {
    Test testCase = new TestSearchModel("testAsynchronousSearch");
    Test timedTest = new TimedTest(testCase, 2000);
    TestSuite suite = new TestSuite( );
    suite.addTest(timedTest);
    return suite;
}
```

In the example above, the total elapsed time is checked once the method under test completes. If the total time exceeds two seconds, the test fails. Another option is for the test to fail immediately if the maximum allowed execution time is exceeded. Here is an example of a timed test that causes immediate failure:

```
public static Test suite( ) {
    Test testCase = new TestSearchModel("testAsynchronousSearch");
    Test timedTest = new TimedTest(testCase, 2000, false);
    TestSuite suite = new TestSuite( );
    suite.addTest(timedTest);
    return suite;
}
```

The constructor in the previous example is overloaded to allow for a third parameter. This parameter specifies whether the timed test should wait for the method under test to complete, or fail immediately if the maximum time allowed is exceeded. A "false" value indicates that the test should fail immediately if the maximum allowed time is exceeded.

Here's an example of the output when a timed test fails.

```
.TimedTest (NON-WAITING): testAsynchronousSearch(com.oreilly.javaxp.junitperf.
TestSearchModel): 1001 ms
F.TimedTest (WAITING): testAsynchronousSearch(com.oreilly.javaxp.junitperf.
TestSearchModel): 1002 ms
F
Time: 2.023
There were 2 failures:
1) testAsynchronousSearch(com.oreilly.javaxp.junitperf.TestSearchModel)junit.
framework.AssertionFailedError: Maximum elapsed time (1000 ms) exceeded!
    at com.clarkware.junitperf.TimedTest.runUntilTimeExpires(Unknown Source)
    at com.clarkware.junitperf.TimedTest.run(Unknown Source)
    at com.oreilly.javaxp.junitperf.TestPerfSearchModel.main(TestPerfSearchModel.
java:48)
2) testAsynchronousSearch(com.oreilly.javaxp.junitperf.TestSearchModel)junit.
framework.AssertionFailedError: Maximum elapsed time exceeded! Expected 1000ms, but
was 1002ms.
    at com.clarkware.junitperf.TimedTest.runUntilTestCompletion(Unknown Source)
    at com.clarkware.junitperf.TimedTest.run(Unknown Source)
    at com.oreilly.javaxp.junitperf.TestPerfSearchModel.main(TestPerfSearchModel.
java:48)

FAILURES!!!
Tests run: 2,  Failures: 2,  Errors: 0
```

The example output shows a timed test that fails immediately and another that waits until the method under test completes. The underlying results are the same—both tests fail—but the printed message is different. A nonwaiting test, or a test that fails immediately, is unable to print the actual time it took to complete the test.

```
Maximum elapsed time (1000 ms) exceeded!
```

On the other hand, a test that fails after the method under test completes provides a better message. This message shows the expected time and the actual time.

```
Maximum elapsed time exceeded! Expected 1000ms, but was 1002ms.
```

 As you can see from the previous output, this test is really close to passing. An important point to make here is that when a test is repeatedly close to passing, you may wish to increase the maximum allowed time by a few milliseconds. Of course, it is important to understand that performance will vary from computer to computer and JVM to JVM. Adjusting the threshold to avoid spurious failure might break the test on another computer.

If you need to view some basic metrics about why a timed test failed, the obvious choice is to construct a timed test that waits for the completion of the method under test. This helps to determine how close or how far away you are from having the test pass. If you are more concerned about the tests executing quickly, construct a timed test that fails immediately.

Example 8-1 shows a complete JUnitPerf timed test. Notice the use of the `public static Test suite( )` method. This is a typical idiom used when writing JUnit tests, and proves invaluable when integrating JUnitPerf tests into an Ant buildfile. We delve into Ant integration in Recipe 8.6.

Example 8-1. JUnitPerf TimedTest

```
package com.oreilly.javaxp.junitperf;

import junit.framework.Test;
import junit.framework.TestSuite;
import com.clarkware.junitperf.TimedTest;

public class TestPerfSearchModel {

    public static Test suite( ) {
        Test testCase = new TestSearchModel("testAsynchronousSearch");
        TestSuite suite = new TestSuite( );
        suite.addTest(new TimedTest(testCase, 2000, false));
        return suite;
    }

    public static void main(String args[]) {
        junit.textui.TestRunner.run(suite( ));
    }
}
```

JUnit's test decoration design brings about some limitations on the precision of a JUnitPerf timed test. The elapsed time recorded by a timed test that decorates a single test method includes the total time of the setUp( ), testXXX( ), and tearDown( ) methods.

If JUnitPerf decorates a TestSuite then the elapsed time recorded by a timed test includes the setUp( ), testXXX( ), and tearDown( ) methods of all Test instances in the TestSuite.

The solution is to adjust the maximum allowed time to accommodate the time spent setting up and tearing down the tests.

See Also

Recipe 8.3 shows how to create a JUnitPerf LoadTest. Recipe 8.6 shows how to use Ant to execute JUnitPerf tests.

8.3   Creating a LoadTest

Problem

You need to make sure that code executes correctly under varying load conditions, such as a large number of concurrent users.

Solution

Decorate an existing JUnit Test with a JUnitPerf LoadTest.

Discussion

A JUnitPerf LoadTest decorates an existing JUnit test to simulate a given number of concurrent users, in which each user may execute the test one or more times. By default, each simulated user executes the test once. For more flexibility, a load test may use a com.clarkware.junitperf.Timer to ramp up the number of concurrent users during test execution. JUnitPerf provides a ConstantTimer and RandomTimer to simulate delays between user requests. By default all threads are started at the same time by constructing a ConstantTimer with a delay of zero milliseconds.

If you need to simulate unique user information, each test must randomly choose a different user ID (for example). This can be accomplished using JUnit's setUp( ) method.

Here is an example that constructs a LoadTest with 100 simultaneous users:

```
public static Test suite() {
    Test testCase = new TestSearchModel("testAsynchronousSearch");
    Test loadTest = new LoadTest(testCase, 100);
```

```
    TestSuite suite = new TestSuite( );
    suite.addTest(loadTest);
    return suite;
}
```

Here is an example that constructs a LoadTest with 100 simultaneous users, in which each user executes the test 10 times:

```
public static Test suite( ) {
    Test testCase = new TestSearchModel("testAsynchronousSearch");
    Test loadTest = new LoadTest(testCase, 100, 10);
    TestSuite suite = new TestSuite( );
    suite.addTest(loadTest);
    return suite;
}
```

And here is an example that constructs a LoadTest with 100 users, in which each user executes the test 10 times, and each user starts at a random interval:

```
public static Test suite( ) {
    Test testCase = new TestSearchModel("testAsynchronousSearch");
    Timer timer = new RandomTimer(1000, 500);
    Test loadTest = new LoadTest(testCase, 100, 10, timer);
    TestSuite suite = new TestSuite( );
    suite.addTest(loadTest);
    return suite;
}
```

The Timer interface defines a single method, getDelay( ), that returns the time in milliseconds-to-wait until the next thread starts executing. The example above constructs a RandomTimer with a delay of 1,000 milliseconds (1 second), with a variation of 500 milliseconds (half a second). This means that a new user is added every one to one and a half seconds.

Be careful when creating timers that wait long periods of time between starting new threads. The longer the wait period, the longer it takes for the test to complete, which may or may not be desirable. If you need to test this type of behavior, you may want to set up a suite of tests that run automatically (perhaps at night).

There are commercial tools available for this type of performance test, but typically they are hard to use. JUnitPerf is simple and elegant, and any developer that knows how to write a JUnit test can sit down and write complex performance tests.

Example 8-2 shows how to create a JUnitPerf load test. As in the previous recipe, the use of the public static Test suite( ) method proves invaluable for integrating JUnitPerf tests into an Ant buildfile. More details on Ant integration are coming up in Recipe 8.6.

Example 8-2. JUnitPerf LoadTest

```
package com.oreilly.javaxp.junitperf;

import junit.framework.Test;
import junit.framework.TestSuite;
import com.clarkware.junitperf.TimedTest;

public class TestPerfSearchModel {

    public static Test suite( ) {
        Test testCase = new TestSearchModel("testAsynchronousSearch");
        Test loadTest = new LoadTest(testCase,
                                     100,
                                     new RandomTimer(1000, 500));
        TestSuite suite = new TestSuite( );
        suite.addTest(loadTest);
        return suite;
    }

    public static void main(String args[]) {
        junit.textui.TestRunner.run(suite( ));
    }
}
```

See Also

Recipe 8.2 shows how to create a JUnitPerf TimedTest. Recipe 8.6 shows how to use Ant to execute JUnitPerf tests.

8.4   Creating a Timed Test for Varying Loads

Problem

You need to test throughput under varying load conditions.

Solution

Decorate your JUnit Test with a JUnitPerf LoadTest to simulate one or more concurrent users, and decorate the load test with a JUnitPerf TimedTest to test the performance of the load.

Discussion

So far we have seen how to create timed and load tests for existing JUnit tests. Now, let's delve into how JUnitPerf can test that varying loads do not impede performance. Specifically, we want to test that the application does not screech to a halt as the number of users increases. The design of JUnitPerf allows us to accomplish this task with ease. Example 8-3 shows how.

Example 8-3. Load and performance testing

```
package com.oreilly.javaxp.junitperf;

import junit.framework.Test;
import junit.framework.TestSuite;
import com.clarkware.junitperf.*;

public class TestPerfSearchModel {

    public static Test suite( ) {
        Test testCase = new TestSearchModel("testAsynchronousSearch");
        Test loadTest = new LoadTest(testCase, 100);
        Test timedTest = new TimedTest(loadTest, 3000, false);

        TestSuite suite = new TestSuite( );
        suite.addTest(timedTest);
        return suite;
    }

    public static void main(String args[]) {
        junit.textui.TestRunner.run(suite( ));
    }
}
```

Remember that JUnitPerf was designed using the decorator pattern. Thus, we are able to decorate tests with other tests. This example decorates a JUnit test with a JUnitPerf load test. The load test is then decorated with a JUnitPerf timed test. Ultimately, the test executes 100 simultaneous users performing an asynchronous search and tests that it completes in less than 3 seconds. In other words, we are testing that the search algorithm handles 100 simultaneous searches in less than three seconds.

See Also

Recipe 8.2 shows how to create a JUnitPerf TimedTest. Recipe 8.3 shows how to create a JUnitPerf LoadTest. Recipe 8.5 shows how to write a stress test. Recipe 8.6 shows how to use Ant to execute JUnitPerf tests.

8.5   Testing Individual Response Times Under Load

Problem

You need to test that a single user's response time is adequate under heavy loads.

Solution

Decorate your JUnit Test with a JUnitPerf TimedTest to simulate one or more concurrent users, and decorate the load test with a JUnitPerf TimedTest to test performance of the load.

Discussion

Testing whether each user experiences adequate response times under varying loads is important. Example 8-4 shows how to write a test that ensures each user (thread) experiences a 3-second response time when there are 100 simultaneous users. If any user takes longer than three seconds the entire test fails. This technique is useful for stress testing, and helps pinpoint the load that causes the code to break down. If there is a bottleneck, each successive user's response time increases. For example, the first user may experience a 2-second response time, while user number 100 experiences a 45-second response time.

Example 8-4. Stress testing

```
package com.oreilly.javaxp.junitperf;

import junit.framework.Test;
import junit.framework.TestSuite;
import com.clarkware.junitperf.*;

public class TestPerfSearchModel {

    public static Test suite() {
        Test testCase = new TestSearchModel("testAsynchronousSearch");
        Test timedTest = new TimedTest(testCase, 3000, false);
        Test loadTest = new LoadTest(timedTest, 100);

        TestSuite suite = new TestSuite();
        suite.addTest(timedTest);
        return suite;
    }

    public static void main(String args[]) {
        junit.textui.TestRunner.run(suite());
    }
}
```

See Also

Recipe 8.2 shows how to create a JUnitPerf TimedTest. Recipe 8.3 shows how to create a JUnitPerf LoadTest. Recipe 8.6 shows how to use Ant to execute JUnitPerf tests.

8.6   Running a TestSuite with Ant

Problem

You want to integrate JUnitPerf tests into your Ant build process.

Solution

Add another target to the Ant buildfile that executes a junit task for all JUnitPerf classes.

Discussion

Ensuring all unit tests execute whenever a code change is made, no matter how trivial the change, is critical for an XP project. We have already seen numerous examples throughout this book discussing how to integrate unit testing into an Ant build process using the junit task, and JUnitPerf is no different. The only twist is that JUnitPerf tests generally take longer to execute than normal JUnit tests because of the varying loads placed on them. Remember that the ultimate goal of a test is to execute as quickly as possible. With this said, it may be better to execute JUnitPerf tests during a nightly build, or perhaps during specified times throughout the day.

No matter how your project chooses to incorporate JUnitPerf tests, the technique is the same: use the junit Ant task. Example 8-5 shows an Ant target for executing only JUnitPerf tests. This example should look similar to what you have seen in other chapters. The only difference is the names of the files to include. This book uses the naming convention "Test" for all JUnit tests, modified to "TestPerf" for JUnitPerf tests so Ant can easily separate normal JUnit tests from JUnitPerf tests.

Example 8-5. Executing JUnitPerf tests using Ant

```
<target name="junitperf" depends="compile">
  <junit printsummary="on" fork="false" haltonfailure="false">
    <classpath refid="classpath.project"/>
    <formatter type="plain" usefile="false"/>
    <batchtest fork="false" todir="${dir.build}">
      <fileset dir="${dir.src}">
        <include name="**/TestPerf*.java"/>
      </fileset>
    </batchtest>
  </junit>
</target>
```

If you examine the examples in the previous recipes you may notice that JUnitPerf classes do not extend or implement any type of JUnit-specific class or interface. So how does the junit Ant task know to execute the class as a bunch of JUnit tests? The answer lies in how the Ant JUnitTestRunner locates the tests to execute. First

JUnitTestRunner uses reflection to look for a suite( ) method. Specifically, it looks for the following method signature:

```
public static junit.framework.Test suite( )
```

If JUnitTestRunner locates this method, the returned Test is executed. Otherwise, JUnitTestRunner uses reflection to find all public methods starting with "test". This little trick allows us to provide continuous integration for any class that provides a valid JUnit suite( ) method.

8.7   Generating JUnitPerf Tests

Problem

You want to use JUnitPerfDoclet, which is an XDoclet code generator created specifically for this book, to generate and execute JUnitPerf tests.

Solution

Mark up your JUnit test methods with JUnitPerfDoclet tags and execute the perfdoclet Ant task.

Discussion

As we were writing this book, we came up with the idea to code-generate JUnitPerf tests to show how to extend the XDoclet framework. This recipe uses that code generator, which is aptly named JUnitPerfDoclet, to create JUnitPerf tests. The concept is simple: mark up existing JUnit tests with JUnitPerfDoclet tags and execute an Ant target to generate the code.

Creating a timed test

Here is how to mark up an existing JUnit test method to create a JUnitPerf TimedTest:

```
/**
 * @junitperf.timedtest maxElapsedTime="2000"
 *                      waitForCompletion="false"
 */
public void testSynchronousSearch( ) {
        // details left out
}
```

The @junitperf.timedtest tag tells JUnitPerfDoclet that it should decorate the testSynchronousSearch( ) method with a JUnitPerf TimedTest.

The maxElapsedTime attribute is mandatory and specifies the maximum time the test method is allowed to execute (the time is in milliseconds) or the test fails.

The `waitForCompletion` attribute is optional and specifies when a failure should occur. If the value is "true", the total elapsed time is checked after the test method completes. A value of "false" causes the test to fail immediately if the test method exceeds the maximum time allowed.

Creating a load test

Here is how to mark up an existing JUnit test method to create a JUnitPerf `LoadTest`:

```
/**
 * @junitperf.loadtest numberOfUsers="100"
 *                     numberOfIterations="3"
 */
public void testAsynchronousSearch( ) {
    // details left out
}
```

The `@junitperf.loadtest` tag tells JUnitPerfDoclet that it should decorate the `testAsynchronousSearch( )` method with a JUnitPerf `LoadTest`.

The `numberOfUsers` attribute is mandatory and indicates the number of users or threads that simultaneously execute the test method.

The `numberOfIterations` attribute is optional. The value is a positive whole number that indicates how many times each user executes the test method.

Generating the code

Example 8-6 shows how to generate the tests. First, a new task definition is created, called perfdoclet. This task is responsible for kick-starting the code generation process. We exclude from the `fileset` any class that begins with "TestPerf" because there may be hand-coded JUnitPerf tests somewhere in the source tree. Finally, the junitperf subtask creates a new JUnitPerf class for each JUnit test case class that contains at least one test method with JUnitPerfDoclet tags. For example, if a JUnit test case class named TestSearch uses JUnitPerfDoclet tags, then the generated JUnit-Perf test class is named `TestPerfTestSearch`.

Example 8-6. JUnitPerfDoclet setup

```
<target name="generate.perf"
    depends="prepare"
    description="Generates the JUnitPerf tests.">
  <taskdef name="perfdoclet" classname="xdoclet.DocletTask">
    <classpath>
      <pathelement location="${dir.lib}/oreilly-junitperf-module.jar"/>
      <pathelement location="${dir.lib}/commons-logging-1.0.jar"/>
      <pathelement path="${env.JUNIT_HOME}/junit.jar"/>
      <pathelement path="${env.XDOCLET_HOME}/lib/xdoclet.jar"/>
      <pathelement path="${env.XDOCLET_HOME}/lib/xjavadoc.jar"/>
    </classpath>
  </taskdef>
```

Example 8-6. JUnitPerfDoclet setup (continued)

```
  <perfdoclet
      destdir="${dir.generated.src}">

    <fileset dir="${dir.src}">
      <include name="**/junitperf/Test*.java"/>
      <exclude name="**/junitperf/TestPerf*.java"/>
    </fileset>

    <junitperf destinationFile="TestPerf{0}.java"/>
  </perfdoclet>
</target>
```

Example 8-7 shows how to execute the performance tests using the junit task. Remember that this book uses the naming convention "TestPerf" to represent JUnit-Perf tests.

Example 8-7. Executing JUnitPerf tests with Ant

```
<target name="junitperf"
    depends="generate.junitperf,compile.generated"
    description="Runs the JUnitPerf tests.">
  <junit printsummary="on" fork="false" haltonfailure="false">
    <classpath refid="classpath.project"/>
    <formatter type="plain" usefile="false"/>
    <batchtest fork="false" todir="${dir.build}">
      <fileset dir="${dir.generated.src}">
        <include name="**/TestPerf*.java"/>
      </fileset>
    </batchtest>
  </junit>
</target>
```

See Also

The last few recipes in Chapter 9 discuss how to extend the XDoclet framework to generate JUnitPerf tests. A good starting point is Recipe 9.8.

CHAPTER 9

XDoclet

9.0 Introduction

XDoclet, available from *http://xdoclet.sourceforge.net,* is an open source tool that extends the Javadoc Doclet API, allowing for the creation of files based on Javadoc @ tags and template files (*.xdt*).

 This chapter uses XDoclet Version 1.2 beta 1, which can be found at *http://xdoclet.sourceforge.net/1.2beta/index.html.* Be sure to check their web site for updated XDoclet releases.

XDoclet provides direct support for generating many different types of files. The most popular use of XDoclet is to generate EJB files such as deployment descriptors, remote and home interfaces, and even vendor-specific deployment descriptors. If XDoclet does not provide what you need, you may define your own @ tags and template files. For ultimate flexibility, new Ant XDoclet tasks and new XDoclet tag handlers may be created, allowing for practically any kind of content.

One of the main goals of XDoclet is providing an active code-generation system through Ant. This means that XDoclet works directly with your Ant buildfile to generate the necessary files your project needs. For example, let's say you are working on an EJB called CustomerBean. Normally, you would have to write a minimum of four files: the bean implementation, remote interface, home interface, and the deployment descriptor. If a new public method is introduced, all four files must be kept in sync or the deployment of the bean fails. With XDoclet you simply write the bean implementation class and mark it up with XDoclet @ tags. During the build process an XDoclet Ant task generates the remaining three files for you. Since all files are based on the single bean implementation class, the files are always in sync.

9.1 Setting Up a Development Environment for Generated Files

Problem

You want to set up your development environment to handle generated files.

Solution

Create two directories at the same level as your source and build tree. The first directory contains generated source code and may be called something like *src-generated*. The second directory contains compiled code for the generated source and may be called something like *build-generated*.

Discussion

The best location for generated source files is in a directory at the same level as your source tree and build tree. Equally important is separating the compiled code for generated source files from the compiled code of nongenerated source files. This provides a convenient, easy to manage directory structure, as shown in Figure 9-1.

Why not place generated files in the source directory?

Placing generated files in the *src* directory causes version control tools to assume new files should be added to the repository, which is simply not true. Generated files should never be versioned, but rather the templates and scripts that are used to generate the files should be versioned.

- DO NOT check generated files into your version control tool.
- DO check the templates and scripts used to generate the files.

Why not place generated files in the build directory?

Placing generated files in the *build* directory has its own problems as well. For starters, the *build* directory, by convention, contains compiled code, not source code. Another important reason to maintain separate directory structures is to keep your Ant buildfile simple and easy to manage. When you want to force code to recompile, simply delete the build directories. If you placed generated source files in the *build* directory, the Ant buildfile would need to exclude those files from being deleted. Introducing a directory specifically for generated files allows the Ant buildfile to remain simple.

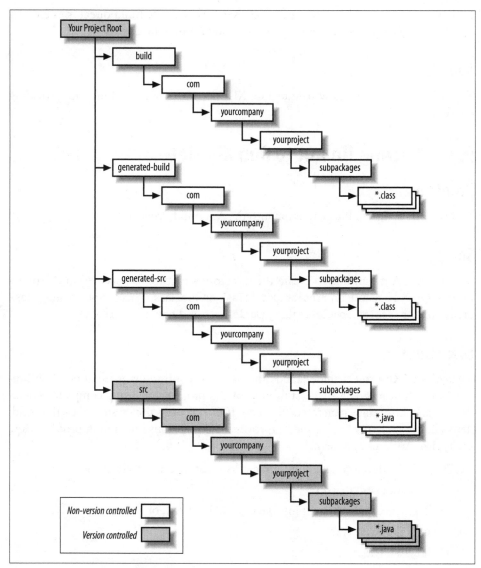

Figure 9-1. Directory structure for generated files

Why not place the compiled generated code in the build directory?

The *build* directory may seem like a natural location for compiled generated code. This type of setup has its problems, though. Developers typically use an IDE for quick development. If a developer rebuilds the entire project through the IDE, then all of the compiled code may be deleted. The IDE has to rebuild all source code, including the generated code. This may not seem like a mammoth task until you are dealing with thousands of generated files. Keeping separate build directories ensures that your development environment remains stable and efficient.

See Also

The next recipe shows how to integrate XDoclet into your Ant buildfile, providing continuous integration.

9.2 Setting Up Ant to Run XDoclet

Problem

You want to integrate file generation into the Ant build process.

Solution

Modify your Ant buildfile to create the directory structure as specified in the previous recipe and execute an xdoclet.DocletTask or subclass. This recipe creates a task definition for xdoclet.modules.ejb.EjbDocletTask and names it ejbdoclet.

Discussion

A successful XP project understands the need for continuous integration. Continuous integration means a successful build of the project, including complete generation of all out-of-date generated files and 100% passing unit tests. With that said, here's how generating source files improves the continuous integration process. Here is a typical Ant build process:

1. Prepare the development environment by creating output directories.
2. Compile out-of-date code.
3. Package the code into a deployable unit (JAR, WAR, or EAR).
4. Execute the JUnit tests.*
5. Deploy to a server.

If any task fails the build should stop and a friendly message should be reported. Code generation adds one more step to this process:

1. Prepare the development environment by creating output directories.
2. Run XDoclet to regenerate out-of-date generated source files.
3. Compile out-of-date code.

---

* For server-side testing, you'll have to deploy before running tests.

4. Package the code into a deployable unit (JAR, WAR, or EAR).

5. Execute the JUnit tests.

6. Deploy to a server.

Adding the code-generation step requires modifying the Ant buildfile. The first step is to define a task definition for an xdoclet.DocletTask task. This recipe uses the xdoclet.modules.ejb.EjbDocletTask class, which extends xdoclet.DocletTask and is provided by XDoclet. When defining the task, a valid classpath must be set up, too. Here is how to define this task:*

```
<taskdef name="ejbdoclet" classname="xdoclet.modules.ejb.EjbDocletTask">
  <classpath>
    <pathelement path="${env.JBOSS_DIST}/client/jboss-j2ee.jar"/>
    <pathelement path="${env.XDOCLET_HOME}/lib/xdoclet.jar"/>
    <pathelement path="${env.XDOCLET_HOME}/lib/xjavadoc.jar"/>
    <pathelement path="${env.XDOCLET_HOME}/lib/xdoclet-ejb-module.jar"/>
    <pathelement location="${dir.lib}/commons-logging-1.0.jar"/>
  </classpath>
</taskdef>
```

Next, set up a few properties that define the development environment. As discussed in the first recipe, the generated source files are placed into the *src-generated* directory specified by the dir.generated.src property, and the compiled generated code gets placed into the *build-generated* directory that is specified by the property dir.generated.build. These directories are at the same level as the *build* and *src* directories, allowing for easy management. Ant properties specify where to place generated deployment descriptors, too.

```
<property name="dir.build" value="build"/>
<property name="dir.src" value="src"/>
<property name="dir.generated.src" value="src-generated"/>
<property name="dir.generated.build" value="build-generated"/>
<property name="dir.ejb.metainf" value="${dir.generated.src}/ejb/META-INF"/>
```

The next step is to create a target that sets up the development environment. Here is a target that creates the build and the generated source directories.

```
<target name="prepare">
  <mkdir dir="${dir.build}"/>
  <mkdir dir="${dir.generated.build}"/>
  <mkdir dir="${dir.generated.src}"/>
  <mkdir dir="${dir.ejb.metainf}"/>
</target>
```

Finally, create a target that invokes the XDoclet Ant task, which in this recipe is the ejbdoclet task. The details of the ejbdoclet task are discussed in recipes to follow. The example below is just one configuration that can be used to generate EJB code.

---

* XDoclet Version 1.2. beta 1 did not include the Jakarta Commons Logging 1.0 JAR file. We included the JAR file in our project's *lib* directory.

```
<ejbdoclet
  ejbspec="2.0"
  destdir="${dir.generated.src}"
  excludedtags="@version,@author,@see"
  force="${force.ejb}">

  <!-- Rename any package called 'ejb' to 'interfaces'. -->
  <packageSubstitution packages="ejb" substituteWith="interfaces"/>

  <fileset dir="${dir.src}">
    <include name="**/ejb/*Bean.java"/>
  </fileset>

  <homeinterface/>
  <remoteinterface/>
  <session/>
  <deploymentdescriptor destdir="${dir.ejb.metainf}" validatexml="true"/>
</ejbdoclet>
```

Here's a target that deletes all generated files:

```
<target name="clean.generated"
    description="Deletes the 'generated.src' and 'generated.build' directories">
  <delete dir="${dir.generated.src}"/>
  <delete dir="${dir.generated.build}"/>
</target>
```

Next is a target that shows how to compile the code, both handwritten and generated. First, this target compiles the handwritten code into the *build* directory. Next, the generated code is compiled into the *build-generated* directory. Finally, the client is compiled into the *build* directory.

```
<target name="compile.ejb" depends="prepare,generate.ejb">
  <!-- compile non-generated server code to the build directory -->
  <javac srcdir="${dir.src}" destdir="${dir.build}">
    <classpath refid="classpath.ejb"/>
    <include name="**/ejbdoclet/ejb/"/>
  </javac>

  <!-- compile generated code to the build-generated directory -->
  <javac srcdir="${dir.generated.src}" destdir="${dir.generated.build}">
    <classpath refid="classpath.ejb"/>
    <include name="**/ejbdoclet/"/>
  </javac>

  <!-- compile non-generated client code to the build directory -->
  <javac srcdir="${dir.src}" destdir="${dir.build}">
    <classpath refid="classpath.ejb"/>
    <include name="**/ejbdoclet/client/"/>
  </javac>
</target>
```

More than likely you will need to create two compilation targets—one for handwritten code and the other for generated code. The only time generated code needs to be recompiled is when generated source file templates change. If you are using XDoclet to generate EJB code, you definitely want to separate out the compilation process once your EJB code becomes solid and does not change often. This dramatically speeds up your builds.

To prevent XDoclet from running again and again, use the Ant uptodate task. For example, generate a temporary file, say *ejbdoclet.done*, and then update the source fileset with the temporary file. If a file is newer than the temp file, XDoclet should regenerate the files; otherwise, skip the XDoclet process.

See Also

Recipe 9.1 discusses where generated source files should go in a development environment. Recipe 9.4 shows how to use XDoclet to generate an EJB deployment descriptor. Recipe 9.6 shows how to generate EJB home and remote interfaces. To download the Jakarta Commons Logging API, visit *http://jakarta.apache.org/commons/logging.html*.

9.3   Regenerating Files That Have Changed

Problem

You want to control when files are regenerated.

Solution

Add the force attribute to any Ant Doclet task.

Discussion

Ant XDoclet tasks, by default, perform dependency-checking on generated files. These checks only regenerate files that are out of date with respect to their corresponding template files. There are times, though, that you may wish to force all generated files to be regenerated. For example, you may wish to do this if you are performing a clean build of the project from scratch, or you have upgraded to a newer version of XDoclet.

All XDoclet tasks, such as ejbdoclet, define an attribute called force. This attribute tells the XDoclet task whether to perform dependency-checking before generating a file. A value of "true" tells the XDoclet task to force generation of all files. A value other than "true" tells the XDoclet task to perform dependency-checking before generating a file. A dependency check simply looks at the timestamp of a source or template file and compares it with the timestamp of its generated files. If a source or template file has a timestamp that is greater than its generated files, then the files are regenerated. Example 9-1 shows how to add the force attribute to any XDoclet task.

Example 9-1. Using the force attribute to control dependency-checking

```
<target name="generate.ejb">
  <ejbdoclet
      ejbspec="2.0"
      destdir="${dir.generated.src}"
      force="${force.ejb}">

  <!-- subtasks left out for brevity -->

  </ejbdoclet>
</target>
```

The force attribute is added to the XDoclet task's list of attributes and its value is defined by the property force.generation. You could set up a property in the build-file that specifies the force attribute value like this:

```
<property name="force.generation" value="true"/>
```

It's not necessary, though. Remember that any value other than "true" turns on dependency-checking. So we can rely on the fact that if Ant cannot find the property ${force.generation}, then the text "${force.generation}" is simply passed as the value, which is definitely not equal to "true". Therefore, dependency-checking is turned on.

Here is how to force all files to be regenerated:

```
ant generate.ejb -Dforce.generation=true
```

And here is how to use dependency-checking (we do nothing special):

```
ant generate.ejb
```

See Also

Recipe 9.1 discusses where generated source files should go in a development environment.

9.4   Generating the EJB Deployment Descriptor

Problem

You want to use XDoclet to generate the EJB deployment descriptor, *ejb-jar.xml*.

Solution

Add the necessary XDoclet tags to your EJB source files and update your Ant build-file to use XDoclet to generate the deployment descriptor.

Discussion

Anyone who has worked with EJBs knows that maintaining deployment descriptors is tedious and often frustrating, especially when dealing with a large number of beans. If a syntax error creeps into the deployment descriptor, you may not know until you have deployed the application to the server. Even then the error messages you receive may or may not be helpful to pinpoint the problem. Another problem is that the deployment descriptors and source files can get out of sync, causing even more deployment frustrations. The solution is to use XDoclet to generate the deployment descriptors whenever an EJB change is made.

Avoiding duplication is a key to simple, maintainable code. XDoclet allows you to make changes in one place and generate all of the tedious, duplicated code.

It is also worth mentioning that XDoclet is immensely less labor-intensive than using point-and-click GUI tools provided by most commercial IDEs. Once the development environment is configured, the Ant build process magically does the dirty work.

XDoclet provides a simple mechanism for generating EJB deployment descriptors. The first step is to mark up the EJB with the necessary XDoclet tags. Example 9-2 shows how this might be done for a stateless session bean.

Example 9-2. Marking up a stateless session bean

```
package com.oreilly.javaxp.xdoclet.ejbdoclet.ejb;

import javax.ejb.SessionBean;

/**
 * @ejb.bean
 *      type="Stateless"
 *      name="PaymentProcessingBean"
 *      jndi-name="ejb/PaymentProcessingBean"
 *      view-type="remote"
 * @ejb.transaction
 *      type="Required"
 * @ejb.transaction-type
 *      type="Container"
 *
 * @author Brian M. Coyner
 */
public abstract class PaymentProcessingBean implements SessionBean {
```

Example 9-2. Marking up a stateless session bean (continued)

```
/**
 * @ejb.interface-method view-type="remote"
 */
public boolean makePayment(String accountNumber, double payment) {
    // perform logic to look up customer and make payment against their
    // account
    return true;
}
}
```

The `@ejb.bean` tag defines information about the bean. This information is used when generating the enterprise-beans section of the deployment descriptor. We define the bean to be a stateless session bean named `PaymentProcessingBean`, with a JNDI name of `ejb/PaymentProcessingBean`. There are numerous other attributes that you may include with this tag that are not shown in this example. See the XDoclet documentation for all possible tags and their usage.

The `@ejb.transaction-type` tag defines how the container should manage the transactions for the bean. Valid values are "Container" and "Bean". The default is "Container".

The `@ejb.transaction` tag defines a single transactional attribute for all methods defined in the bean. Valid values are "NotSupported", "Supports", "Required", "RequiresNew", "Mandatory", or "Never". The attribute may be omitted if different methods in the bean need different transactional attributes. The `@author` tag was left to show that you can mix and match XDoclet tags with other tags.

The next step is to tell the `ejbdoclet` task to generate the deployment descriptor. Here is an example:

```
<ejbdoclet
    ejbspec="2.0"
    destdir="${dir.generated.src}"
    excludedtags="@author"
    force="${force.ejb}">

    <!-- other subtasks left out for brevity -->

    <deploymentdescriptor destdir="${dir.ejb.metainf}" validateXML="true"/>
</ejbdoclet>
```

The `deploymentdescriptor` subtask tells XDoclet to generate the deployment descriptor file (*ejb-jar.xml*) and write it to a directory defined by the property `dir.ejb.metainf`. Setting the optional attribute `validateXML` to "true" validates the generated XML file against its DTD or XML Schema.

Now let's look at the generated *ejb-jar.xml* file.[*]

---

[*] This example has been cleaned up for this recipe because the actual generated file is not nicely formatted.

```xml
<?xml version="1.0" encoding="UTF-8"?>
<!DOCTYPE ejb-jar
  PUBLIC "-//Sun Microsystems, Inc.//DTD Enterprise JavaBeans 2.0//EN"
  "http://java.sun.com/dtd/ejb-jar_2_0.dtd">

<ejb-jar >
  <description>No Description.</description>
  <display-name>Generated by XDoclet</display-name>
  <enterprise-beans>
    <session>
      <description><![CDATA[No Description.]]></description>
      <ejb-name>PaymentProcessingBean</ejb-name>
      <home>
        com.oreilly.javaxp.xdoclet.ejbdoclet.interfaces.PaymentProcessingBeanHome
      </home>
      <remote>
        com.oreilly.javaxp.xdoclet.ejbdoclet.interfaces.PaymentProcessingBean
      </remote>
      <ejb-class>
        com.oreilly.javaxp.xdoclet.ejbdoclet.ejb.PaymentProcessingBeanSession
      </ejb-class>
      <session-type>Stateless</session-type>
      <transaction-type>Container</transaction-type>
    </session>
  </enterprise-beans>

  <assembly-descriptor>
    <container-transaction>
      <method>
        <ejb-name>PaymentProcessingBean</ejb-name>
        <method-name>*</method-name>
      </method>
      <trans-attribute>Required</trans-attribute>
    </container-transaction>
  </assembly-descriptor>
</ejb-jar>
```

XDoclet frees you from having to manage the deployment descriptor yourself. You simply mark up your EJB class with the necessary tags, execute the ejbdoclet task, and deploy your application. The majority of the time you never have to bother looking at the deployment descriptor.

See Also

Recipe 9.6 shows how to generate the home and remote interfaces, removing yet another tedious task from EJB development.

9.5   Specifying Different EJB Specifications

Problem

You need to change the EJB specification used when generating EJB files.

Solution

Change the ejbdoclet attribute ejbspec to "1.1" or "2.0".

Discussion

By default, the current version of the ejbdoclet task creates files based on the 2.0 version of the EJB specification. If you need to change this to an earlier version of the EJB specification, simply change the ejbdoclet attribute ejbspec. Here's an example:

```
<ejbdoclet
    ejbspec="1.1"
    destdir="${dir.generated.src}"
    force="${force.ejb}">

  <!-- all subtasks left out for brevity -->
</ejbdoclet>
```

 The only supported EJB specifications are 1.1 and 2.0.

If your project must run on 1.1 and 2.0-compliant servers, the build process can emit multiple versions of the application, one for each specification.

See Also

Recipe 9.4 shows how to generate an EJB deployment descriptor.

9.6   Generating EJB Home and Remote Interfaces

Problem

You need XDoclet to generate the EJB home and remote interfaces each time your bean class changes.

Solution

Mark up your bean implementation class with the necessary XDoclet tags and use XDoclet to generate the home and remote interfaces.

Discussion

Writing EJB home and remote interfaces is a cumbersome task. The remote, home, and bean code must stay in sync or the deployment of the bean fails. Depending on the server, you may or may not receive suitable error messages. Let's look at an example of what needs to be written if XDoclet is not used.

Example 9-3 shows an example of a hand-coded remote interface. When writing remote interfaces, ensure that each method throws java.rmi.RemoteException. This may not seem like a huge task but the first time you forget to add the exception to the throws clause you will wish you never wrote this interface.

Example 9-3. Hand-coded remote interface

```
package com.oreilly.javaxp.xdoclet.ejbdoclet.ejb;

import javax.ejb.EJBObject;
import java.rmi.RemoteException;

public interface PaymentProcessingBean extends EJBObject {

    public boolean makePayment(String accountNumber, double payment)
            throws RemoteException;
}
```

Example 9-4 shows an example of a hand-coded home interface. The home interface provides a view into the container for creating, finding, and removing beans. You must ensure that all "create" methods throw javax.ejb.CreateException, that "finder" methods throw javax.ejb.FinderException, and all methods throw RemoteException. Once again, this may not seem like a daunting task—but the first time you forget is the last time you will want to write this code.

Example 9-4. Hand-coded home interface

```
package com.oreilly.javaxp.xdoclet.ejbdoclet.ejb;

import java.rmi.RemoteException;
import javax.ejb.EJBHome;
import javax.ejb.CreateException;

public interface PaymentProcessingBeanHome extends EJBHome {

    public PaymentProcessingBean create()
            throws CreateException, RemoteException;
}
```

Finally, Example 9-5 shows the bean implementation. The bean implementation, in this example, extends javax.ejb.SessionBean and provides empty implementations of the SessionBean interface methods. Also notice the ejbCreate( ) method. This method is added because the home interface defined a create method called create( ). Failure to add this method causes runtime problems.

Example 9-5. Bean implementation

```
package com.oreilly.javaxp.xdoclet.ejbdoclet.ejb;

import javax.ejb.SessionBean;

public class PaymentProcessingBean implements SessionBean {

    public boolean makePayment(String accountNumber, double payment) {
        // perform logic to look up customer and make payment against their
        // account
        return true;
    }

    /**
     * Not part of the SessionBean interface. This method exists because the
     * home interface defined a method called create( ).
     */
    public void ejbCreate( ) {
    }

    public void ejbActivate( ) throws EJBException, RemoteException {
    }

    public void ejbPassivate( ) throws EJBException, RemoteException {
    }

    public void ejbRemove( ) throws EJBException, RemoteException {
    }

    public void setSessionContext(SessionContext sessionContext)
            throws EJBException, RemoteException {
    }
}
```

The previous example is simple but helps exemplify the cumbersome tasks that take attention away from what really matters—writing the bean! Now, let us turn our attention to automatically generating the home and remote interfaces using XDoclet.

Using XDoclet to generate home and remote interfaces requires marking up the bean implementation with XDoclet tags. Use Ant to execute the XDoclet engine to generate the files. Example 9-6 shows the marked-up bean implementation.

Example 9-6. Marked-up PaymentProcessingBean

```
/**
 * @ejb.bean
 *     type="Stateless"
 *     name="PaymentProcessingBean"
 *     jndi-name="ejb/PaymentProcessingBean"
 *     view-type="remote"
 * @ejb.transaction
 *     type="Required"
 * @ejb.transaction-type
 *     type="Container"
 *
 * @author Brian M. Coyner
 */
public abstract class PaymentProcessingBean implements SessionBean {

    /**
     * @ejb.interface-method view-type="remote"
     */
    public boolean makePayment(String accountNumber, double payment) {
        // perform logic to look up customer and make payment against their
        // account
        return true;
    }
}
```

This is the only source file you have to write. In this example, the @ejb.interface-method is the only tag specified for the makePayment() method, which simply tells XDoclet that this method should be included in the remote interface. Another important aspect to this example is that it is declared abstract. Thus, we do not have to directly implement any of the SessionBean methods or add the ejbCreate() method, but rather we rely on XDoclet to provide a subclass of the bean to provide the implementations. Example 9-7 shows the generated session bean.[*]

Example 9-7. Generated session bean

```
/*
 * Generated by XDoclet - Do not edit!
 */
package com.oreilly.javaxp.xdoclet.ejbdoclet.ejb;

/**
 * Session layer for PaymentProcessingBean.
 */
public class PaymentProcessingBeanSession
        extends com.oreilly.javaxp.xdoclet.ejbdoclet.ejb.PaymentProcessingBean
        implements javax.ejb.SessionBean {
    public void ejbActivate() {
    }
```

---

[*] This example has been reformatted to print nicely on the page.

Example 9-7. Generated session bean (continued)

```
    public void ejbPassivate() {
    }

    public void setSessionContext(javax.ejb.SessionContext ctx) {
    }

    public void unsetSessionContext() {
    }

    public void ejbRemove() {
    }

    public void ejbCreate() throws javax.ejb.CreateException {
    }
}
```

Example 9-8 shows how to set up the Ant buildfile to generate the home and remote interfaces, as well as providing a subclass of our bean containing implementations of the SessionBean interface methods.

Example 9-8. Using Ant to generate EJB files

```
<target name="generate.ejb" description="Generates EJB specific files.">
  <taskdef name="ejbdoclet" classname="xdoclet.modules.ejb.EjbDocletTask">
    <classpath>
      <pathelement path="${env.JBOSS_DIST}/client/jboss-j2ee.jar"/>
      <pathelement path="${env.XDOCLET_HOME}/lib/xdoclet.jar"/>
      <pathelement path="${env.XDOCLET_HOME}/lib/xjavadoc.jar"/>
      <pathelement path="${env.XDOCLET_HOME}/lib/xdoclet-ejb-module.jar"/>
      <pathelement location="${dir.lib}/commons-logging-1.0.jar"/>
    </classpath>
  </taskdef>

  <ejbdoclet
      ejbspec="2.0"
      destdir="${dir.generated.src}"
      excludedtags="@version,@author,@see"
      force="${force.ejb}">

    <!-- Rename any package called 'ejb' to 'interfaces'. -->
    <packageSubstitution packages="ejb" substituteWith="interfaces"/>

    <fileset dir="${dir.src}">
      <include name="**/ejb/*Bean.java"/>
    </fileset>

    <homeinterface/>
    <remoteinterface/>
    <session/>
    <deploymentdescriptor destdir="${dir.ejb.metainf}" validatexml="true"/>
  </ejbdoclet>
</target>
```

The destdir attribute specifies the destination directory for all generated files. Next, the fileset specifies which files should be included or excluded from the generation process. This recipe is only interested in looking at Java source files that end with *Bean.java*.

 Consistent naming conventions serve two purposes. First, they make your code more maintainable. Second, consistency facilitates automation. Specifying that all bean implementation classes must end in *Bean.java* allows the Ant buildfile to remain simple and easy to understand. Without strict naming conventions, this task and others like it would be nearly impossible.

Here are three subtasks responsible for generating a single file for each bean: the homeinterface subtask is responsible for generating the EJB home interface; the remoteinterface subtask is responsible for generating the EJB remote interface.; and the session subtask is responsible for extending each SessionBean implementation class (our PaymentProcessBean class) and providing default implementations of the SessionBean interface methods and the ejbCreate( ) method. Each EJB subtask uses a pre-existing template file supplied in *xdoclet-ejb-module.jar*; thus, no extra work is needed on our part.

Once this task is integrated into the Ant build process, the days of creating and maintaining the mundane and frustrating aspects of EJB code are long gone. Also gone are the days of using point-and-click wizards that require human intervention. Ant and XDoclet completely automate EJB code generation. Once your build process is set up you can forget about EJB deployment and focus on solving business problems.

See Also

Recipe 9.4 shows how to use XDoclet to generate the EJB deployment descriptor.

9.7 Creating and Executing a Custom Template

Problem

You want to write and execute a custom XDoclet template file (*.xdt*).

Solution

Create an *.xdt* file that contains the necessary XDoclet template tags to generate the desired output. Finally, update your Ant buildfile to execute the template subtask via the xdoclet.DocletTask task.

Discussion

Using XDoclet to generate EJB files is fairly straightforward because the templates are already written. The challenge occurs when you want to create a custom template to generate a specific file. Knowing where to look up information on custom templates and deciphering that information can be a difficult task.

XDoclet templates are at the core of XDoclet's extensibility, and XDoclet provides a plethora of built-in template tags for us to use. Template tags control how and what information is generated. Template tags are broken down into two categories, block and content.

Block

Block tags are used for iterating and performing logic, which is synonymous with for loops and if statements. The snippet below shows how to iterate through all classes using the built-in Class template tag:

```
<XDtClass:forAllClasses>
</XDtClass:forAllClasses>
```

The next snippet shows how to check if a method contains a specific @ tag using the built-in Method template tag. In this example we are checking for "deprecated":

```
<XDtMethod:ifHasMethodTag tagName="deprecated">
</XDtMethod:ifHasMethodTag>
```

Content

Content tags are used for outputting information. These tags are synonymous with getter methods that return a string. Content tags never contain nested information. The snippet below shows how to output the current method name using the built-in Method template tag.

```
<XDtMethod:methodName/>
```

A template tag is very similar to an XML tag. The first part of the tag represents the namespace. For example, XDtMethod is a namespace. The part directly after the namespace represents the tag name. For example, methodName is a tag name. By convention all namespaces begin with "XDt". This prefix is not directly part of the namespace and is stripped off by XDoclet when the template is being parsed.

Now, let's delve into creating a custom template. Example 9-9 shows a custom template used to generate a code-deprecation report. The custom template uses template tags defined by XDoclet. The first step is to create a new template file and add it to your project. This recipe creates a new template file called *deprecation-report.xdt* and places it in the *resources* directory. This template generates a report of all classes and methods marked as deprecated. Take note that the tagName attribute omits the @ character.

Example 9-9. deprecation-report.xdt template file

```
Deprecated Classes and Methods
-------------------------------
<XDtClass:forAllClasses>
  +++ <XDtClass:fullClassName/>
  <XDtClass:ifHasClassTag tagName="deprecated">
      WARNING: This class is deprecated.
      NOTE: <XDtClass:classTagValue tagName="deprecated"/>
  </XDtClass:ifHasClassTag>

  <XDtClass:ifDoesntHaveClassTag tagName="deprecated">
      DEPRECATED METHODS
      ------------------
    <XDtMethod:forAllMethods>
      <XDtMethod:ifHasMethodTag tagName="deprecated">
        METHOD: <XDtMethod:methodName/>(<XDtParameter:parameterList/>)
          NOTE: <XDtMethod:methodTagValue tagName="deprecated"/>
      </XDtMethod:ifHasMethodTag>
    </XDtMethod:forAllMethods>
  </XDtClass:ifDoesntHaveClassTag>
</XDtClass:forAllClasses>
```

Example 9-10 shows an updated Ant buildfile that executes the new template.

Example 9-10. Executing a custom template

```
<target name="deprecation.report"
    description="Generates a Deprecation Report."
    depends="prepare">

  <taskdef name="deprecateddoclet" classname="xdoclet.DocletTask">
    <classpath>
      <pathelement path="${env.XDOCLET_HOME}/lib/xdoclet.jar"/>
      <pathelement path="${env.XDOCLET_HOME}/lib/xjavadoc.jar"/>
      <pathelement location="${dir.lib}/commons-logging-1.0.jar"/>
    </classpath>
  </taskdef>

  <deprecateddoclet
      destdir="${dir.build}">

    <fileset dir="${dir.src}">
      <include name="**/deprecation/"/>
    </fileset>

    <template
        templateFile="${dir.build}/${deprecation.template}"
        destinationFile="deprecation-report.txt"/>
  </deprecateddoclet>
</target>
```

The first step is to set up a task definition called deprecateddoclet for the class xdoclet.DocletTask. The DocletTask is the base class for all Ant XDoclet tasks. This class can be used directly to execute a custom template file when a subclass is not required.

The fileset specifies which files should be included or excluded from the generation process.

Finally, the template subtask specifies which template file to use and the name of the file to generate.* This subtask is used to apply generic templates (in this example it is the template file *deprecation-report.xdt*) to produce any type of text output.

Here is what an example report might look like:

```
Deprecated Classes and Methods
-------------------------------

  +++ com.oreilly.javaxp.xdoclet.deprecation.Employee

      DEPRECATED METHODS
      ------------------
      METHOD: getEmployeeId( )
        NOTE: use {@link #getId}.
      METHOD: setEmployeeId(long)
        NOTE: use {@link #setId}.

  +++ com.oreilly.javaxp.xdoclet.deprecation.Person
      WARNING: This class is deprecated.
      NOTE: No replacement for this class.
```

See Also

The tags used in this recipe only scratch the surface of what XDoclet provides. For a complete listing of all XDoclet template tags, see *http://xdoclet.sourceforge.net/1.2beta/templates/index.html*.

9.8   Extending XDoclet to Generate Custom Files

Problem

You would like to extend XDoclet to generate custom files.

---

* Adding the substring "{0}" to the destinationFile attribute tells XDoclet to generate a new file for each processed class. Omitting the substring "{0}" creates a single file, which is useful for generating a comprehensive report or deployment descriptor.

Solution

There are five main steps needed to create a custom XDoclet extension. XDoclet refers to custom extensions as modules. A *module* is a JAR file with a specific naming convention and structure. See Recipe 9.13 for more information on modules. Here are the steps:

1. Create an Ant task and subtask to invoke your XDoclet code generator from an Ant buildfile.

2. Create an XDoclet tag handler class to perform logic and generate snippets of code.

3. Create an XDoclet template file (*.xdt*) for mixing snippets of Java code with XDoclet tag handlers to generate a complete file.

4. Create an *xdoclet.xml* file that defines the relationships of tasks and subtasks, as well as specifying a tag handlers namespace.

5. Package the new XDoclet code generator into a new JAR file, known as a module.

Discussion

Creating a custom code generator is not as dire as you may think. The key is to take each step one at a time and build the code generator in small chunks. There are five main steps needed to complete an entire custom code generator, and each of these steps is broken into its own recipe.

The following recipes build a code generator for creating JUnitPerf test classes based on custom XDoclet @ tags. The new @ tags are used to mark up existing JUnit tests to control the type of JUnitPerf test to create. This example is realistic because JUnit-Perf tests build upon existing JUnit tests. By simply marking up a JUnit test with specific @ tags, a JUnitPerf test can be generated and executed through Ant. The code generator is aptly named `JUnitPerfDoclet`.[*]

See Also

Recipe 9.9 shows how to create a custom Ant Doclet subtask to generate JUnitPerf tests. Recipe 9.10 shows how to create the JUnitPerfDoclet tag handler class to perform simple logic and generate snippets of code. Recipe 9.11 shows how to create a custom template file that uses the JUnitPerfDoclet tag handler. Recipe 9.12 shows how to create an XDoclet *xdoclet.xml* file used to define information about your code generator. Recipe 9.13 shows how to package JUnitPerfDoclet into a JAR module. Chapter 8 provides information on the JUnitPerf tool and how to update your Ant buildfile to invoke JUnitPerfDoclet.

---

[*] At the time of this writing, a tool to generate JUnitPerf tests did not exist.

9.9   Creating an Ant XDoclet Task

Problem

You want to create an Ant XDoclet task and subtask to generate a new type of file.

Solution

Extend `xdoclet.DocletTask` to create the main task, if necessary, and extend `xdoclet.TemplateSubTask` to create one or more subtasks.

Discussion

This recipe is the first part of a five-part recipe. It describes the steps needed to create a new Ant XDoclet task and subtask. We are going to create tasks for the `JUnitPerfDoclet` code generator.

 JUnitPerfDoclet does not need a main XDoclet task. Specifically, we do not need to extend `xdoclet.DocletTask` because no extra functionality needs to be added. All of the functionality needed by JUnitPerf-Doclet lies in the subtask. For completeness, this recipe shows how to create a Doclet task.

Creating an Ant XDoclet task

The first step is to create the main Ant XDoclet task. This task is much like the ejbdoclet task, serving as an entry point into the XDoclet engine.

Here are the steps needed to create an Ant XDoclet task:

1. Create a new Java source file and give it a name. For this example, create a *YourNewDocletTask.java* file and add it to your project.

2. Add the following import:

   ```
   import xdoclet.DocletTask;
   ```

3. Extend the `DocletTask` class:

   ```
   public class YourNewDocletTask extends DocletTask {
   ```

4. Add the necessary public getter and setter methods for attributes your task defines. For example, if your new task defines an attribute called `validId`, then you would have this setter method:

   ```
   public void setValidId(String id) {
       this.id = id;
   }
   ```

5. Optionally, you may override the `validateOptions()` method if you need to validate your task.

Typically, you override this method to ensure that the user has set the proper attributes. Here's an example:

```
protected void validateOptions() throws BuildException {
    super.validateOptions();

    if (this.id == null || "".equals(this.id)) {
        throw new BuildException("You must specify a valid 'id' attribute.");
    }
}
```

You should call `super.validateOptions()` to allow the base class a chance to perform validation, too. If any error occurs an `org.apache.tools.ant.BuildException` should be thrown.

Another interesting feature of XDoclet is the `checkClass(String class)` method. This method tries to load a class specified by the given `class` parameter using `Class.forName()`, and if the class is not on the classpath then a nice error message is printed to the console. The classpath is the one defined for the Ant task definition. This is a major improvement over earlier versions of XDoclet, where you were left sifting through Java reflection errors. Here is an example:

```
protected void validateOptions() throws BuildException {
    super.validateOptions();

    if (this.id == null || "".equals(this.id)) {
        throw new BuildException("You must specify a valid 'id' attribute.");
    }

    checkClass("com.oreilly.javaxp.xdoclet.SomeClassThatYouWant");
}
```

Creating the Ant Doclet subtask

Now let's delve into creating the JUnitPerfDoclet subtask, `JUnitPerfDocletSubTask`. This subtask is responsible for the code generation process.

1. Create a new Java source file called *JUnitPerfDocletSubTask.java* and add it to your project.

2. Add the following imports:

```
import xdoclet.TemplateSubTask;
import xdoclet.XDocletException;
```

3. Extend the `xdoclet.TemplateSubTask` class:

```
public class JUnitPerfDocletSubTask extends TemplateSubTask {
```

The `TemplateSubTask` provides the hooks necessary for XDoclet to locate a template file and start the code generation process.

4. Set up a few constants:

```
public static final String DEFAULT_TEMPLATE =
        "/com/oreilly/javaxp/xdoclet/perf/junitperf.j";
private static final String DEFAULT_JUNIT_PERF_PATTERN =
        "TestPerf{0}.java";
```

It is a good idea to set up constants that define default values the subtask needs. The constants defined above are values specifying the JUnitPerfDoclet template file and the pattern used for the classname and filename of the generated code.

5. Add a default constructor:

```
public JUnitPerfDocletSubTask() {
    setDestinationFile(DEFAULT_JUNIT_PERF_PATTERN);
    setTemplateURL(getClass().getResource(DEFAULT_TEMPLATE));
}
```

A constructor should set up any default values. The only two attributes needed for our subtask are the destination file and template file. The `TemplateSubTask` class defines both of these attributes.

The destination file attribute specifies the name of the generated file. If this attribute contains the substring "{0}" then XDoclet generates a new file for each source file processed. If the substring "{0}" is omitted, only one output file is generated for all source files processed. Let's look at an example.

If the value of the destination file attribute is `TestPerf{0}.java` and the current class being processed is `Customer`, then XDoclet generates a new file named *TestPerfCustomer.java*. The name of the current class being processed is substituted in place of the substring "{0}". If you are familiar with the `java.text` package, you may have guessed that XDoclet uses the `java.text.MessageFormat` class to achieve the substitution. The next recipe shows how to use this technique.

The template file attribute specifies where to locate the *.xdt* file. JUnitPerf-Doclet, by default, loads the *junitperf.xdt* template file from the classpath.

6. Override the `validateOptions()` method to validate one or more attributes:

```
public void validateOptions() throws XDocletException {
    super.validateOptions();

    if (getDestinationFile().indexOf("{0}") == -1) {
        throw new XDocletException(
            "The '" + getSubTaskName() +
            "' Ant Doclet Subtask attribute 'destinationFile' " +
            "must contain the substring '{0}', which serves as a " +
            "place holder JUnit Test name.");
    }
}
```

Here the `validateOptions()` method is overridden to ensure that the "destinationFile" attribute contains the substring "{0}". An `XDocletException` is thrown with a friendly message if the "destinationFile" attribute does not contain the "{0}" substring. The subtask `validationOptions()` method throws an `XDocletException` not a `BuildException`. This allows the main task to handle all `XDocletExceptions` before halting the process.

It is important to call `super.validateOptions()`. It ensures that the base class gets a chance to perform validation it requires.

7. The last method to implement is a convenience method for the JUnitPerf tag handler class (this class is written in the next recipe):

```
public String getJUnitPerfPattern() {
    return getDestinationFile().
            substring(0, getDestinationFile().indexOf(".java"));
}
```

This method strips off the file extension, and it is used by the JUnitPerfTagHandler.className() method. The next recipe examines why this is important.

Example 9-11 shows the complete example.

Example 9-11. JUnitPerfDocletSubTask

```java
package com.oreilly.javaxp.xdoclet.perf;

import xdoclet.TemplateSubTask;
import xdoclet.XDocletException;

public class JUnitPerfDocletSubTask extends TemplateSubTask {

    public static final String DEFAULT_TEMPLATE =
            "/com/oreilly/javaxp/xdoclet/perf/junitperf.j";
    public static final String DEFAULT_JUNIT_PERF_PATTERN =
            "TestPerf{0}.java";

    public JUnitPerfDocletSubTask() {
        setDestinationFile(DEFAULT_JUNIT_PERF_PATTERN);
        setTemplateURL(getClass().getResource(DEFAULT_TEMPLATE));
    }

    /**
     * Used by {@link JUnitPerfTagHandler} to generate the new class name.
     * Before returning the '.java' extension is stripped off.
     *
     * @return the JUnitPerf file pattern with the '.java' extension removed.
     */
    public String getJUnitPerfPattern() {
        return getDestinationFile().
                substring(0, getDestinationFile().indexOf(".java"));
    }

    /**
     * Overridden to validate the 'destinationFile' attribute. This attribute
     * must include a '{0}', which serves as a place holder for the JUnit
     * test name.
     */
    public void validateOptions() throws XDocletException {
        super.validateOptions();

        if (getDestinationFile().indexOf("{0}") == -1) {
            throw new XDocletException(
```

Example 9-11. JUnitPerfDocletSubTask (continued)

```
                         "The '" + getSubTaskName( ) +
                         "' Ant Doclet Subtask attribute 'destinationFile' " +
                         "must contain the substring '{0}', which serves as a " +
                         "place holder JUnit test name.");
          }
       }
}
```

See Also

Recipe 9.10 shows how to create the JUnitPerfDoclet tag handler class to perform simple logic and generate snippets of code. Recipe 9.11 shows how to create a custom template file that uses the JUnitPerfDoclet tag handler. Recipe 9.12 shows how to create an XDoclet *xdoclet.xml* file used to define information about your code generator. Recipe 9.13 shows how to package JUnitPerfDoclet into a JAR module. Chapter 8 provides information on the JUnitPerf tool and how to update your Ant buildfile to invoke JUnitPerfDoclet.

9.10   Creating an XDoclet Tag Handler

Problem

You want to create a new XDoclet Tag Handler.

Solution

Extend the xdoclet.XDocletTagSupport class; write public methods that perform logic and generate content. The methods are referenced in an XDoclet template file (*.xdt*).

Discussion

The previous recipe created a custom Ant XDoclet subtask, providing an entry point into our custom code generator. Now it is time to write the tag handler class, which is responsible for generating snippets of content and performing simple logic.

There are no methods that must be overridden or directly implemented when creating a custom tag handler. Rather, you create public methods that a template file references.

Let's see how to write the tag handler class JUnitPerfTagHandler:

1. Create a new Java source file called *JUnitPerfTagHandler.java* and add it to your project.
2. Add the following imports:

```
import xdoclet.XDocletException;
import xdoclet.XDocletTagSupport;
import xdoclet.tagshandler.TypeTagsHandler;
import java.text.MessageFormat;
```

3. Extend the XDocletTagSupport class:

```
public class JUnitPerfTagHandler extends XDocletTagSupport {
```

4. Add public methods to generate snippets of content and to perform logic.

Step three deserves further explanation. There are two categories of methods used in a tag handler class: block and content.

Block

Block methods are used for iterating and performing logic, which is synonymous with for loops and if statements. A block method accepts a single parameter containing any content that should be parsed if a condition is met. The generate(String) method is provided by the base class and used to continue processing nested content, if necessary.

The code snippet below shows how to check if the current class being evaluated is an instance of junit.framework.TestCase. This method shows an example usage of the XDoclet utility class TypeTagsHandler.

```
public void ifIsTestCase(String template) throws XDocletException {
    if (TypeTagsHandler.isOfType(getCurrentClass(),
                                 "junit.framework.TestCase",
                                 TypeTagsHandler.TYPE_HIERARCHY)) {
        generate(template);
    }
}
```

 This method is never referenced in the *junitperf.xdt* file; rather, it is shown here for illustration purposes.

Content

Content tags are used for outputting information. These tags are synonymous with getter methods that return a string. Content tags never contain nested information. The snippet below shows how to generate the JUnitPerf test classname.

```
public String className() throws XDocletException {
    JUnitPerfDocletSubTask task = (JUnitPerfDocletSubTask)
            getDocletContext().getActiveSubTask();

    String currentJUnitTest = getCurrentClass().getName();
    return MessageFormat.format(task.getJUnitPerfPattern(),
                                new Object[] { currentJUnitTest });
}
```

The example above has a few interesting details that deserve some attention. First, the call to getDocletContext( ) returns an instance of an xdoclet.DocletContext class. A DocletContext object contains information passed to the Ant XDoclet task in the buildfile. For example, the DocletContext object contains the destination directory, whether or not the 'force' attribute is set, the active subtask,[*] and numerous other attributes. Here we retrieve the active subtask, which we know must be a JUnitPerfDocletSubTask because it is the only subtask we created. Next, we retrieve the name of the class that is currently being parsed by XDoclet, which should be the classname of a JUnit test. Once we have the current JUnit classname we need to generate the JUnitPerf test class name. This is done using the java.text.MessageFormat class to perform a text substitution between the classname pattern and the classname of the JUnit test. The classname pattern is retrieved using the getJUnitPerfPattern( ) method on the subtask. Recall that this is the value of the "destinationFile" attribute set in the Ant buildfile, but without the filename extension. Let's take a look at a simple example. Suppose the JUnitPerf pattern is "TestPerf{0}", and the name of the current JUnit test class name is "TestExample". The output of MessageFormat.format( ), using these values as parameters, yields "TestPerfTestExample".

Example 9-12 shows the full implementation of the JUnitPerfTagHandler class.

Example 9-12. JUnitPerfTagHandler

```
package com.oreilly.javaxp.xdoclet.perf;

import xdoclet.XDocletException;
import xdoclet.XDocletTagSupport;
import xdoclet.tagshandler.TypeTagsHandler;

import java.text.MessageFormat;

/**
 * Provides a window into the junitperf.xdt template file. The instance
 * methods can be used in the template file to retrieve or perform
 * logic. See the junitperf.xdt file for how these methods are referenced.
 */
public class JUnitPerfTagHandler extends XDocletTagSupport {

    public static final String TIMED_TEST = "junitperf.timedtest";
    public static final String LOAD_TEST = "junitperf.loadtest";
    public static final String WAIT_FOR_COMPLETION = "waitForCompletion";
    public static final String NUMBER_OF_USERS = "numberOfUsers";
    public static final String NUMBER_OF_ITERATIONS = "numberOfIterations";
    public static final String MAX_ELAPSED_TIME = "maxElapsedTime";

    /**
     * If the current class being evaluated extends <code>TestCase</code>
     * then process the data contained in the given parameter.
     *
     * @param template the current block of text to be parsed.
     */
```

---

[*] An active subtask is the Ant subtask currently being processed. Remember that an Ant task may have multiple subtasks.

Example 9-12. JUnitPerfTagHandler (continued)

```
public void ifIsTestCase(String template) throws XDocletException {
    if (TypeTagsHandler.isOfType(getCurrentClass(),
                                 "junit.framework.TestCase",
                                 TypeTagsHandler.TYPE_HIERARCHY)) {
        generate(template);
    }
}

/**
 * This shows an example of a content-level method that returns
 * the name of the generated class. See the junitperf.xdt file for
 * an example of how to use this method.
 *
 * <p>
 * This method shows how to use the active Ant subtask to retrieve
 * attributes defined in the Ant buildfile. Here we extract out the
 * 'jUnitPerfPattern' attribute.
 * </p>
 *
 * @return the new name of the generated class.
 */
public String className() throws XDocletException {
    JUnitPerfDocletSubTask task = (JUnitPerfDocletSubTask)
            getDocletContext().getActiveSubTask();

    String currentJUnitTest = getCurrentClass().getName();
    return MessageFormat.format(task.getJUnitPerfPattern(),
                                new Object[]{currentJUnitTest});
}

/**
 * This method shows an example of how to use XDoclet to output
 * code that instantiates an object.
 *
 * @return a line of code that instantiates a new JUnitPerf <code>
 * TimedTest</code>.
 */
public String timedTest() throws XDocletException {
    return "new TimedTest(" + getJUnitConstructor() +
            ", " + getMaxElapsedTime() +
            ", " + getWaitForCompletion() + ");";
}

/**
 * This method shows an example of how to use XDoclet to output
 * code that instantiates an object.
 *
 * @return a line of code that instantiates a new JUnitPerf <code>
 * LoadTest</code>.
 */
public String loadTest() throws XDocletException {
    return "new LoadTest(" + getJUnitConstructor() +
```

Example 9-12. JUnitPerfTagHandler (continued)

```
                     ", " + getNumberOfUsers() +
                     ", " + getNumberOfIterations() + ");";
    }

    /**
     * Helper method that retrieves the current class being evaluated. This
     * class should be an instance of a JUnit <code>TestCase</code> and
     * therefore we pass a single parameter, which is the current method name
     * being evaluated. This produces a new instance of a <code>TestCase</code>
     * that executes a single JUnit test method. For example:
     * <code>new TestExample("testExampleLoad");</code> might be
     * the output of the method.
     *
     * @return a line of code that constructs a new <code>TestCase</code>
     * method for executing a single JUnit test method.
     */
    private String getJUnitConstructor() {
        return "new " + getCurrentClass().getName() + "(\"" +
                getCurrentMethod().getName() + "\")";
    }

    /**
     * Helper method that retrieves the number of users to use for a
     * <code>LoadTest</code>.
     *
     * @return the number of users to use for a load test. This is a mandatory
     * XDoclet tag parameter (attribute).
     * @throws XDocletException if this attribute does not exist in the
     * source file; it's mandatory!
     */
    private String getNumberOfUsers() throws XDocletException {
        return getTagValue(XDocletTagSupport.FOR_METHOD,
                           LOAD_TEST,
                           NUMBER_OF_USERS,
                           null,
                           null,
                           false,
                           true);
    }

    /**
     * Helper method that retrieves the number of iterations each user
     * of a <code>LoadTest</code> must execute.
     *
     * @return the number of iterations to use for a load test. If the
     * value is not specified in the source file a default value of
     * 1 is used.
     */
    private String getNumberOfIterations() throws XDocletException {
        return getTagValue(XDocletTagSupport.FOR_METHOD,
                           LOAD_TEST,
                           NUMBER_OF_ITERATIONS,
```

Example 9-12. JUnitPerfTagHandler (continued)

```
                                    null,
                                    "1",
                                    false,
                                    false);
    }

    /**
     * Helper method that retrieves the max allowed time for a <code>
     * TimedTest</code> to execute. This is another example of a mandatory
     * attribute.
     *
     * @return the max allowed time for a test to execute.
     * @throws XDocletException
     */
    private String getMaxElapsedTime() throws XDocletException {
        return getTagValue(XDocletTagSupport.FOR_METHOD,
                            TIMED_TEST,
                            MAX_ELAPSED_TIME,
                            null,
                            null,
                            false,
                            true);
    }

    /**
     * Helper method that retrieves whether or not the <code>TimedTest</code>
     * should wait for the JUnit test method to complete before throwing
     * an exception if the time has elapsed. This method shows an example
     * of setting up two valid default values.
     *
     * @return 'true' if the timed test should wait for completion of the
     * JUnit test method before throwing an exception; 'false' if an
     * exception should be raised immediately.
     */
    private String getWaitForCompletion() throws XDocletException {
        return getTagValue(XDocletTagSupport.FOR_METHOD,
                            TIMED_TEST,
                            WAIT_FOR_COMPLETION,
                            "true,false",
                            "false",
                            false,
                            false);
    }
}
```

See Also

Recipe 9.9 shows how to create a custom Ant Doclet subtask to generate JUnitPerf
tests. Recipe 9.11 shows how to create a custom template file that uses the JUnitPerf-
Doclet tag handler. Recipe 9.12 shows how to create an XDoclet *xdoclet.xml* file used

to define information about your code generator. Recipe 9.13 shows how to package JUnitPerfDoclet into a JAR module. Chapter 8 provides information on the JUnit-Perf tool and how to update your Ant buildfile to invoke JUnitPerfDoclet.

9.11 Creating a Template File

Problem

You want to create a new template file (*.xdt*) that uses the `JUnitPerfTagHandler` class created in the previous recipe.

Solution

Create a template file called *junitperf.xdt*.

Discussion

XDoclet template files mix snippets of Java code and XML-style tags. These tags refer to XDoclet tag handler classes.

Instead of jumping directly into the completed example, it is best if we walk through each step of how the example template file is created. This example can be modified if your coding conventions differ or if you want to add extra functionality.

First, the template creates the package statement:

```
package <XDtPackage:packageName/>;
```

> XDoclet prefixes all namespaces with "XDt", and is not part of the actual namespace specified in the *xdoclet.xml* file. In order to reference the "Perf" namespace, you would use "XDtPerf". This is simply a convention that XDoclet uses.

Next, we add the import statements.

```
import com.clarkware.junitperf.*;
import junit.framework.*;
```

These are the only import statements that we need. Here is how to include import statements from the class being parsed (if you need them):

```
<XDtClass:importedList currentClass="&lt;XDtClass:className/&gt;"/>
```

> It's not a strict requirement to use entity references such as < and > when nesting greater-than and less-than symbols, but it does make the file easier to read, in our opinion. You are free to write this too: currentClass="<XDtClass:className/>"

For fun, any class comments are copied from the JUnit test.

```
/**
<XDtClass:classCommentTags indent="0"/> */
```

Let's look at our first `JUnitPerfTagHandler` class, which is referenced by the namespace "XDtPerf". The next recipe shows how to define a namespace for a tag handler class. This snippet maps directly to the `JUnitPerfTagHandler.className()` method.

```
public class <XDtPerf:className/> {
```

We create the start of the `suite()` method and a new `TestSuite` for the JUnitPerf tests.

```
public static Test suite() {
    TestSuite suite = new TestSuite();
```

It's time to create the JUnitPerf tests. We start by iterating all methods of the JUnit test being parsed. Recall that since the "destinationFile" attribute has a value that contains the substring "{0}", XDoclet generates output for multiple files. Specifically, this means that the template file is executed for each JUnit test class that is parsed. The attribute "superclasses" is set to "false", indicating that superclasses should not be evaluated—probably what we want most of the time.

```
<XDtMethod:forAllMethods superclasses="false">
```

Now, the next snippet evaluates each method's Javadoc, looking for the tag `junitperf.timedtest`. If a method has this tag, the nested content is evaluated. Otherwise, it is skipped. The nested content simply creates a new JUnitPerf `TimedTest` and adds it to the `TestSuite`. The template tag `XDtPerf:timedTest` references the `JUnitPerfTagHandler.timedTest()` method to create a line of code that constructs a new JUnitPerf `TimedTest`.

```
<XDtMethod:ifHasMethodTag tagName="junitperf.timedtest">
    Test timedTest = <XDtPerf:timedTest/>
    suite.addTest(timedTest);
</XDtMethod:ifHasMethodTag>
```

This next snippet is identical to the previous snippet, except that now we are looking for the tag `junitperf.loadtest`.

```
<XDtMethod:ifHasMethodTag tagName="junitperf.loadtest">
    Test loadTest = <XDtPerf:loadTest/>
    suite.addTest(loadTest);
</XDtMethod:ifHasMethodTag>
```

Example 9-13 shows a complete template file that can be used to generate JUnitPerf code.

Example 9-13. JUnitPerfDoclet template file

```
package <XDtPackage:packageName/>;

import com.clarkware.junitperf.*;
import junit.framework.*;
```

Example 9-13. JUnitPerfDoclet template file (continued)

```
/**
 <XDtClass:classCommentTags indent="0"/> */
public class <XDtPerf:className/> {

    public static Test suite( ) {
        TestSuite suite = new TestSuite( );

        <XDtMethod:forAllMethods superclasses="false">
            <XDtMethod:ifHasMethodTag tagName="junitperf.timedtest">
        Test timedTest = <XDtPerf:timedTest/>
        suite.addTest(timedTest);
            </XDtMethod:ifHasMethodTag>
            <XDtMethod:ifHasMethodTag tagName="junitperf.loadtest">
        Test loadTest = <XDtPerf:loadTest/>
        suite.addTest(loadTest);
            </XDtMethod:ifHasMethodTag>
        </XDtMethod:forAllMethods>

        return suite;
    }
}
```

See Also

Recipe 9.9 shows how to create a custom Ant Doclet subtask to generate JUnitPerf tests. Recipe 9.10 shows how to create the JUnitPerfDoclet tag handler class to perform simple logic and generate snippets of code. Recipe 9.12 shows how to create an XDoclet *xdoclet.xml* file used to define information about your code generator. Recipe 9.13 shows how to package JUnitPerfDoclet into a JAR module. Chapter 8 provides information on the JUnitPerf tool and how to update your Ant buildfile to invoke JUnitPerfDoclet.

9.12   Creating an XDoclet xdoclet.xml File

Problem

You need to create a new XDoclet *xdoclet.xml* file for a custom code generator.

Solution

Mark up your sub tasks with @ant.element tags and your tag handler classes with @xdoclet.taghandler tags. Add an Ant target to your buildfile that executes XDoclet's template subtask with XDoclet's *xdoclet-xml.xdt* template file.

Discussion

XDoclet 1.2 code generators require a deployment descriptor named *xdoclet.xml*. This file defines the namespace for an XDoclet tag handler class used in a template file, and defines the subtasks that are valid for a single XDoclet task. The file must exist in the *meta-inf* directory of your code generator's JAR file. The JAR file is known as an XDoclet module. Modules are discussed in more detail in the next recipe.

Example 9-14 shows how to mark up an XDoclet subtask. The only tag needed is an @ant.element tag. This tag defines two mandatory attributes: name and parent. The name attribute specifies the subtask name to use in the Ant buildfile. The parent attribute specifies the Ant XDoclet task that is allowed to execute the subtask. Remember that we do not need a subclass of xdoclet.DocletTask; therefore, we use DocletTask as the parent.

Example 9-14. Marked-up XDoclet subtask

```
/**
 * @ant.element
 *     name="junitperf"
 *     parent="xdoclet.DocletTask"
 *
 * @author Brian M. Coyner
 */
```

Example 9-15 shows how to mark up an XDoclet tag handler class. The only tag needed is an @xdoclet.taghandler tag with the mandatory attribute namespace. The namespace attribute tells the template file, which in our example is *junitperf.xdt*, the namespace to use when referencing this tag handler. Remember that template files, by convention, always include 'XDt' as part of the namespace. You should never include 'XDt' when defining the namespace here.

Example 9-15. Marked-up XDoclet tag handler

```
/**
 * @xdoclet.taghandler namespace="Perf"
 *
 * @author Brian M. Coyner
 */
public class JUnitPerfTagHandler extends XDocletTagSupport {
```

Now that our files are marked up, we need to generate the *xdoclet.xml* file. Example 9-16 shows how to use XDoclet's *xdoclet-xml.xdt* template file[*] to generate the *xdoclet.xml* file for the JUnitPerfDoclet code generator. This example is similar to the example in Recipe 9.7. The only major difference is the template file being used.

---

[*] As of XDoclet 1.2 beta, the *xdoclet-xml.xdt* template file is not available in the binary distribution. You will need to download the source distribution and look in the *src/modules* directory for this file.

Example 9-16. Generating the xdoclet.xml file

```
<target name="generate.xdoclet.xml">
  <taskdef name="xdoclet" classname="xdoclet.DocletTask">
    <classpath>
      <pathelement path="${env.XDOCLET_HOME}/lib/xdoclet.jar"/>
      <pathelement path="${env.XDOCLET_HOME}/lib/xjavadoc.jar"/>
      <pathelement location="${dir.lib}/commons-logging-1.0.jar"/>
    </classpath>
  </taskdef>

  <xdoclet
      destdir="${dir.build}">

    <fileset dir="${dir.src}">
      <include name="**/perf/"/>
      <exclude name="**/perf/Test*.java"/>
    </fileset>

    <template
        templateFile="${dir.resources}/xdoclet-xml.xdt"
        destinationFile="xdoclet.xml"/>
  </xdoclet>
</target>
```

After executing this target, an *xdoclet.xml* file should exist in the *build* directory. Here is the generated file:

```
<?xml version="1.0" encoding="UTF-8"?>

<!--
<!DOCTYPE xdoclet-module PUBLIC "-//XDoclet Team//DTD XDoclet Module 1.0//EN" "http:/
/xdoclet.sourceforge.net/dtd/xdoclet-module_1_0.dtd">
-->

<xdoclet-module>
    <!--
    com.oreilly.javaxp.xdoclet.perf.JUnitPerfDocletSubTask
    com.oreilly.javaxp.xdoclet.perf.JUnitPerfTagHandler
    -->

    <taghandler
        namespace="Perf"
        class="com.oreilly.javaxp.xdoclet.perf.JUnitPerfTagHandler"/>

    <subtask
        name="junitperf"
        implementation-class="com.oreilly.javaxp.xdoclet.perf.JUnitPerfDocletSubTask"
        parent-task-class="xdoclet.DocletTask"/>
</xdoclet-module>
```

See Also

Recipe 9.9 shows how to create a custom Ant Doclet subtask to generate JUnitPerf tests. Recipe 9.10 shows how to create the JUnitPerfDoclet tag handler class to perform simple logic and generate snippets of code. Recipe 9.11 shows how to create a custom template file that uses the JUnitPerfDoclet tag handler. Recipe 9.13 shows how to package JUnitPerfDoclet into a JAR module. Chapter 8 provides information on the JUnitPerf tool and how to update your Ant buildfile to invoke JUnitPerfDoclet.

9.13 Creating an XDoclet Module

Problem

You have created a custom XDoclet code generator and now you need to create an XDoclet module.

Solution

Add an Ant jar task to your buildfile that packages up the code generator's class files, template files, and *xdoclet.xml* file.

Discussion

XDoclet 1.2 code generators are packaged into JAR files known as modules. Modules are nothing more than a JAR file with a well-defined structure. It is the same process as packaging up a WAR or EAR file, only an XDoclet module is much simpler.

Example 9-17 shows an Ant target, `jar.perf.module`, that creates an XDoclet module. There are two special considerations for creating a module. First, the name of the JAR file should end with "module". This is only a convention, but it should be followed. Second, the *xdoclet.xml* must be placed in the *meta-inf* directory of the JAR file. This step is required for XDoclet to map template namespaces and parent task and subtask relationships. It is easy to do, using jar's `metainf` subtask.

Example 9-17. Creating an XDoclet module

```
<target name="jar.perf.module" depends="compile.perf,generate.xdoclet.xml">
  <jar jarfile="${dir.build}/oreilly-junitperf-module.jar">
    <fileset dir="${dir.build}">
      <include name="**/perf/"/>
      <exclude name="**/xdoclet.xml"/>
    </fileset>
    <metainf dir="${dir.build}" includes="xdoclet.xml"/>
  </jar>
</target>
```

See Also

Recipe 9.9 shows how to create a custom Ant Doclet subtask to generate JUnitPerf tests. Recipe 9.10 shows how to create the JUnitPerfDoclet tag handler class to perform simple logic and generate snippets of code. Recipe 9.11 shows how to create a custom template file that uses the JUnitPerfDoclet tag handler. Recipe 9.12 shows how to create an XDoclet *xdoclet.xml* file used to define information about your code generator. Chapter 8 provides information on the JUnitPerf tool and how to update your Ant buildfile to invoke JUnitPerfDoclet.

CHAPTER 10

Tomcat and JBoss

10.0 Introduction

Tomcat, available from *http://jakarta.apache.org/tomcat*, is an open source servlet container and the official reference implementation for Java Servlet and JavaServer Pages technologies. Table 10-1 shows Tomcat versions and the specification that each version adheres to. All recipes in this chapter assume Tomcat 4.1.x.

Table 10-1. Tomcat versions and specifications

Tomcat version	Servlet specification	JSP specification
5.0.x (Not yet released)	2.4 (Work-in-progress at Sun)	2.0
4.1.x	2.3	1.2
3.3.1	2.2	1.1

JBoss, available from *http://www.jboss.org*, is an open source EJB container. JBoss is extremely specification-compliant, making it well suited for application-server neutral development. JBoss also supports hot deploying applications, including web application WAR files. JBoss is not a servlet container. JBoss can embed a servlet container, though. For example, you can configure JBoss to use Tomcat.

10.1 Managing Web Applications Deployed to Tomcat

Problem

You want to manage your web applications deployed to Tomcat.

Solution

Tomcat's Manager application provides the tools necessary to deploy, undeploy, list currently loaded web applications, and start and stop a web application, along with numerous other tasks.

Discussion

Tomcat ships with a built-in application to manage web applications. By default, this web application is installed on the context path */manager*, and from here on we refer to it as the *Manager* application. The ability to deploy and undeploy a web application while the server is running is critical for any production or testing environment. For example, if there is a new version of a web application to install and the server does not support hot deploying, you must stop and restart the server before the new web application is loaded. Other running web applications are stopped, which is unacceptable in a production environment. Also, the ability to make and test small code changes quickly is critical because it takes too long to restart most servers.

The Manager application requires an authenticated user who has a *manager* role. For good reason—you do not want a would-be hacker on the Internet to install web applications, or possibly worse, remove installed web applications.

First, you need to set up a username and password, if an appropriate one does not already exist, and assign the *manager* role to it. By default, Tomcat is configured to look up authentication and authorization data from the file *$CATALINA_HOME/conf/tomcat-users.xml*. Here is how to set up a new user who has access to the Manager application:

```
<user username="javaxp" password="secret" roles="manager"/>
```

Once you have Tomcat set up with the appropriate authentication and authorization information, you may start up Tomcat and access the Manager application.

See Also

Recipe 10.2 shows how to hot deploy a web application to Tomcat. 10.3 shows how to remove a web application from Tomcat. 10.9 shows how to deploy a web application to JBoss.

10.2 Hot-Deploying to Tomcat

Problem

You want to install a new version of a web application without stopping and restarting Tomcat.

Solution

Tomcat provides an Ant task called InstallTask that uploads and deploys a WAR file to Tomcat using Tomcat's Manager application.

Discussion

Deploying a new web application to a running server is critical for test-first development because it takes too long to restart most servers. Example 10-1 shows how to use Tomcat's InstallTask, aptly named install, to hot deploy. A new target, deploy, invokes the install task.

 Like all Ant taskdefs, you are responsible for giving the task a name. The name is not specified by the task. For example, you could name a task BrianCoyner.

Before deploying the web application, a new WAR file must be generated, the server must be started, and the old web application must be removed (if it exists). Recipes later in this chapter delve into more details on the dependency targets.

Example 10-1. Hot-deploying to Tomcat

```
<target name="deploy" depends="war,start.tomcat,undeploy">
  <taskdef name="install" classname="org.apache.catalina.ant.InstallTask">
    <classpath>
      <path location="${env.CATALINA_HOME}/server/lib/catalina-ant.jar"/>
    </classpath>
  </taskdef>

  <pathconvert dirsep="/" property="fullWarDir">
    <path>
      <pathelement location="${dir.build}/${webapp.context.name}.war"/>
    </path>
  </pathconvert>

  <install
      url="${url.manager}"
      username="${username.manager}"
      password="${password.manager}"
      path="/${webapp.context.name}"
      war="jar:file:/${fullWarDir}!/"/>
</target>
```

First, create a task definition so Ant knows about the install task. The task is found at *$CATALINA_HOME/server/lib/catalina-ant.jar*, where *$CATALINA_HOME* is the base directory for Tomcat. Next, the full path of the WAR file being deployed is stored in the property fullWarDir. This is done using Ant's pathconvert task. Finally, the install task is executed. The install task defines five attributes:

1. The url attribute specifies the location of the Manager application. By default, Tomcat installs the application on the context path */manager*. For example, the URL might be *http://localhost:8080/manager*.

2. The username attribute specifies the name of the user who wishes to use the Manager application.

3. The password attribute specifies a password for authenticating the username with the Manager application.

4. The path attribute specifies the context path to install the web application.

5. The war attribute specifies an absolute path to the WAR file being deployed and takes on a URL that complies with the class java.net.JarURLConnection.

 The install task fails if there is an existing web application installed on the current context path. Failure causes the build processes to halt. Before deploying the new WAR file, you must remove the old instance. Recipe 10.3 shows how to do this.

See Also

Recipe 10.3 discusses removing an existing application from Tomcat using the Manager application.

10.3   Removing a Web Application from Tomcat

Problem

You want to remove an old version of a web application without stopping and restarting Tomcat.

Solution

Tomcat provides an Ant task called RemoveTask that removes a WAR file to Tomcat using Tomcat's Manager web application.

Discussion

Before deploying a new version of a web application, Tomcat requires the current version of the web application be removed from the context path. This requirement is somewhat frustrating because the Ant build process must first ensure that the current web application is removed before trying to deploy; otherwise, the build process fails. Example 10-2 shows how to use Tomcat's RemoveTask, aptly named remove, to remove a web application from a given context path. A new target, undeploy, invokes the remove task. This target only executes if the property is.webapp.deployed is "true". The init target sets this property to "true" if there is a web application installed on the context path. Recipe 10.4 delves into how this is done.

Example 10-2. Removing a web application from Tomcat

```
<target name="undeploy" depends="init" if="is.webapp.deployed">
  <taskdef name="remove" classname="org.apache.catalina.ant.RemoveTask">
    <classpath>
      <path location="${env.CATALINA_HOME}/server/lib/catalina-ant.jar"/>
    </classpath>
  </taskdef>

  <remove
      url="${url.manager}"
      username="${username.manager}"
      password="${password.manager}"
      path="/${webapp.context.name}"/>
</target>
```

First, create a task definition so Ant knows about the remove task. The task is found at *$CATALINA_HOME/server/lib/catalina-ant.jar*, where *$CATALINA_HOME* is the base directory for Tomcat. Next, the remove task is executed and removes the web application from Tomcat on a specific context path. The remove task defines four attributes:

1. The url attribute specifies the location of the Manager web application. By default, Tomcat installs this on the context path */manager*. For example, the URL might be *http://localhost:8080/manager*.

2. The username attribute specifies the name of the user who wishes to use the Manager application.

3. The password attribute specifies a password for authenticating the username with the Manager application.

4. The path attribute specifies the context path of the web application to remove.

 The remove task fails if there is not an existing web application installed on the current context path. Failure causes the build processes to halt. Before trying to remove the web application, check to see if it exists. Recipe 10.4 shows how to do this.

See Also

Recipe 10.4 shows how to determine if Tomcat is started and if a web application is deployed on a given context path.

10.4   Checking If a Web Application Is Deployed

Problem

You need to check if a web application is installed on a particular context path.

Solution

Create an Ant target that sets a property if a given context path contains an installed web application. This target should execute before trying to remove the web application.

Discussion

Tomcat's Manager application fails when trying to remove a web application that does not exist. It's frustrating because the Ant build process must check if the web application is installed before attempting to remove it. Luckily, the solution is simple. Example 10-3 shows an init target that checks if the web application is installed on a given context path. The init target sets two properties: is.tomcat.started and is.webapp.deployed. The condition task sets is.tomcat.started to "true" if the nested subtask http returns a valid HTTP response code.* The condition task sets is.webapp.deployed to "true" if Tomcat is started and the nested http subtask returns a valid response code. A valid response code means that some type of success occurred when opening a connection to the URL. If a failure occurs, the URL is assumed to be invalid.

Example 10-3. Checking if a web application exists on a given context path

```
<target name="init">
  <condition property="is.tomcat.started">
    <http url="${host}:${port}"/>
  </condition>

  <condition property="is.webapp.deployed">
    <and>
      <isset property="is.tomcat.started"/>
      <http url="${host}:${port}/${webapp.context.name}"/>
    </and>
  </condition>
</target>
```

---

* Response codes 400 and above represent errors according to the HTTP 1.1 specification. This specification is available in RFC 2616 at *http://www.ietf.org/rfc/rfc2616.txt*. Response codes below 400 indicate some sort of success.

See Also

10.3 discusses how to use Tomcat's Manager application to remove a web application from a context path.

10.5 Starting Tomcat with Ant

Problem

You want to start Tomcat using Ant.

Solution

Create a target that invokes the custom Ant task `com.oreilly.javaxp.tomcat.tasks.StartTomcatTask`.

Discussion

Typically, a server is started from a command prompt using a predefined script distributed with the server. To facilitate test-first programming, we need the ability to start Tomcat from Ant. Specifically, the Ant build process needs to start Tomcat and *wait* for Tomcat to become available before continuing. As of this writing, there is no generic way to solve this problem. So we created a new Ant task called `StartTomcatTask` to provide the functionality needed.

Example 10-4 shows the `AbstractTomcatTask`, which is the base class for the `StartTomcatTask` (Example 10-5) and `StopTomcatTask` (Recipe 10.6). This task extends Ant's `Task`, and is directly referenced in a buildfile.

Example 10-4. AbstractTomcatTask

```
package com.oreilly.javaxp.tomcat.tasks;

import org.apache.tools.ant.BuildException;
import org.apache.tools.ant.Task;

public abstract class AbstractTomcatTask extends Task {

    private TomcatSupport tomcatSupport;

    /**
     * Overrides the base class implementation to instantiate the
     * <code>TomcatSupport</code> class.
     */
    public void init() {
        this.tomcatSupport =
                new TomcatSupport(this, getScriptToExecute(), isStarting());
    }
```

Example 10-4. AbstractTomcatTask (continued)

```
/**
 * @return the name of the script to execute. For Tomcat 4.0 and
 * higher a valid filename might be 'startup'. The name of the script
 * should <strong>not</strong> include the extension.
 */
public abstract String getScriptToExecute();

/**
 * @return true if Tomcat is being started; false if Tomcat is being
 * stopped.
 */
public abstract boolean isStarting();

/**
 * Called by Ant to start the execution of the target.
 */
public void execute() throws BuildException {
    this.tomcatSupport.execute();
}

/**
 * Called by Ant to set the attribute 'testURL'. This attribute is
 * referenced in the buildfile.
 *
 * @param testURL a URL that is used to connect to Tomcat. This URL
 * is used to validate that Tomcat is running.
 */
public void setTestURL(String testURL) {
    this.tomcatSupport.setTestURL(testURL);
}

/**
 * Called by Ant to set the attribute 'catalinaHome'. This attribute is
 * referenced in the buildfile.
 *
 * @param catalinaHome the full path to where Tomcat is installed.
 */
public void setCatalinaHome(String catalinaHome) {
    this.tomcatSupport.setCatalinaHome(catalinaHome);
}

/**
 * @param timeout a number representing the timeout in
 * milliseconds. The timeout must be greater than 10 seconds
 * (10000 ms) and less than 60 seconds (60000 ms).
 */
public void setTimeout(String timeout) {
    try {
        long temp = Long.parseLong(timeout);
        if (temp >= 10000 && temp <= 60000) {
            this.tomcatSupport.setTimeout(temp);
        } else {
```

Example 10-4. AbstractTomcatTask (continued)

```
            throw new BuildException("Invalid 'timeout' value: "
                + timeout + ". The timeout must be between " +
                "10000 and 60000.");
        }
    } catch (NumberFormatException nfe) {
        throw new BuildException("Invalid 'timeout' value: " + timeout);
    }
  }
}
```

This task defines three attributes:

1. The testURL attribute specifies a URL that is used to determine when the server is started. For example, *http://localhost:8080*.

2. The catalinaHome attribute specifies where Tomcat is installed. This is the same as the environment variable *CATALINA_HOME*.

3. The timeout attribute specifies how long the task should wait before failing. Typically, Tomcat starts in 10–15 seconds, depending on the computer. Anything over 60 seconds is too long.

Example 10-5 shows the StartTomcatTask. This task extends from Abstract-TomcatTask and provides the implementation for the getScriptToExecute() and isStarting() methods.

Example 10-5. StartTomcatTask

```
package com.oreilly.javaxp.tomcat.tasks;

public class StartTomcatTask extends AbstractTomcatTask {

    /**
     * @return the script name "startup" without any extension.
     */
    public String getScriptToExecute() {
        return "startup";
    }

    public boolean isStarting() {
        return true;
    }
}
```

Example 10-6 shows the support class TomcatSupport used by the new task.

Example 10-6. TomcatSupport class

```
package com.oreilly.javaxp.tomcat.tasks;

import org.apache.tools.ant.BuildException;
import org.apache.tools.ant.Project;
import org.apache.tools.ant.Task;
```

Example 10-6. TomcatSupport class (continued)

```java
import java.io.ByteArrayOutputStream;
import java.io.File;
import java.io.IOException;
import java.io.PrintWriter;
import java.net.HttpURLConnection;
import java.net.MalformedURLException;
import java.net.URL;

public class TomcatSupport {

    private Task task;
    private URL testURL;
    private String catalinaHome;
    private String scriptToExecute;
    private long timeout;
    private boolean isStarting;

    /**
     * @param task the task that invoked this class. It's used only
     * for logging.
     * @param scriptToExecute the Tomcat 4.1.12 script used to start
     * or stop the server.
     */
    public TomcatSupport(Task task,
                         String scriptToExecute,
                         boolean isStarting) {
        this.task = task;
        this.scriptToExecute = scriptToExecute;
        this.isStarting = isStarting;

        // I have a pretty slow machine and this seems to be long enough.
        this.timeout = 20000;
    }

    /**
     * Executes a Tomcat script to start or stop the server.
     */
    public void execute( ) throws BuildException {

        // if the server is up and we are trying to start it then return
        // if the server is down and we are tryint to stop it then return
        if (isTomcatRunning( ) == this.isStarting) {
            if (this.isStarting) {
                this.task.log("Tomcat is already started!");
            } else {
                this.task.log("Tomcat is *not* running!");
            }
            return;
        }

        runScript( );
```

Example 10-6. TomcatSupport class (continued)

```
        boolean didTimeout = true;
        this.timeout = System.currentTimeMillis( ) + this.timeout;
        while (System.currentTimeMillis( ) < this.timeout) {
            sleep(500);
            if (isTomcatRunning( ) == this.isStarting) {
                didTimeout = false;
                break;
            }
        }

        if (didTimeout) {
            throw new BuildException("The server was not started " +
                    "successfully. Please make sure that your buildfile " +
                    "specifies a long enough timeout period AND that " +
                    "your environment is setup correctly.");
        }

        if (this.isStarting) {
            this.task.log("Tomcat is started!");
        } else {
            this.task.log("Tomcat is stopped!");
        }
    }

    public void runScript( ) throws BuildException {
        validateScript(this.catalinaHome, this.scriptToExecute);

        this.task.log((this.isStarting ? "Starting" : "Stopping") +
                " Tomcat...");

        try {
            Runtime.getRuntime( ).exec(this.catalinaHome +
                    File.separator + "bin" + File.separator +
                    this.scriptToExecute);
        } catch (IOException e) {
            throw new BuildException(e);
        }
    }

    public void setTestURL(String testURL) {
        try {
            this.testURL = new URL(testURL);
        } catch (MalformedURLException e) {
            throw new BuildException("Invalid URL: " + testURL);
        }
    }

    public void setCatalinaHome(String catalinaHome) {
        this.catalinaHome = catalinaHome;
    }
```

Example 10-6. TomcatSupport class (continued)

```java
    public void setScriptToExecute(String scriptToExecute) {
        this.scriptToExecute = scriptToExecute;
    }

    public void setTimeout(long timeout) {
        this.timeout = timeout;
    }

    private boolean isTomcatRunning() {

        HttpURLConnection conn = null;
        try {
            conn = (HttpURLConnection) this.testURL.openConnection();
            conn.connect();
            isURLValid(conn);
            return true;
        } catch (IOException e) {
            logException(e);
            return false;
        } finally {
            if (conn != null) {
                conn.disconnect();
            }
        }
    }

    private boolean isURLValid(HttpURLConnection conn) {
        int responseCode = 0;
        try {
            responseCode = conn.getResponseCode();
            // Response Codes 400 and above represent errors according
            // to the HTTP 1.1 specification available in RFC 2616 at
            // http://www.ietf.org/rfc/rfc2616.txt
            return (responseCode >= 100 && responseCode < 400);
        } catch (IOException e) {
            logException(e);
            return false;
        }
    }

    private void logException(Exception e) {
        ByteArrayOutputStream baos = new ByteArrayOutputStream();
        PrintWriter writer = new PrintWriter(baos);
        e.printStackTrace(writer);
        writer.close();
        this.task.log(new String(baos.toByteArray()), Project.MSG_DEBUG);
    }

    private void sleep(long ms) {
        try {
            Thread.sleep(ms);
```

Example 10-6. TomcatSupport class (continued)

```
        } catch (InterruptedException e) {
        }
    }

    private static void validateScript(String path, String script) {
        File file = new File(path + File.separator + "bin" +
            File.separator + script);
        if (!file.exists() || file.isDirectory()) {
            throw new BuildException("Invalid File: " +
                file.getAbsolutePath( ));
        }
    }
}
```

The execute method drives this support class, and is called from the
StartTomcatTask.execute( ) method. Here are the main steps this method executes:

1. Invoke the method isTomcatRunning( ) to determine if Tomcat is already started.
   If so, then exit the method.

2. The runScript( ) method is executed to start Tomcat. Tomcat is started in a new
   JVM courtesy of Tomcat's startup script.

3. Keep invoking the isTomcatRunning( ) method until the timeout is exceeded or
   Tomcat is started.

4. Once the server is started, the execute( ) method relinquishes control to Ant and
   the other tasks are allowed to execute if the timeout has not been exceeded. If
   the task timed out, the build process stops.

Example 10-7 shows how to use this task in an Ant buildfile.

Example 10-7. Starting Tomcat through Ant

```
<target name="start.tomcat">
  <taskdef name="starttomcat"
      classname="com.oreilly.javaxp.tomcat.tasks.StartTomcatTask">
    <classpath>
      <path location="${dir.build}"/>
    </classpath>
  </taskdef>

  <starttomcat
      testURL="${host}:${port}"
      catalinaHome="${env.CATALINA_HOME}"
      timeout="30000"/>
</target>
```

See Also

Recipe 10.6 shows how to use the custom task StopTomcatTask to stop Tomcat from
an Ant buildfile. This task patiently waits until the server is completely stopped
before relinquishing control to other Ant targets.

10.6   Stopping Tomcat with Ant

Problem

You want to stop Tomcat using Ant.

Solution

Create a target that invokes the custom Ant task `com.oreilly.javaxp.tomcat.tasks.StopTomcatTask`.

Discussion

Typically, a server is stopped from a command prompt using a predefined script distributed with the server. Since we have a new task to start Tomcat, it only seems fitting to provide a way to stop Tomcat, too. The ability to stop Tomcat is very useful from within an Ant buildfile, especially if we need to ensure that Tomcat is stopped before allowing any other Ant targets to execute. Example 10-8 shows the `StopTomcatTask` class. This new task extends `AbstractTomcatTask`, which we saw in Recipe 10.5, and causes Tomcat to shutdown. The task patiently waits until Tomcat is stopped before relinquishing control to other tasks.

An alternative approach is executing Tomcat's shutdown script with Ant's exec task. This approach works fine if you do not care if and when Tomcat actually stops. The same holds true for starting Tomcat.

Example 10-8. StopTomcatTask class

```
package com.oreilly.javaxp.tomcat.tasks;

public class StopTomcatTask extends AbstractTomcatTask {

    public String getScriptToExecute() {
        return "shutdown";
    }

    public boolean isStarting() {
        return false;
    }
}
```

Example 10-9 shows how to use this task in an Ant buildfile.

Example 10-9. Stopping Tomcat with Ant

```
<target name="stop.tomcat">
  <taskdef name="stoptomcat"
     classname="com.oreilly.javaxp.tomcat.tasks.StopTomcatTask">
    <classpath>
```

Example 10-9. Stopping Tomcat with Ant (continued)

```
        <path location="${dir.build}"/>
    </classpath>
  </taskdef>

  <stoptomcat
      testURL="${host}:${port}"
      catalinaHome="${env.CATALINA_HOME}"
      timeout="10000"/>
</target>
```

10.7 Setting Up Ant to Use Tomcat's Manager Web Application

Problem

You want to set up your Ant buildfile to use Tomcat's Manager application.

Solution

Create an Ant buildfile that invokes Ant targets to start and stop Tomcat, along with targets to install and remove web applications from Tomcat.

Discussion

Setting up a consistent build process is extremely important, especially if you are dealing with application servers that must be running during portions of the build process. For example, Chapter 7 discusses how to write unit tests that execute in a running server. In order for the tests to execute, a server must be started (in this case, Tomcat). To facilitate this process, a buildfile needs to ensure that the server is started before invoking any tasks that require a running server. Figure 10-1 shows a graphical view of the Ant buildfile. Earlier recipes discuss each target, minus the war target and its dependencies.

The following targets are executed in the following order when a user types **ant deploy** on the command line:

1. The prepare target executes first to set up the build environment.
2. The compile target compiles the out-of-date code.
3. The war target creates a .*war* file that is ultimately deployed to Tomcat.
4. The start.tomcat uses a custom Ant task to start the server. The build process patiently waits until Tomcat successfully starts or the task times out.
5. The init target sets two properties: is.tomcat.started and is.webapp.deployed.
6. If the property is.webapp.deployed is "true", the undeploy target is invoked.
7. Finally, the deploy target is invoked to deploy the new WAR file.

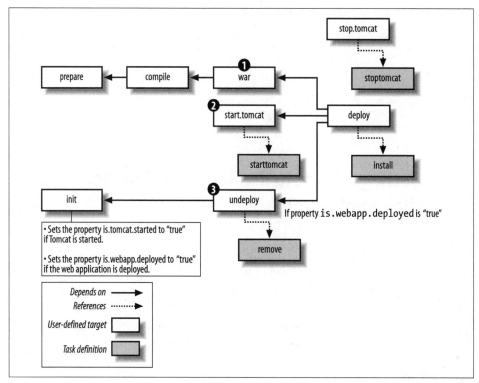

Figure 10-1. Graphical view of an Ant buildfile

See Also

The next recipe shows how to set up your Ant buildfile to hot deploy applications to JBoss. Recipe 10.9 discusses how to hot-deploy web applications to JBoss.

10.8   Hot-Deploying to JBoss

Problem

You want to deploy a new EAR or WAR file to JBoss.

Solution

Copy a new EAR to the *deploy* directory within the server environment that JBoss was started with.

Discussion

JBoss provides a simple mechanism to hot deploy: simply copy a new EAR file to the *deploy* directory within the server environment that JBoss was started with. This process is different from Tomcat; Tomcat requires the use of the Manager application. JBoss simply keeps tabs on the appropriate *deploy* directory, and when something new is discovered, it's deployed. If an old application exists then it is removed.

Here is an Ant target named deploy that copies an EAR file to JBoss, which is automatically installed:

```
<target name="deploy" depends="ear"
    description="Builds and deploys the project to JBoss.">
  <copy file="${dir.build}/${ear.file}" todir="${dir.jboss.deploy}"/>
</target>
```

The same target could be duplicated to copy a WAR file, too. The todir attribute is extremely important. The Ant property dir.jboss.deploy is defined as a well-known location within JBoss. Specifically, JBoss scans a directory for new deployed applications within the server environment that JBoss was started with. JBoss has three main default server environments:

minimal
> The bare minimum needed to start JBoss 3.x. This environment contains only logging, JNDI, and a URL deployment scanner for hot deploying. An EJB container, JMS, and other services are not available.

default
> The default server environment. This environment contains all services except for clustering and RMI\IIOP.

all
> This environment provides all services available with the JBoss server.

This recipe simply uses the default server environment. Here are the Ant properties needed to set up the JBoss server environment and deployment directory:

```
<property name="jboss.server.config" value="default"/>
<property name="dir.jboss.deploy"
    value="${env.JBOSS_DIST}/server/${jboss.server.config}/deploy"/>
```

Copying an EAR to the appropriate directory allows JBoss to automatically deploy your new application.

See Also

10.2 shows how to use Tomcat's Manager web application to hot-deploy.

10.9   Hot-Deploying a Web Application to JBoss

Problem

You want to use JBoss to hot-deploy a web application WAR file.

Solution

Copy a new WAR to the *deploy* directory within the server environment that JBoss was started with. Of course, you also need to ensure that JBoss is configured with a servlet container.

Discussion

A lot of developers use JBoss with a compliant servlet container, such as Tomcat, to receive the benefits of automatic hot-deploying. JBoss is intelligent enough to scan the *deploy* directory for WAR files, too, and deploy them to the servlet container. This ability removes the need for managing a complex Ant buildfile that we saw earlier in this chapter.

 JBoss is not a servlet container. JBoss can embed a servlet container, though. For example, you can configure JBoss to use Tomcat.

Recipe 10.8 shows how to deploy an EAR file to JBoss. The same techniques apply for WAR files, too.

See Also

Recipe 10.8 shows how set up your Ant buildfile for deploying applications to JBoss.

10.10 Testing Against Multiple Servers

Problem

You want to set up your Ant build process to deploy and test your code against multiple servers.

Solution

Set up your Ant buildfile to deploy and execute your server-side test suite for multiple servers.

Discussion

Throughout this book, we have discussed numerous approaches for testing server-side code. This chapter discusses hot-deploying applications to a running server in order to facilitate test-first development. Hot deploying is critical because it takes too long to restart most servers. Setting up your Ant buildfile to hot deploy to Tomcat takes a little effort, but you will save time throughout the project because you will be writing testable code in a stable environment. Hot deploying to JBoss is easy. Simply drop an EAR or WAR file into the appropriate *deploy* directory. Once the Ant build-file is set up, you can simply execute an Ant target that packages your applications, including tests, and deploys them to multiple servers. Next, Ant executes the tests within each server. This ensures that your application is server neutral. For example, you could package and deploy to Tomcat and JBoss/Tomcat.

See Also

Recipe 10.2 shows how to hot deploy to Tomcat. Recipes 10.8 and 10.9 discuss how to hot deploy to JBoss.

CHAPTER 11
Additional Topics

11.0   Introduction

This chapter highlights a handful of tools that were not covered earlier in this book. We also suggest a few techniques for testing EJB code, which is not readily testable in most cases. A quick visit to *http://www.junit.org* reveals that there are dozens of specialized tools for testing; unfortunately, we cannot cover them all.

11.1   Testing XML Files

Problem

You want to write unit tests for XML files.

Solution

Use XMLUnit.

Discussion

Suppose you have a Java class that generates an XML document and you want to write unit tests to ensure the XML data is correct. Your first inclination might be to compare the XML to a string. If the text is equal, you know the XML is correct. While this works, it is highly fragile and fails in cases where ignorable whitespace is the only difference between two XML documents. Consider this unit test:

```
public void testPersonXml( ) {
    String xml = new Person("Tanner", "Burke").toXml( );
    assertEquals("<person><name>Tanner Burke</name></person>", xml);
}
```

This test only works if the XML is formatted exactly as you expect. Unfortunately, the following XML contains the same data, but it causes the test to fail:

```
<person>
  <name>Tanner Burke</name>
</person>
```

Example 11-1 shows how to use XMLUnit to test your XML without worrying about whitespace differences.

Example 11-1. Simple XMLUnit test

```
public class TestPersonXml extends XMLTestCase {

    ...

    public void testPersonXml() {
        String xml = new Person("Tanner", "Burke").toXml();

        setIgnoreWhitespace(true);
        assertXMLEquals("<person><name>Tanner Burke</name></person>", xml);
    }
}
```

XMLUnit also supports the following types of XML tests:

- Validating against a DTD
- Transforming via XSLT and checking the results
- Evaluating XPath expressions and checking the results
- Treating badly formed HTML as XML and running tests
- Using the DOM API to traverse and test XML documents

See Also

XMLUnit is available at *http://xmlunit.sourceforge.net*.

11.2   Enterprise JavaBeans Testing Tools

Problem

You want to write tests for Enterprise JavaBeans components.

Solution

Try out ServletTestCase or J2EEUnit.

Discussion

Testing EJB code is challenging because beans only work in the context of an application server. In order to test these beans, your tests must either invoke bean methods through remote interfaces, or be deployed alongside the beans and run on the server.

While you can always write client unit tests that test your EJBs through their remote interfaces, performance may suffer due to the remote calls. The two tools mentioned in this recipe run in a servlet container, typically removing the remote method call overhead. In most cases, particularly in testing environments, the servlet container runs in the same JVM as the EJB container. The shared JVM gives these server-side tests the desired performance boost.

ServletTestCase

ServletTestCase is a small application for creating and testing server side code. Your tests extend from `junit.framework.ejb.ServerTestCase` and you simply add `testXXX()` just as if you were writing a normal JUnit test. The tests are then deployed to your servlet container along with the ServletTestCase application. The tests are executed using Ant's junit task.

J2EEUnit

J2EEUnit is a framework for testing server-side code. J2EEUnit uses a servlet as an entry point for executing your EJB tests. Unlike ServletTestCase, you write J2EEUnit tests by extending `junit.framework.TestCase`. You use the `setUp()` method to retrieve a reference to an EJB. Here's an example:

```
protected void setUp() throws Exception {
    Context jndiContext = new InitialContext();
    Object obj = jndiContext.lookup("java:comp/env/ejb/CustomerBean");
    CustomerHome home = (CustomerHome)
            PortableRemoteObject.narrow(obj, CustomerHome.class);
    this.customer = home.create();
}
```

Here's a simple test method:

```
public void testGetAccountNumber() throws Exception {
    assertEquals("Account Number.",
                "12345",
                this.customer.getAccountNumber());
}
```

You use `org.junitee.anttask.JUnitEETask` Ant task to execute the tests.

See Also

ServletTestCase is available at *http://www.junit.org/news/extension/j2ee/index.htm*. J2EEUnit is available at *http://junitee.sourceforge.net*.

11.3 Avoiding EJB Testing

Problem

You want to test server-side business logic but avoid the complexity of EJB deployment and remote method calls.

Solution

Decouple business logic from EJBs, facilitating dedicated unit testing without an application server.

Discussion

Example 11-2 shows a code fragment from a stateless session bean. In order to test this bean, you must deploy it to an application server. The deployment steps make your Ant buildfile more complex and slow you down as you write tests, deploy, run your tests, and change your code.

Example 11-2. Part of a stateless session bean

```
public class AccountBean implements SessionBean {
    // a bunch of EJB methods
    public void ejbCreate() { ... }
    public void ejbActivate() { ... }
    public void ejbPassivate() { ... }
    etc...

    public double getBalanceAsOf(Date date) {
        // fetch data
        ...
        // apply interest
        ...
        // deduct bank fees
        ...
    }
}
```

Fortunately, we can refactor EJBs so they do not require as much testing. If business logic is decoupled from the beans, you can write tests against the business logic without first deploying to an application server. This capability drastically simplifies your tests, while making the whole test-driven development cycle faster.

Example 11-3 shows the improved bean.

Example 11-3. Refactored stateless session bean

```
public class AccountBean implements SessionBean {
    // a bunch of EJB methods
    public void ejbCreate() { ... }
    public void ejbActivate() { ... }
    public void ejbPassivate() { ... }
    etc...

    public double getBalanceAsOf(Date date) {
        // delegate to a businss object
        return AccountBO.getBalanceAsOf(date);
    }
}
```

The business logic now resides in a dedicated class called AccountBO. In addition to testing benefits, AccountBO is now reusable by other beans and perhaps even by servlets or client code. We don't show AccountBO because it is just an ordinary Java class with a static method. You can test it using JUnit just like any other class.

See Also

This technique was first mentioned in Recipe 6.7.

11.4   Testing Swing GUIs

Problem

You want to use a specialized toolkit for testing Swing GUI code.

Solution

Try out Abbot, Pounder, Jemmy, or JFCUnit.

Discussion

Testing GUI code is challenging. You locate GUI components, simulate user input, and capture the actual output to test against your expected output. You must also deal with threading issues, because many Swing events are delivered asynchronously on the event queue.

Minimizing dependency on GUI tests is always your first line of defense. You should make every effort to modularize your GUI code so that data models can be tested independently from the GUI. You can also write many tests against individual panels and components. But at some point, you may find that you have to run tests against the entire user interface in order to fully simulate how the user works with your application. This is where specialized GUI testing tool enter the picture.

Abbot

Abbot is a testing framework that builds on functionality offered by the java.awt.Robot class. In Abbot, you create testing scripts that locate components, perform actions, and then assert that the GUI is in the correct state. These scripts are your automated GUI tests. Although you can use the Abbot API to write tests programmatically, Abbot scripts are normally used for testing.

You generally create a script by running your application while Abbot Recorders capture all events and generate the script for you. Then use the Costello script editor to change and customize your scripts. Next, insert assertions and tests into your scripts. Then run Abbot scripts through JUnit using the ScriptTestCase and ScriptTestSuite classes, or you can run them interactively using the Costello script editor.

Pounder

Pounder is another recording/playback tool, much along the same lines as Abbot. You record scripts by running your application in the Pounder tool, and then play them back using the Player class. After the script completes, you can use normal Java code, rather than assertions in the scripts, to assert that the various GUI components are in the expected state. For example:

```
public void testLoginFrame() throws Exception {
    Player player = new Player("scripts/login/badUserName.pnd");
    LoginFrame loginFrame = (LoginFrame) player.play();

    assertEquals("joe", loginFrame.getUserNameField().getText());
    etc...
}
```

Jemmy

Jemmy is a NetBeans module for testing GUI components, but is also designed for use as a standalone class library. Unlike Abbot and Pounder, Jemmy is not a recording and playback tool. Instead, Jemmy includes a comprehensive Java API for dealing with Swing user interfaces.

One advantage of a tool like Jemmy is its ability to locate components based on their content, rather than requiring the exposure of the accessor methods in the panels and frames being tested. Without Jemmy's searching capabilities, you would either have to write your own searching methods, or else write a lot of methods in your GUI code like getFirstNameField() that would allow your unit test to locate fields and run tests against them.

JFCUnit

JFCUnit is similar in concept to Jemmy; it is another Java class library for writing Swing unit tests. Like Jemmy, JFCUnit allows you to programmatically locate windows and components within those windows, deliver events, and then test component states in a thread-safe way.

See Also

Abbot is available at *http://abbot.sourceforge.net*. Pounder is available at *http://pounder.sourceforge.net*. Jemmy is available at *http://jemmy.netbeans.org*. JFCUnit is available at *http://jfcunit.sourceforge.net*.

11.5 Testing Private Methods

Problem

You can't test certain methods because they're private and your test can't get to them.

Solution

Refactor the functionality into standalone classes or make the methods package scope.

Discussion

Suppose you have the following code:

```
public class Widget {
    public void draw(Graphics g) {
        computeCoordinates();
        // paint the component
    }
    private void computeCoordinates() {
        // some complex logic here
    }
}
```

The real complexity lies in the `computeCoordinates()` method, but tests cannot call the method directly because it is private. You could write tests against the `draw()` method, but such tests might be slow and would be more complicated than necessary. You might have to wait while the widget paints itself on screen, or you might have to create mock `Graphics` objects. Making the `computeGraphics()` method package-scope is a simple fix and makes it easy for tests in the same package to call the method. We use this approach in many of our classes and it works well.

Increasing visibility in order to facilitate testing is not without drawbacks. Good designs seek to minimize visibility of fields and methods. By making this method package-scope, any other class in the same package can now call it. This can increase coupling and increase overall application complexity. While we find ourselves using this technique from time to time, it is often an indicator that something needs changing in the design.

 Hard-to-test code is a "smell" suggesting that the design can be improved.

Rather than increasing the visibility of methods, investigate refactoring into new classes. These classes encapsulate the desired functionality and are testable on their own. In our previous example, you might create a class called `CoordinateCalculator` that does the work formerly found in the `computeCoordinates()` method.

Incidentally, standalone helper classes can be reused throughout an application, while private utility methods are only good for a single class. This is an example of how testing and refactoring lead to better designs.

See Also

Recipe 6.7 discusses how to break up large methods into smaller, testable methods.

Index

We'd like to hear your suggestions for improving our indexes. Send email to *index@oreilly.com*.

About the Authors

Eric M. Burke is an O'Reilly author and a Principal Software Engineer with Object Computing, Inc. in St. Louis, MO. He specializes in Java, and his job duties include consulting, training, and public-speaking engagements. When he is not working at the computer, Eric enjoys woodworking and home improvement projects. Eric can be reached at *burke_e@yahoo.com.*

Brian M. Coyner is a Senior Software Engineer with Object Computing, Inc., in St. Louis, MO. He has a B.S. in Computer Science from Southeast Missouri State University, and specializes in Java training and consulting. When he is not working, which is rare, Brian enjoys playing the guitar and spending time with his family

Colophon

Our look is the result of reader comments, our own experimentation, and feedback from distribution channels. Distinctive covers complement our distinctive approach to technical topics, breathing personality and life into potentially dry subjects.

The animal on the cover of *Java Extreme Programming Cookbook* is a bison. American Bison (*Bison bison*) are the largest land mammals in North America. Prior to European colonization, an estimated 30 to 70 million animals roamed the continent in vast herds. Bison were recklessly overhunted until, in the late 1800s, approximately 1,500 remained. Now bison are legally protected in Yellowstone National Park and on preserves such as the National Bison Refuge in Montana. The development of commerical bison ranching has also played a role in increasing the North American Bison population, which has grown to over 350,000 animals.

Colleen Gorman was the production editor and the copyeditor for *Java Extreme Programming Cookbook*. Mary Brady, Brian Sawyer, and Mary Anne Weeks Mayo provided quality control. Tom Dinse wrote the index.

Hanna Dyer designed the cover of this book, based on a series design by Edie Freedman. The cover image is a 19th-century engraving from the Dover Pictorial Archive. Emma Colby produced the cover layout with QuarkXPress 4.1 using Adobe's ITC Garamond font.

Bret Kerr designed the interior layout, based on a series design by David Futato. This book was converted by Joe Wizda to FrameMaker 5.5.6 with a format conversion tool created by Erik Ray, Jason McIntosh, Neil Walls, and Mike Sierra that uses Perl and XML technologies. The text font is Linotype Birka; the heading font is Adobe Myriad Condensed; and the code font is LucasFont's TheSans Mono Condensed. The illustrations that appear in the book were produced by Robert Romano and Jessamyn Read using Macromedia FreeHand 9 and Adobe Photoshop 6. This colophon was written by Colleen Gorman.